D0324260

Managing Labor Migration in the Twenty-first Century

Managing Labor Migration in the Twenty-first Century

Philip Martin, Manolo Abella, and Christiane Kuptsch

Yale University Press

New Haven and London

Set in Adobe Garamond with Stone Sans types by The Composing Room of Michigan, Inc.
Printed in the United States of America by Vail-Ballou Press, Binghamton, New York.

Library of Congress Cataloging-in-Publication Data

Martin, Philip L., 1949–
Managing labor migration in the twenty-first century / Philip Martin, Manolo Abella, and Christiane Kuptsch.
p. cm. — (Global management series)
Includes bibliographical references and index.
ISBN-13: 978-0-300-10904-7 (cloth (13-digit) : alk. paper)
ISBN-10: 0-300-10904-0 (cloth (10-digit) : alk. paper)
1. Alien labor. 2. Alien labor—Government policy. I. Abella, Manolo I. II. Kuptsch, Christiane. III. Title. IV. Series.
HD6300.M345 2005
331.6′2—dc22

2005010347

A catalogue record for this book is available from the British Library.

The paper in this book meets the guidelines for permanence and durability of the Committee on Production Guidelines for Book Longevity of the Council on Library Resources.

10 9 8 7 6 5 4 3 2 1

To Roger Böhning, chief of the Migrant Branch of the International Labor Organization between 1982 and 1998, and a leader in understanding international labor migration and protecting migrants

Man is of all sorts of luggage the most difficult to be transported.
—Adam Smith

Contents

Preface

José González left his village in Oaxaca, traveled north by bus through Mexico, and found a smuggler to guide him over the Mexican-U.S. border and through the Arizona desert to Phoenix. From Phoenix, a van took him to a town in Iowa with a meatpacking plant that was always hiring new workers. José bought a driver's license and green card from a man he met in the bodega—the store serving the immigrant community—presented his documents at the meatpacking plant, and, after a morning orientation that included watching a safety video and getting a lesson on sharpening knives, went to work, earning $8 an hour for cutting the large pieces of meat that passed in front of him into smaller pieces. If José stays on the "dis-assembly line" for at least sixty days, his cousin Manuel, who told him about the job and lent him the money to pay the smuggler, will receive a $200 referral payment.

Binrod Ilahi studied computer science at an Indian institute of technology. An ethnic Indian who had emigrated to the United States came to his school and told him how to find a U.S. employer who would hire him with an H-1B visa. During the six years that Binrod could stay in the United States, the recruiter assured him that his U.S. employer would sponsor Binrod for an immigrant visa, which would allow Binrod to live and work anywhere in the country and, after five years, to become a naturalized citizen. Binrod got the visa, and his parents, who wanted him to marry before he left, placed an ad for a spouse that emphasized Binrod's H-1B, which raised the dowry price the bride's parents would be expected to pay to Binrod's family.

Zheng Yang, in Fujian, China, had several relatives in New York City who told him that if he could get to New York, a job would be waiting. They warned Zheng that work in the land of opportunity would be hard, but he could expect to earn at least $1,500 a month. Zheng found a snakehead—a smuggler of illegal immigrants—who agreed to put Zheng and twenty-five other migrants into a shipping container that took a month to travel from China to New York. Zheng borrowed $20,000 to pay the smuggler, climbed into the container, and set off. When he arrived in New York, the snakehead's accomplices demanded more money and held a knife to his throat as he called his relatives in Fujian, pleading for more money to save his life. A month after he left China, Zheng found himself illegally in New York City and in debt for $25,000, but confident that he could pay off his debts within two years.

Christina Galvez was a nurse in Manila who earned $300 a month but dreamed of earning ten times as much abroad. She went to a recruiting agency, got a contract for an overseas job, and bid her family farewell. Christina flew to Chicago and, after going to work at a large downtown hospital, soon learned why Americans shunned her overnight nursing job. The hospital was far from safe and affordable housing, forcing Christina to either share an expensive apartment nearby with six others or take risky late-night rides to work on public transit. Like the other migrant nurses, Christina was a good and reliable worker who volunteered for overtime, and she hoped that the purgatory of her first U.S. job would be followed by higher wages and easier work elsewhere.

This is a book about the people who cross national borders to work. The world's ninety million migrant workers constitute 3 percent of the global workforce, and migrant experiences range from red carpet welcomes for some computer programmers to red card detention and deportation for some apprehended unauthorized workers. International migration for employment is increasing, and in this book we explain that countries and companies need to learn to better manage labor migration so that it contributes to prosperity and equality between the nation-states that send and receive migrants. The alternative, which would have some nations producing workers for others and make labor transfers a permanent business, is too reminiscent of slavery to be a global goal.

We aim to provide a road map for understanding the causes and impacts of international migrant workers and to point the way to sustainable labor migration policies. The roots of what is sometimes seen as out-of-control migration in labor-receiving countries lie primarily within their borders, often in previous colonization or guest worker programs. Industrial democracies such as Britain, France, Spain, and Portugal had colonies that sent migrants to the mother countries, and Austria, Germany, and Switzerland recruited guest workers from Turkey and Yugoslavia to fill vacant jobs in the 1960s. Fast population growth and slow economic development encouraged people in poorer countries, especially the young, to emigrate for a better life, and the communications and transportation networks that evolved to bridge borders made it ever easier for migrant workers to move over borders for jobs, even in defiance of recruitment stops and stepped-up border and interior controls. Finally, the rights available to all residents helped migrants to stay abroad, as they applied for asylum or used other means to avoid immediate removal. However, attempting to manage migration by manipulating the rights of migrants, the response of most governments, is a problematic way to deal with labor migration.

The world's largest international labor migration, workers moving from Mexico to the United States, provides an example of how recruitment can set labor migration in motion. On September 29, 1942, the first bracero workers arrived by train from Mexico to work on U.S. farms. Some twenty-two years and almost five million bracero admissions later, President John F. Kennedy persuaded Congress to end the bracero program, agreeing with U.S. unions and churches that braceros in the fields slowed the upward mobility of Mexican-Americans, just as government-sanctioned discrimination had held back African-Americans. Recruitment set Mexican-U.S. migration in motion, and fast population growth combined with slow economic growth in rural Mexico increased emigration pressures. Networks evolved to link U.S. farmers and rural Mexicans, and they bridged the border so well that forty years after the bracero program ended, almost 10 percent of 110 million persons born in Mexico have migrated to the United States, including 5 million in the 1990s. The United States responded to this upsurge in legal and unauthorized Mexican-U.S. migration by expanding the border patrol to more than eleven thousand agents and curtailing the right of noncitizens and unauthorized foreigners to welfare and other social service benefits.

In Germany, the millionth guest worker, Armando Sa. Rodrigues from Vale de Madeiros, Portugal, was greeted with a brass band and a motorcycle at the Cologne train station on September 10, 1964. The ceremony symbolized the contributions of guest workers to the German economic miracle in the 1960s, but as the guest workers grew more diverse and settled, their recruitment was stopped in 1973. Meanwhile, southern European nations such as Greece and Portugal joined the European Union (EU) and soon grew fast enough to raise wages and reduce emigration pressures, but emigration pressures remained high in non-EU countries such as Turkey and Yugoslavia. Four decades after the Cologne train station ceremony, Germany has more than seven million partially integrated foreign residents and is attempting to change popular perceptions that immigrants impose costs rather than benefits with an immigration policy that favors the arrival of highly educated newcomers.

The United States, Germany, and the other industrial democracies developed new guest worker programs in the 1990s; most included features that aimed to avoid the "mistakes" of the past by keeping foreign workers temporary, to ensure that they were truly guests who left after a few months or years. If the old guest worker programs can be likened to shotguns that sprayed workers throughout the labor market under a single set of rules, the new guest worker programs are more like rifles aiming to fill job vacancies in particular labor market niches under rules that often vary with the education of the migrant and the industry and occupation in which she works. For example, computer programmers and other professionals are often allowed or encouraged to stay as immigrants, while farm workers and seasonal laborers are sometimes subject to rules that aim to rotate them out of the country after a few months.

Despite the proliferation of guest worker programs, there are more unauthorized than legal foreign workers in most industrial democracies, which raises the major question we tackle in this book—how should the rising number of migrants be managed? Our focus is on the industrial democracies in North America and western Europe, where managing labor migration is particularly important because a large share of labor force growth in societies with low fertility must come from foreigners: in western Europe practically all labor force growth is due to immigration, as is about 40 percent of such growth in the United States and Canada. If migrant workers settle and become indistinguishable from the native born, immigration can enrich destination countries. If migrants settle and do not integrate successfully, unemployment may rise and social cohesion may weaken.

The processes for admitting and employing migrants affect their prospects for upward mobility, the wages and working conditions of native workers and migrants, and the way in which host societies integrate newcomers. One way to envision the impacts of migrants is to remember that a major achievement of the industrial democracies over the past half-century has been the creation of diamond-shaped societies, with the wide middle representing the large middle class. Globalization has helped to squeeze the middle class, pushing people up or down the earnings ladder in a manner that could yield hourglass-shaped and more unequal societies. Current labor migration patterns reinforce this trend toward inequality because migrants tend to be either professionals at the top of the hourglass, such as Indian computer programmers, or unskilled workers at the bottom, such as Mexican farm workers.

Since migration is increasingly important for labor force growth in industrial countries and may increase inequality between richer and poorer nations, what blocks policy changes that could head off future problems? The answer is that the debate about migration is often dominated by groups with the extreme positions of "no borders" or "no immigrants." The "no borders" position is exemplified by the *Wall Street Journal*'s call in a 1986 editorial, repeated in 1990, for a five-word amendment to the U.S. Constitution: "There shall be open borders." The open-borders argument rests on several foundations, including the putative need of aging societies for fresh blood, the difficulty of keeping migrants out, and the need to provide shelter to refugees as well as to share wealth with the world's poor by offering them jobs. The "no immigrants" position, exemplified by the Federation for American Immigration Reform (FAIR), asserts, among other things, that there is no shortage of workers, only a shortage of wages, and that the world's poor can benefit by producing and exporting goods rather than emigrating.

Managing Labor Migration in the Twenty-first Century provides a middle-of-the-road guide to labor migration issues. We explain why the number of migrants moving from developing to industrial countries will continue rising, and we survey migration patterns around the world. We next turn to the two fastest-growing types of migrants: professionals, such as nurses and computer programmers, and unskilled workers, who pick crops, work in private households, and clean buildings or wash dishes in restaurant kitchens. In Part III we turn to south-south migration, recognizing that 40 percent of the world's migrants move from one developing country to another; we focus on the case of Thailand, a southeast Asian Tiger economy that has more than a million migrants from neighboring countries. In the concluding chapter we compare migration-related flows to other global flows, emphasizing that the volume of remittances—money sent home by migrants abroad—surpassed official development assistance (ODA) in the mid-1990s and was double ODA in 2004. With labor becoming a significant export of more developing countries, the three R's associated with migration—recruitment, remittances, and returns—take on greater importance. The trick is to use labor migration to accelerate stay-at-home development and allow migration pressures to ebb naturally.

As Adam Smith observed more than two hundred years ago, "Man is of all sorts of luggage the most difficult to be transported." The labor market is complex in every society because workers cannot be separated from their work, making the exchange of effort for reward a complex economic transaction, and far more complex when it extends over national borders. In this book we lay out a road map for managing labor migration so that it contributes to the convergence between nation-states needed for peace and prosperity in a globalizing world.

One of the major lessons from evaluating migration policies is that the unintended consequences of moving people over borders are often more important than the intended effects, as when guest workers become immigrants. Unintended consequences need not be bad, and this book is a welcome unintended consequence of our efforts to chart a road map for sustainable labor migration policies in preparation for the International Labor Organization (ILO)'s June 2004 conference that focused on migrant workers.

We are indebted to Jean-Pierre Laviec and the ILO's International Institute for Labour Studies (IILS) for making our collaboration possible. Piyasiri Wickramasekara and the other ILO migration specialists read parts of the manuscript and provided useful comments, as did participants in several IILS-organized workshops and seminars in which the ideas presented here were discussed. We are responsible for any errors, and the views expressed are our own.

Abella and Kuptsch would like to thank their families and ILO colleagues for their support in completing the manuscript. Martin's work on migrant workers has been supported by the German Marshall Fund of the United States and the Rosenberg, Farm, and Giannini Foundations.

Part I Global Migration

Who is a migrant, and which countries send and receive migrants? In Chapter 1 we review migrant definitions and trends, highlighting the fact that there were 175 million migrants in 2000. Several factors discourage international migration, including inertia, government controls, and economic development, but growing demographic and economic differences between nations nonetheless are encouraging many people to cross national borders in hope of a better life. These differences, combined with revolutions in communications, transportation, and the rights of individuals vis-à-vis governments, promise more migrants in the twenty-first century.

In many cases, countries facing common problems learn from each other, searching for best practices to improve the downtown areas of cities, to move people efficiently in urban areas, or to deal with environmental issues. To find best practices that might be copied or adapted, we need to know how countries deal with migration issues, and in Chapter 2 we survey migration patterns in the major countries and regions of the world. Most of the world's countries are senders of migrants, receivers of migrants, or places through which migrants transit, and many are all three, but most migrants come from and go to relatively few countries, leaving countries such as Mexico and the Philippines and migrating to countries such as the United States and Saudi Arabia.

1 Why International Migration?

The United Nations Population Division defines international migrants as persons outside their country of birth or citizenship for twelve months or more, regardless of the reason for moving or legal status abroad. No country defines migrants in this way: in the United States, for example, residents born in other countries are divided into various categories. A naturalized citizen is one who was born outside the United States and typically has been in the United States for at least five years before taking the citizenship oath. A legal immigrant is someone who has not become a U.S. citizen and may have arrived yesterday or thirty years ago. Nonimmigrants, including students, foreign workers, and tourists, may have been in the United States several years or several days, while unauthorized foreigners similarly have been in the country for varying periods.

In a world of about two hundred sovereign nation-states, each of which issues passports and regulates who can cross its borders and stay, there were 175 million migrants in 2000, including 110 million, or 63 percent, in what the United Nations calls "more developed" regions: Europe and North America, Australia and New Zealand, Japan, and the ex-Soviet Union "where it is presented as a separate area." Since 1960 the share of migrants in more-developed countries has risen, while the share in less-developed countries has fallen, largely because of immigration and slow population growth in more-developed countries.

Is the number of migrants too many, too few, or just right? Those who think there are too many migrants note that if the world's 175 million migrants were gathered as one "nation," it would be the sixth-most populous, after China, India, the United States, Indonesia, and Brazil, and ahead of Russia and Pakistan. If the 110 million migrants in more-developed countries were one nation, they would be the fourth-most populous industrial country, after the United States, Russia, and Japan, and ahead of Germany. Low birthrates and almost daily stories of migrants dying as they try to walk across the Arizona desert into the United States or cross the Mediterranean to Spain or Italy in small boats characterize an age of migration, an era in which most migrants are moving from developing countries in Africa, Asia, and Latin America to North America and Europe.

The number of migrants is rising faster than the global population, a response to the fall of communism, wars that produce refugees, as in Yugoslavia and Afghanistan, the approval of the North American Free Trade Agreement, and the Asian economic miracle.[1] Table 1.1 shows that the migrant share of the global population has risen from a low of 2.2 percent in 1970 to 2.9 percent in 1990 and 2000. Developed countries have more migrants than developing countries, and the share of migrants in their populations has almost tripled in the past forty years.

Many recent migration flows were unanticipated, and they led to efforts by receiving countries to reduce the influx of migrants. For example, in response to the influx of migrants fleeing Balkan wars and seeking asylum in Europe in the 1990s, many European countries offered only temporary protected status to Yugoslavs, in the hope that migrants who did not have a secure residence status would be easier to persuade to return once peace was achieved. To deal with migrants from more distant trouble spots such as Iraq, many European countries adopted policies that required those seeking refuge to apply for asylum in the first safe country they reached, so that an Iraqi reaching Austria via Hungary could have his asylum application in Austria rejected and be returned to Hungary.

The increase in the number of migrants in many industrial countries has slowed, demonstrating that governments have considerable control over entries and stays. However, modes of entry into industrial countries have changed, with most asylum applicants in Europe, for example, believed to have been

Table 1.1. International Migrants and Global Population, 1960–2000

	Global Population (billions)			International Migrants (millions)			Migrants as Percentage of Population		
	World	MD[a] (%)	LD[a] (%)	World	MD[a] (%)	LD[a] (%)	World	MD[a]	LD[a]
1960	3.0	0.9 (31%)	2.1 (69%)	75.9	32.1 (42%)	43.8 (58%)	2.5	3.4	2.1
1970	3.7	1.1 (29%)	2.6 (71%)	81.5	38.2 (47%)	43.2 (53%)	2.2	3.6	1.6
1980	4.4	1.1 (26%)	3.3 (74%)	99.8	47.8 (48%)	52.1 (52%)	2.3	4.2	1.6
1990	5.3	1.2 (23%)	4.0 (77%)	154.0	89.7 (58%)	64.3 (42%)	2.9	7.4	1.6
2000	6.1	1.3 (21%)	4.8 (79%)	174.9	110.3 (63%)	64.6 (37%)	2.9	8.7	1.3

[a]MD: more-developed (Europe, North America, Australia, New Zealand, Japan, and the former USSR; LD: less-developed.

Source: Population Division, DESA, United Nations. Trends in Total Migrant Stock by Sex, 1990–2000, 2003 Revision, POP/DB/MIG/Rev. 2003.

smuggled over borders in order to ask for refuge from persecution at home (Futo and Jandl, 2004). New destinations for migrants have emerged, especially middle-income developing countries surrounded by poorer countries, such as Thailand and Malaysia, which receive most of their migrants from Myanmar (Burma) and Indonesia, respectively. Such south-south migration is little studied, and our chapter on Thailand highlights the dilemmas involved in having to develop a capacity to manage migration seemingly overnight.

A migrant crosses a geographic boundary and stays away from "home" for at least twelve months, but international movement and minimum stay abroad are the only characteristics that migrants share. Migrants cross borders for many reasons, including to escape persecution, to work, to study, or to visit or join family members. Once in destination countries, migrants have a variety of statuses, from naturalized citizen to legal immigrant to irregular migrant. The international community has long recognized that workers away from home can be vulnerable to abuse, and has developed standards to protect them. For example, in postwar Europe, uneven economic growth promoted labor migration from south to north, and the International Labor Organization (ILO)'s Convention 97 (1949) outlined protections for the "migrant for employment," defined as "a person who migrates from one country to another with a view to being employed otherwise than on his own account." The document established the fundamental principle in most migrant conventions—equality of treatment, meaning that migrant workers are to be treated like other workers in the countries in which they work.[2]

FACTORS MOTIVATING MIGRATION

Migration is as old as humankind wandering in search of food, but international migration across regulated national borders is a relatively recent development, since it was only in the early twentieth century that the system of nation-states, passports, and visas developed to regulate the international flow of people (Torpey, 1999). Because of inertia, controls, and hopes for improvement and opportunity at home, long-distance international migration is the rarest type of movement. Inertia is the number one form of migration control simply because most people do not want to move away from family and friends. Governments have significant capacity to regulate migration, and they do, requiring passports and visas from visitors and establishing border controls to determine who enters and remains. Historical experience, such as European migration to the Americas, or the contemporary conditions in Ireland, Italy,

Spain, and South Korea, demonstrate that the migration transition can turn a country from an emigration to an immigration area with just a few decades of rapid economic growth.

Migration responds to differences, and two major categories of differences prompt people to move: economic and noneconomic (Massey et al., 1998). The factors that encourage a migrant to cross borders can usually be grouped into three categories: demand-pull in destination areas, supply-push in origin areas, and network factors that link them (see Table 1.2). This framework makes it possible to distinguish economic migrants who are encouraged to migrate because of a demand for their labor abroad from noneconomic migrants who cross borders to join family members settled abroad. A person in rural Mexico, for example, may be recruited to work in U.S. agriculture by a recruiter who offers a job, a demand-pull factor.[3] The potential migrant may not have a job at home, or may have failing crops, and thus be willing to move, a supply-push factor. Networks or links across borders help migrants to move, as when a potential migrant obtains information about work and wages in the United States from a previous migrant, decides to migrate from Mexico with the help of a smuggler, and, once in the United States, stays with the family members likely to help him to get a job.

The three types of factors encouraging migration do not usually have equal weights in any individual or family situation, and the importance of each factor can change over time. Generally, demand-pull and supply-push factors are strongest at the start of a migration flow, and network factors become more important as migration streams mature. The first guest workers tend to be re-

Table 1.2. Determinants of Migration: Factors Encouraging an Individual to Migrate

Type of Migrant	Demand-Pull	Supply-Push	Network/Other
Economic	Labor recruitment; e.g., guest workers	Un- or underemployment; low wages; e.g., farmers whose crops fail	Job and wage information flows; e.g., sons following fathers
Noneconomic	Family unification; e.g., family members join spouse	Flight from war and persecution; e.g., displaced persons and refugees/asylum seekers	Communications; transportation; assistance organizations; desire for new experience/adventure

Note: These examples are illustrative. Individuals contemplating migration may be encouraged to move by all three factors. The importance of pull, push, and network factors can change over time.

cruited, often in rural areas where unemployment and underemployment are high. But after some migrants return to their areas of origin with savings, network factors may become more important in sustaining migration, so that even employed workers in a mature migration stream, such as Mexico to the United States, may leave their jobs to earn higher U.S. wages (Zahnheiser, 1999).

The number of foreign workers often becomes larger than planned. For example, after Taiwanese construction firms requested foreign workers for high-priority national infrastructure projects, the government in October 1989 approved the entry of forty-four thousand foreign construction workers. The ceiling was gradually raised, manufacturing and private households were permitted to employ migrants, and now there are more than three hundred thousand foreign workers in Taiwan. Joseph Lee (2004, 4) explains: "The purpose of importing foreign workers, as set by the government, was strictly to relieve the labor shortage in the construction and labor-intensive industries." As other industries requested and won permission to recruit and employ migrants, the "need" for migrants expanded, and their number grew larger than anticipated.

Family unification is the most important noneconomic factor encouraging migration. Pioneer migrants go abroad and, if they find jobs and supportive employers, many migrants have their families join them. The migration literature often uses a nautical metaphor to explain family unification: a pioneer becomes an anchor migrant who sends for family members, producing follow-on chain migration. Most European countries allow family unification for legal foreign residents who have been residents at least a year and can support the family members they wish to have join them. The United States, by contrast, has a complex family unification system. On the one hand this system has a broader concept of family, allowing grandparents as well as adult sons and daughters and adult brothers and sisters of U.S. citizen residents to obtain immigrant visas, but on the other hand it limits the number of such visas available, so that the wait for family unification visas can be, in extreme cases, a decade or more.

Refugees and asylum seekers also move for noneconomic reasons. Refugees are persons outside their countries of citizenship who are unable or unwilling to return because they face persecution.[4] They often stay in camps near their countries of origin until the situation in their home countries changes or until they are resettled in another country. Asylum seekers arrive in a country and ask to be recognized as refugees: if they are so recognized, they are usually allowed to resettle in the country and begin their lives anew. Most asylum applicants are not found to be in need of protection, but many nonetheless stay, especially in western Europe. A U.N. agency, the United Nations High Commissioner for Refugees, issues an annual report on refugees, and in 2003 the agency reported that there were 9.7 million refugees and an additional 7.4 million persons of concern, such as recently returned refugees, asylum applicants, and internally displaced persons.

International migration is a result of demographic, economic, and other differences between countries. These differences are widening, promising more international migration in the twenty-first century. Demographic trends provide an example. The world's population reached six billion in October 1999 and is growing by 1.4 percent, or eighty-four million, per year, with 97 percent of global population growth in developing countries.[5] Population density varies greatly but is higher in developing than in developed countries—51 persons per square kilometer in low- and middle-income countries versus 29 in the high-income countries. Will people move from more–densely to less–densely populated places in the twenty-first century, much as the nineteenth century was marked by migration from more–densely populated Europe to the Americas and Oceania?

A comparison of the demographic evolution of Europe and Africa is instructive. In 1800 Europe had about 20 percent of the world's one billion people and Africa 8 percent. In 2000 the populations of these two continents were almost equal—Europe had 728 million residents and Africa 800 million, giving each continent 12 to 13 percent of the world's population. If current trends continue, the populations of Europe and Africa will diverge. Europe is projected to shrink to 660 million by 2050, giving it 7 percent of the world's 9 billion residents, while Africa is projected to expand to 1.8 billion, or 20 percent of the world's residents. If history repeats itself, there could be migration from demographically expanding Africa to other parts of the world.

Economic differences between countries are widening, encouraging migration for higher incomes and jobs. The world's gross domestic product (GDP) was $30 trillion in 2000, making the average value of goods and services produced $5,000 per person per year, but there was significant variation: the range was from $100 per person per year in Ethiopia to $38,000 in Switzerland. When countries are grouped by their per capita GDPs, the gap between high-income countries, where per capita GDPs are $9,300 or more per person per year, and low- (below $750 per person per year) and middle-income countries has been widening, with very few low- and middle-income countries climbing into the high-income ranks.[6] In 1975 per capita GDPs in the high-income countries were forty-one times greater than those in low-income countries, and eight times greater than in middle-income countries. A quarter-century later, the per capita GDPs of high-income countries were sixty-six times those in low-income countries and fourteen times those in middle-income countries. Rising per capita income differences help to explain why so many migrants from low- and middle-income countries take big risks to enter high-income countries, sometimes turning to smugglers or buying false documents.

A second dimension to increasing economic differences, poverty among farmers, adds to international migration pressures. Of the world's labor force of 3 billion in 2000, 2.6 billion workers were in the low- and middle-income countries. In low- and middle-income countries, half of the workforce, comprising some 1.3 billion persons, is employed in agriculture, usually as small farmers, and many are taxed despite the fact that farmers have lower than average incomes.[7] Farm-nonfarm income gaps encourage rural-urban migration, helping to explain why the urban share of the population in low- and middle-income countries rose from 32 to 42 percent between 1980 and 2000.

Many industrial countries had a "Great Migration" off the land in the 1950s and 1960s, and similar migrations are under way in many major emigration countries, including China, Mexico, and Turkey. The Great Migration has three implications for international labor migration. First, ex-farmers everywhere are most likely to accept so-called 3-D (dirty, dangerous, difficult) jobs in urban areas, either inside their countries or abroad. This is evident in Chinese coastal cities, where internal rural-urban migrants fill 3-D jobs, and abroad, where Chinese migrants are employed in industries that range from services to sweatshops. Second, farmers leaving agriculture often make physical as well as cultural transitions by moving to cities, and many are willing to go overseas if there is recruitment or a migration infrastructure to help them to cross borders. For example, Turks leaving eastern Turkey or Mexicans leaving southern Mexico may find adaptation in Berlin or Fresno as easy as integration in larger cities within their countries. Third, if rural-urban migrants move to cities within their countries, they get one step closer to the country's exits, since it is usually easiest to obtain visas and documents for legal migration, or to make arrangements for illegal migration, in the cities of developing countries.

Rising demographic and economic differences between countries, combined with rural-urban migration within countries, promise more economically motivated migration. Security and human rights differences add to migration pressures. After the global conflict between capitalism and communism ended in the early 1990s, local conflicts erupted in many areas, leading to separatist movements, new nations, and more migrants, as in the former Yugoslavia and the former Soviet Union. The emergence of new nations is almost always accompanied by migration, as populations are reshuffled so that the "right" people are inside the "right" borders. Governments sometimes send migrants to areas later rent by separatist feelings or movements, and if the area later breaks away and forms a new nation, these migrants and their descendants can become international migrants without moving again, as with Russians who were sent to the Baltics or Indonesians sent to East Timor. After independence, new governments have established rules that in some cases made it difficult for residents born in the country to be considered citizens.

There is also a more mechanical reason for increased international migration: the existence of more nation-states means more international borders to cross. There were 191 generally recognized nation-states in 2000, up from 43 in 1900.[8] As a result, some Africans who continue traditional seasonal migrations, for example, have become international migrants by traversing ex-colonies. The number of new nation-states has increased much faster than the number of regional agreements, such as the European Union (EU), that permit freedom of movement.

Differences encourage migration, but it takes networks or links to persuade people to move. Migration networks are a broad concept and include factors that enable people to learn about opportunities abroad before employing the migration infrastructure that enables migrants to cross national borders, find jobs, and stay abroad (Massey et al., 1998; Waldinger and Lichter, 2003). Networks have been shaped and strengthened by three major revolutions in the past half-century: in communications, in transportation, and in rights. The communications revolution helps potential migrants to learn about opportunities abroad. The best information often comes from migrants established abroad, who can provide family and friends at home with information in a context they understand. Many people in developing countries see movies and television programs produced in high-income countries. Some believe that if they can get into countries with such wealth, they can share it, which is why such television shows as *Dallas* and *Dynasty* may spur migration toward the United States from all corners of the world.[9]

The transportation revolution highlights the declining cost of long-distance travel. British migrants unable to pay passage to the colonies in the eighteenth century often indentured themselves, signing contracts that obliged them to work for three to six years for whomever met the shipping cost and paid the captain for one-way transportation. Transportation costs today are far less, typically less than $2,500 to travel anywhere in the world legally, and $1,000 to $20,000 for unauthorized migration. Most studies suggest that migrants today are able to retire their relocation debts faster than before; even those who paid high smuggling fees can usually repay them within two or three years (Kwong, 1998; Kyle and Koslowski, 2001).

The rights revolution reflects the spread of individual rights and entitlements that allow some foreigners to stay abroad. Many governments have ratified conventions promulgated by the United Nations, the ILO, and other groups that commit them to guarantee basic human rights to all persons within their borders, including due process, emergency health care, and sometimes housing and food while they are awaiting decisions on their applications for asylum. This means that individuals who allege that they face persecution at home are given an opportunity to explain why, and if one judge does not believe them, they may receive benefits while their appeal is pending, a process that can take several years. Most European countries have social safety net programs that provide housing, food, and health care for asylum applicants, making it easier for migrants in Europe to stay there, at least for several years.

There is little that countries experiencing "unwanted immigration" can do in the short term about the demographic, economic, and security differences that promote migration, and they have little power or desire to reverse the communications and transportation revolutions that, as a by-product of connecting people in the global village, inform migrants about opportunities abroad and make it less costly for them to travel. Governments create and enforce rights, and the default policy instrument to manage migration in the 1990s was new or modified legal restriction of the rights of migrants. As noted, many European governments reacted to the influx of asylum seekers by establishing rules that made application for asylum more difficult for some foreigners, such as those who came from "safe" countries or transited safe countries in which they could have sought refuge. Such middle-income countries as Thailand receiving migrants have also adjusted migrant rights in an effort to manage migration, often tolerating the presence of unauthorized migrants in economic booms and stepping up restrictive enforcement during recession.

The challenge and opportunity are to find better ways to manage labor migration, the major type of international migration. The review of global migration patterns and issues in Chapter 2 makes it clear that governments in most countries believe they have a "migration problem," in the sense that many or most of their migrants arrive outside established channels of entry and many are employed outside official programs for foreign workers. The question is whether countries should step up enforcement and other efforts to put migrants into established channels, or whether they should modify or develop new channels to deal with migration realities. There is not likely to be a common response to the gap between migration policies and realities across countries, since each has a different set of circumstances and different expectations about migration.

2 Global Migration Patterns and Issues

Almost all countries participate in the migration system as countries of origin, transit, or destination, and many play all three roles. However, perceptions of migration problems differ markedly between countries (Stalker, 1999). Canada and the United States are classic countries of immigration that have been shaped by newcomers from many countries, and they continue to plan for the arrival and integration of immigrants despite the fact that, in the U.S. case, 30 percent of foreign-born residents are unauthorized. Most European countries, by contrast, are reluctant countries of immigration, accepting the return of people from former colonies and guest workers who settled, but not developing immigration systems that include, for example, applications to immigrate on the Internet (Weiner, 1995).

Asia was a relative latecomer to labor migration. Many Asian nations sent migrants to the Middle East after oil prices rose in the 1970s, and later to other Asian nations as guest workers and trainees. Several Asian countries sent mostly female migrants abroad, such as Filipinos, Indonesians, and Sri Lankans who work as domestic helpers in such Persian Gulf countries as Kuwait and Saudi Arabia. The Middle East is also a special case, with migrants constituting 70 to 90 percent of private sector workers in most oil-exporting countries. As a result, many of the Gulf oil-exporting nations have tried—so far with limited success—to "nationalize" their workforces by prohibiting the employment of migrants in particular industries and occupations.

Africa has long been associated with seasonal labor migration across borders drawn by colonial powers, but nationalism has sharpened differences between natives and migrants in some of the relatively richer countries that receive migrants, such as the Ivory Coast and South Africa. Africa, which has an eighth of the world's people and a quarter of the world's refugees, has witnessed several dramatic and large-scale refugee movements, as in the Great Lakes region in the mid-1990s and in western Sudan in 2004.

In previous centuries Latin America and the Caribbean islands received settlers and slaves, who intermixed with native peoples. Most Latin American countries today are emigration areas, and some have large percentages of their natives abroad. About 20 percent of those born in El Salvador, for example, are in the United States, and 10 to 20 percent of those born in the Caribbean countries of Cuba, the Dominican Republic, and Jamaica have emigrated. There is migration between Latin American countries, as from Haiti to Dominican Republic, but in South America economic troubles have redirected much of the labor migration that took Bolivians to Argentina and Colombians to Venezuela; migrants from both sending and receiving countries in South America now migrate to Europe and North America. Oceania includes the traditional immigration countries Australia and New Zealand as well as Pacific islands, many of which face unique immigration, economic, and environmental issues.

MIGRATION IN EUROPE

Most European societies were shaped by emigration to the Americas—about sixty million Europeans emigrated between 1820 and 1914.[1] During this great Atlantic migration, there was also significant migration from east to west within Europe, as from Poland to Germany. Two world wars led to the creation of new nation-states, and to the subsequent exchange of people who wound up in the "wrong" country when borders were redrawn, as exemplified by the exchange of Greeks and Turks in the 1920s and the migration of ethnic Germans to West Germany after World War II.

Some economically motivated migration after World War II was from rural to urban areas within a European country, and some took migrants from territories and colonies to the home country, such as from Algeria to France, or from India and Pakistan to the United Kingdom (Castles and Miller, 2003, 73–4). More than 600,000 Algerians lived in France by 1970, and thousands more moved to "metropolitan France" as French citizens from west Africa and other overseas departments and territories before these became independent, leaving no data on their movement. London Transport recruited workers from Commonwealth nations in the Caribbean and South Asia, and there were more than 500,000 new Commonwealth migrants in the United Kingdom by the early 1960s. The Netherlands received "repatriates" from its Indonesian territories as well as from Suriname in South America.

Many of the movements from colonies to the mother country were economically motivated, and so were the guest worker flows that soon dominated migration from former colonies. Rapid postwar recovery in northern European countries that did not have colonies, including Germany, Switzerland, and the Scandinavian countries, prompted the recruitment of guest workers in southern Europe, where economic recovery was slower. Most governments that launched guest worker programs assumed that Yugoslav and Turkish workers would rotate in and out of their labor markets, working for a year or two and then returning home to be replaced by other migrants if guest workers were still needed. However, most guest workers were in fact probationary immigrants, entitled to unify their families if their Dutch or German employers requested that their initial one-year work and residence permits be renewed. The attraction of having their work permits renewed and thereby gaining the right to have family members with them gave migrants a powerful incentive to satisfy employers.

Most guest workers returned home after a year or two as assumed by the rotation model that European governments embraced, but many settled and unified their families, giving European countries populations and labor forces that today include 5 to 10 percent foreigners. Even though 1960s guest workers were primarily men, foreign populations today are more evenly balanced between men and women as a result of family unification and births to settled migrants. In 2001 there were about 21 million foreigners in the major western European countries, and half were in the labor force. The percentage of foreign residents was highest in Luxembourg, which has only 500,000 residents, fewer than a medium-sized city, and varies from under 3 percent in Italy and Spain to 20 percent in Switzerland.

Today, foreign worker shares of the labor force are similar to foreign resident shares of the population. However, during the guest worker era of the 1960s,

Table 2.1. Foreigners and Foreign Workers in Western Europe, 2001

	Population (in millions)		Labor Force (in thousands)	
	Total	Foreign (%)	Total	Foreign (%)
Austria	8.132	0.764 (9.4%)	3,940	387 (9.8%)
Belgium	10.226	0.847 (8.3%)	4,448	357 (8.0%)
Denmark	5.359	0.267 (5.00%)	2,862	104 (3.6%)
France	59.188	3.263 (5.50%)	26,967	1,612 (6.0%)
Germany	81.351	7.319 (9.00%)	39,690	3,511 (8.8%)
Ireland	3.839	0.151 (3.90%)	1,782	101 (5.7)
Italy	57.348	1.363 (2.40%)	23,901	801 (3.4%)
Luxembourg	0.443	0.167 (37.70%)	282	83 (29.4%)
Netherlands	15.987	0.690 (4.30%)	8,150	295 (3.6%)
Norway	4.514	0.186 (4.10%)	2,361	80 (3.4%)
Spain	40.266	1.109 (2.80%)	17,854	490 (2.7%)
Sweden	8.896	0.476 (5.40%)	4,465	205 (4.6%)
Switzerland	7.233	1.419 (19.60%)	4,262	864 (20.3%)
U.K.	59.756	2.587 (4.30%)	29,470	1,406 (4.8%)
Total	362.538	20.608 (8.70%)	170,434	10,296 (8.2%)

Source: OECD. Trends in International Migration, 2003 (SOPEMI). Paris. Pp. 44, 50.

almost all of the foreigners living in European countries were in the labor force, since it was only by being employed that foreigners could enter these mostly nonimmigration countries. There are several special countries. In Luxembourg, many of the foreign residents are not foreign workers, and the foreign share of the population is larger than the foreign share of the workforce. Countries with relatively large shares of seasonal foreign workers, including Austria and Italy, have foreign worker shares that are higher than their foreign resident shares (see Table 2.1).

Foreign populations in Europe cannot be compared directly with the foreign-born share of the population or labor force in countries shaped by immigration, such as Canada and the United States. Many European countries report data by citizenship, and some allow citizenship to be conferred by blood, not place of birth. This means that there can be "second-generation" foreigners in many European countries, but not in Canada or the United States. For example, almost 20 percent of the "foreigners" in Germany were born in Germany.[2] On the other hand, Germany considers ethnic Germans—persons born in eastern Europe and the former Soviet Union who have German parents or grandparents—to be Germans, so the three million ethnic Germans who moved to Germany in the 1980s and 1990s are not considered to be immigrants, even though they were born outside Germany and in many cases do not speak German.

The economic impacts of foreigners and foreign workers are often debated in Europe and are kept in the news by high unemployment rates and high rates of dependence on social assistance. During the peak years of guest worker recruitment, 1961–1973, foreign workers were generally considered an economic plus for receiving countries, and they simultaneously served the political goal of accelerating economic integration within the European Economic Community (EEC; European Union after 1993). Unemployment in the northern countries such as Germany that recruited guest workers on behalf of their labor-short employers was very low—the number of vacant jobs often exceeded the number of unemployed workers—and undervalued European currencies in a world of fixed exchange rates encouraged investment of domestic and foreign capital in France, Germany, and other European countries in order to create more jobs in manufacturing goods for domestic consumption and export markets (Schiller et al., 1967). It seemed impossible to get more workers locally in the 1960s because the Great Migration off the land was largely completed, a baby boom made it hard to raise female labor force participation rates, and the expansion of education and retirement systems delayed the labor force entry of some young workers and encouraged the retirement of older workers.

Recruiting workers in southern Europe, where a labor surplus prevailed, seemed to make eminent economic and political sense (Kindleberger, 1967). If unemployed Italians, Greeks, and Turks migrated north, unemployment would be reduced, and the remittances from migrants abroad would provide the capital needed for economic development and job creation in southern Europe. Returning migrants with training and experience would be the productive factory workers needed to accelerate development in this mutual benefits of labor migration scenario.

Migration realities were different. During the 1966–1967 recession, when most migrants had just arrived, the rotation model functioned as expected. Laid-off migrants hoping to wait out the recession returned home, where living costs were cheaper, keeping the unemployment rate lower than it would otherwise have been in northern Europe (Martin, 2004). However, the oil crisis of 1973–1974 largely stopped the recruitment of additional guest workers from outside the EEC (EU), as many governments worried about a creeping structural dependence on migrant workers, and the decade after the end of recruitment was marked by guest workers unifying their families, which most had the right to do.

This time migrants did not return home, since unemployment also had risen in their countries of origin, and they feared that if they returned home, they would be unable to migrate again to richer countries to work. Countries such as France and Germany encouraged returns by offering departure bonus payments and discouraged family unification by prohibiting spouses from working for several years after arrival, but this effort to prevent family unification and settlement largely failed to inspire large-scale returns. In 1973, 65 percent of the foreigners in Germany were in the labor force; by 1983, only 38 percent were (see Figure 2.1).

The 1980s were marked by often contradictory efforts to deal with the settlement of foreign workers and their families (Martin, 2004). For example, German leaders insisted that Germany was not a country of immigration, and that foreigners should be encouraged to return to their countries of origin, but simultaneously pledged to integrate those who decided to stay. Debates over what to do about the growing number of foreign children in school reflected similar contradictions: some schools taught children in their parents' language to ease their integration into home countries anticipating return, while others taught in the host country's language to ease the transition from school to work, anticipating settlement. Immigration problems were met with ad hoc fixes. For example, when there was an upsurge in asylum applicants from Turkey after a military coup in the early 1980s, Germany and other countries with established Turkish populations found an easy remedy—require Turks to obtain visas to travel to Germany—and the problem seemed to be solved.

The fall of the Berlin Wall in 1989 unleashed a new wave of east-west migration. This migration, often economically motivated but reflected in an upsurge of asylum seekers, contributed to the perception that migrants were arriving not to work but to take advantage of generous social safety nets. By 1992, more than one thousand foreigners a day were applying for asylum in Germany. Although 80–90 percent of the asylum applications were ultimately rejected, from the time they applied until their cases were decided, they were entitled to housing, food, and pocket money that were paid for by local taxpayers. The German government distributed asylum applicants around the country, and many cities had asylum homes in which young men prohibited from working stood around drinking beer, a perfect recipe for an antimigrant backlash.

Meanwhile, the unemployment rates of foreigners often were twice those of native workers, and second- and third-generation foreigners educated in

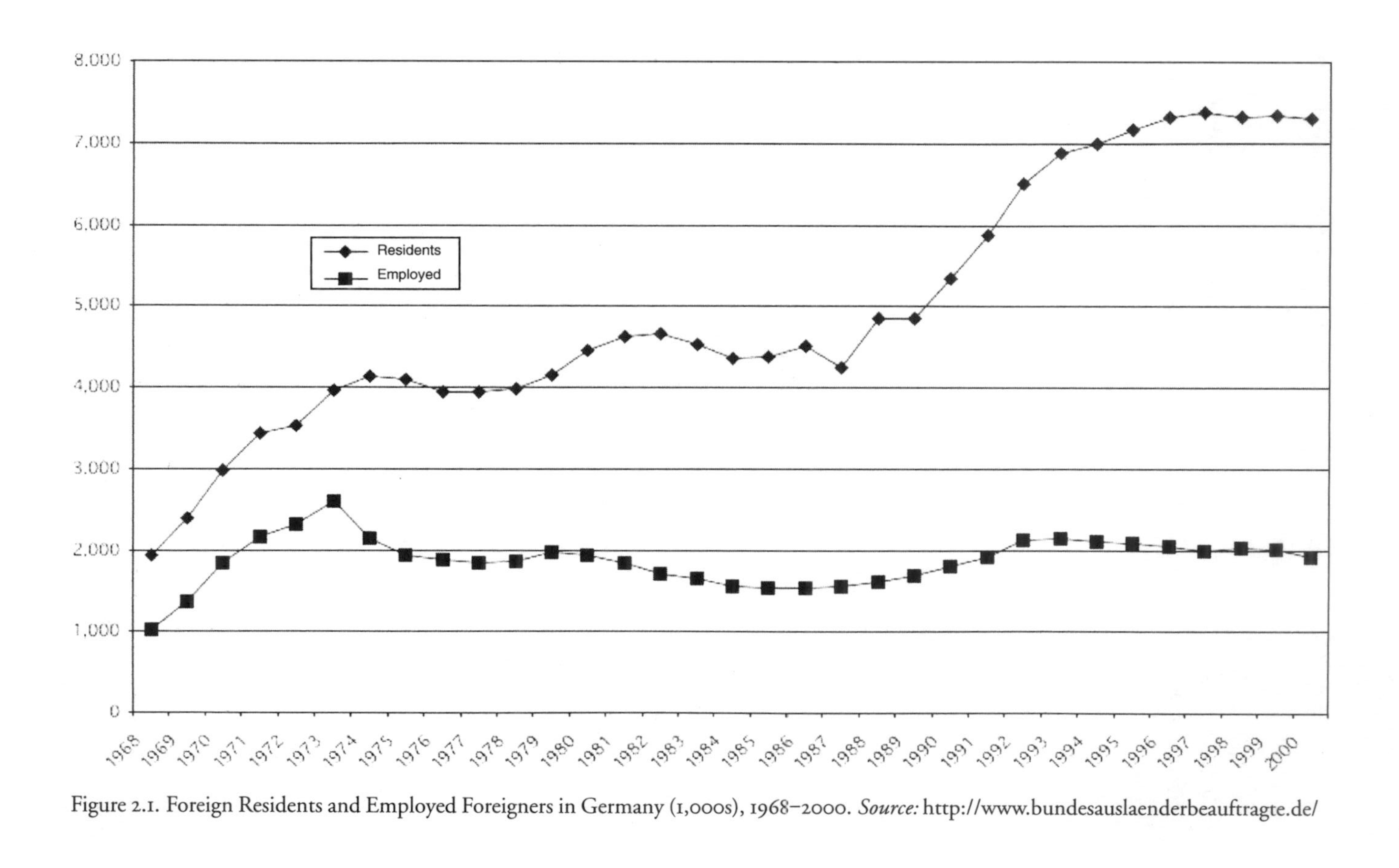

Figure 2.1. Foreign Residents and Employed Foreigners in Germany (1,000s), 1968–2000. *Source:* http://www.bundesauslaenderbeauftragte.de/

France, Germany, and the Netherlands were having trouble finding jobs. Migrant advocates argued that the problems of foreigners were due to discrimination and urged governments to introduce affirmative action and similar efforts to help migrants find and keep good jobs. Anti-immigrant politicians, on the other hand, argued that unemployed foreigners and those who committed crimes should be expelled.

The sense that many foreigners have arrived to take advantage of generous host societies and that those who have settled may be a potential threat because they are not well integrated into the host culture has produced a curious debate in twenty-first-century Europe. Many European leaders believe that immigration is needed to prevent populations and labor forces from declining, and to avoid having to make drastic cuts in social security systems that depend on having current workers support retirees.

However, immigration would have to increase massively to stabilize populations, labor forces, and social security systems, a difficult prospect because of incomplete integration of current migrants. The United Nations projected the immigration levels that would be necessary to avoid population declines, to maintain the working age population, and to maintain the ratio of fifteen- to sixty-four-year-olds to residents sixty-five and older. Using 1995 as the base year, when the Big Four EU countries—France, Germany, Italy, and the United Kingdom—had two-thirds of EU residents and received about 88 percent of EU immigrants, the United Nations projected that if these four countries were to maintain their 1995 populations at current fertility rates, they would have to almost triple immigration levels, from 237,000 a year to 677,000 a year, with the greatest increase required in Italy. To maintain their 1995 labor forces the Big Four would have to increase immigration to 1.1 million a year. In order to "save social security"—maintain the ratio of persons fifteen to sixty-four years old to persons sixty-five and older—they would have to increase immigration thirty-sevenfold, to almost 9 million a year (see Table 2.2).

Most Europeans do not want more immigration, and certainly not levels of immigration that could remake them in a relatively short time. To illustrate the opposition to more migration, it is instructive to see how the established EU-15 countries dealt with the accession of ten eastern European countries on May 1, 2004. Countries such as Poland and Hungary have lower wages and higher unemployment rates than Germany and Austria, but studies of potential migration from the accession countries projected only modest additional migration—one projected that an additional 335,000 workers might migrate west the first year, with the number of migrants shrinking to 160,000 a year by

Table 2.2. Immigration Required to Avoid Population Decline, 2000–2050

	Immigration (in thousands)			
	Actual 1995	Needed to Maintain 1995 Population[a]	Needed to Maintain 1995 Working-Age Population[a]	Needed to Maintain 1995 Population Support Ratio[ab]
EU (15 countries)	270	949 (4)	1,588 (6)	13,480 (50)
Big 4 EU	237	677 (3)	1,093 (5)	8,884 (37)
France	7	29 (4)	109 (16)	1,792 (256)
Germany	204	344 (2)	487 (2)	3,630 (18)
Italy	6	251 (42)	372 (62)	2,268 (378)
United Kingdom	20	53 (3)	125 (6)	1,194 (60)
Other EU	33	272 (8)	495 (15)	4,596 (139)
United States	760	128 (0.2)	359 (0.5)	11,851 (16)

[a]Figure in parentheses represents multiple of 1995 immigration.
[b]Ratio of persons ages 15–64 to those ages 65 or older.
Source: United Nations, "Replacement Migration: Is It a Solution to Declining and Aging Population?"

2010.[3] This was too much migration for most of the EU-15. They insisted on a seven-year transition period during which individual countries cannot block the travel of Poles and Hungarians west: freedom of travel is guaranteed to EU nationals, but freedom of movement for employment can be delayed for up to seven years after entry.

Fear of too much migration is a key factor in the ambivalence many Europeans feel toward the prospect of Turkey's joining the EU. The European Union plans to add more member nations, expanding from the current twenty-five to perhaps thirty or thirty-five, and was scheduled to begin accession negotiations with Turkey in fall 2005. Turkey occupies a unique position: its territory lies mostly in Asia and, historically, Turkey has served as both a barrier and a bridge between Europe and Asia (Teitelbaum and Martin, 2003). If Turkey were admitted to the EU, it would be the largest country in land area and the second-largest after Germany in terms of population. Turks in the past proved eager to migrate for employment—more than a million were on waiting lists to go to Europe as guest workers in 1973, when recruitment was stopped—and many Europeans fear that if Turks had freedom of movement rights, Europe would be overrun by migrants. Interviews with Turks in the late 1980s, when an earlier application by Turkey for EU membership was rebuffed, suggested that perhaps 20 percent of Turks might migrate to try for jobs in Europe, double the 10 percent who migrated between 1963 and 1973 (Martin, 1991).

Despite popular opposition to increased immigration, several European countries have taken steps to open doors to migrants, especially highly skilled professionals. During the high-tech economic boom of the late 1990s, many European employers complained of shortages of computer programmers, and governments in France, Germany, and other European countries responded with new programs to facilitate the entry of non-EU computer professionals, or eased rules to allow foreign students who graduated from local universities to remain and work. For example, in response to employer assertions that there was a shortage of seventy-five thousand information technology (IT) workers, the German government approved a "green card" program that offered up to twenty thousand five-year work permits to non-EU computer professionals who were paid at least DM100,000 ($45,000) a year.[4]

The number of green cards issued was far less than expected, but the green card program did help to change the tenor of the immigration debate in Germany by emphasizing that immigrants can benefit Germans as well as themselves. The political parties that dominated the government between 1982 and 1998—the Christian Democratic Union and the Christian Social Union

(CDU-CSU)—had insisted that "Deutschland ist kein Einwanderungsland," Germany is not a country of immigration. They were replaced by a Social Democratic Party–Green coalition government in 1998 that made opening Germany to immigrants one of its top domestic priorities. An independent commission urged an immigration system in its July 2001 report and also recommended new steps to encourage the integration of settled foreigners into Germany. The SPD-Green government got a bill incorporating the commission's recommendations through Parliament in 2002, but the procedure by which the upper house approved the bill was later found to be unconstitutional.

The SPD-Green government in mid-2004 compromised with the opposition on Germany's first law that anticipates the arrival and settlement of foreigners. Beginning in 2005, foreigners who are under forty-five and invest at least one million euros and create at least ten jobs, as well as scientists and professionals earning at least E84,000 a year, can immigrate. Foreign students graduating from German universities can stay in Germany for one year and, if they find a job, receive a residence and work permit. The integration side of the law requires settled foreigners who are unemployed and dependent on social assistance to take steps to learn German.[5] For example, unemployed foreign residents in Germany less than six years can be ordered to leave if they do not enroll in and pass a course of three hundred hours in basic German and German law and culture.

Even as countries such as Germany and the United Kingdom develop immigration policies that reflect domestic concerns, the EU is developing policies to strengthen cooperation between member states to prevent illegal migration and to handle asylum seekers. The EU divides public policy issues into three areas or pillars: first-pillar issues are those for which the EU takes the lead in establishing policy, such as agriculture; second-pillar issues are those on which national governments take the lead, such as defense; and third-pillar issues are those for which the EU coordinates efforts to harmonize national policies, such as in immigration and asylum.

The EU has discussed migration issues repeatedly, and progress toward a unionwide migration policy can be seen as a glass half-full or half-empty. On the one hand, the EU developed the so-called Schengen agreement, signed in 1985 and in force since 1995, to establish a single external border around member countries, coordinate visa issuance policies, and maintain a database accessible to border control officers. A Spanish consulate may issue a "Schengen visa" to a Colombian headed to Germany, French authorities may check the

Colombian in Paris as she changes flights, but the Colombian arrives in Germany without ever being checked by German immigration officials. The Schengen agreement should eventually lead to a United States of Europe in which crossing national borders within the EU will be as free of controls as traveling between U.S. states.

The EU is also attempting to coordinate the asylum policies of member states. The 1951 Geneva Convention defines a refugee as a person who, "owing to a well-founded fear of being persecuted for reasons of race, religion, nationality, membership in a particular social group, or political opinion, is outside the country of his nationality, and is unable to, or owing to such fear, is unwilling to avail himself of the protection of that country." In most European countries, a foreigner applying for asylum is given a chance to explain to authorities why he faces persecution at home and to appeal a negative decision; the goal is to ensure that foreigners are not returned to persecution, which was the fate, for example, of some of those trying to escape the Nazis. While asylum applicants await the first and appeal decisions, most European countries offer them housing and food, but most do not allow them to work.

When the number of asylum applications skyrocketed, many governments complained of "compassion fatigue," and most took steps to limit and streamline the asylum application and adjudication process. EU leaders meeting in Dublin agreed to establish minimum standards for dealing with asylum seekers, to make one EU country's decision on the need for asylum binding on other EU countries, and to establish a system for determining which country is responsible for dealing with a particular asylum applicant. In line with the Dublin Convention of 1990, the EU established a database to fingerprint asylum applicants, so that government officials can quickly check and see whether the applicant already has applied in another country, and the union developed a fund to assist countries that receive large numbers of applicants.[6] However, EU leaders cannot agree on whether asylum applicants should be sent to safe camps outside the EU near their countries of origin, or whether to link foreign aid to cooperation in dealing with migration.[7]

Optimists surveying the Schengen and Dublin agreements emphasize how much coordination the EU has fostered between national governments on migration issues, with most governments now accepting that the EU will take the lead in migration policy development. The 1997 Treaty of Amsterdam called for common EU migration and asylum policies by 2004 and laid out a procedure under which majority voting would replace the need for unanimity on migration policy decisions, so that single countries no longer can block EU-wide migration decisions.[8] Many EU leaders expect the EU soon to develop immigration rules and set an annual quota, thus imitating the U.S. system of opening doors for family unification, employment, and other immigrants.

Pessimists emphasize that there are still frequent disputes between EU member countries on migration issues, as during 2001–2002, when France allowed a center for migrants to be opened in an old warehouse used to store equipment to build the Eurotunnel under the English Channel. Every night, hundreds of migrants from the camp cut or scaled fences that protected the trains headed to England and attempted to slip onto them in order to apply for asylum in Dover. The British asked the French government to close the camp at Sangatte, while the French advised the British to revise policies that gave asylum applicants housing, food, and pocket money. The camp was finally closed in November 2002, but the Red Cross estimated that forty-two thousand of the fifty thousand people who passed through Sangatte made it to England.[9]

Europe, the source of most of the world's migrants in the nineteenth century, appears likely to be a major destination for migrants in the twenty-first century. Most European leaders welcome the prospect of more migration and see the challenge as one of persuading aging voters to accept the need for newcomers. Sweden's Prime Minister Goran Persson said, "[We need] to persuade the voters that economic migration will be a prerequisite for welfare and wealth—that they [migrants] will contribute, not be a burden."[10] However, with unemployment rates for foreigners double or triple natives' rates, and with elderly voters often resisting the changes that accompany migration, opening Europe to immigration runs the risk that anti-immigrant politicians could come to power or at least scare established politicians, as have Jean-Marie Le Pen's National Front party in France or the List Pim Fortuyn party in the Netherlands.[11]

MIGRATION IN NORTH AMERICA

The North American migration system includes the world's major emigration and immigration destinations, whether defined in volume terms (migration between Mexico and the United States averaged 230,000 legal immigrants a year in the 1990s, plus 300,000 unauthorized settlers) or in per capita terms (between 10 and 20 percent of persons born in the Dominican Republic and El Salvador have emigrated, and Canada aims to increase its population by 1 percent a year via immigration). Migration in North America has demographic and economic impacts in both sending and receiving areas. For example, Canada and the United States have some of the fastest-growing populations among industrial countries, and many of the Latin American and Caribbean countries are very dependent on remittances from their nationals abroad.

Canadian Policy

Canada admitted 229,000 immigrants in 2002, when it had 31 million residents, and is one of the few countries receiving fewer immigrants than desired. Then–Prime Minister Jean Chretien in July 2002 said: "The population is not growing as fast as it should. And it's why we have a very open immigration policy. And we're working to reform it. Because we don't achieve as many immigrants as we would like to have in the Canadian economy."

Canada has three major avenues of entry for legal immigrants: economic or independent skilled workers, 56 percent of the flow in 2000; family unification, 31 percent; and refugees, 13 percent.[12] The leading countries of origin of Canadian immigrants were China, 15 percent of immigrants; India, 9 percent; and Pakistan and the Philippines, 5 percent each. About three-fourths of immigrants to Canada settle in three cities—Toronto, Montreal, and Vancouver.

Canada's Immigration Act of 1976 established a point system to select economic or independent immigrants. As revised in 2003, it assesses potential immigrants against six criteria on which applicants must score at least 67 points (out of a maximum of 100) to be granted an immigrant visa. For example, language skills (knowing English and/or French) can earn an applicant a maximum 24 points, while education beyond a bachelor's degree can earn a potential immigrant up to 25 points. An additional educational training factor is worth up to 21 points.[13]

Canadian public opinion suggests more satisfaction with migration than in almost any other industrial country, but migration policies are nonetheless changing. Perhaps the biggest change is in the administration of the program. In the United States the federal government decides who has priority to immigrate, but in Canada provinces can sign agreements with the federal government that give them authority to select at least some of their immigrants. Quebec has long selected immigrants wanting to join its French-speaking community, and the sparsely populated midwestern and Atlantic provinces have also begun to look to immigrants as a way to stabilize their populations.

A second issue is the economic integration of immigrants. All countries want their newcomers to find jobs, earn money, and pay taxes. Many immigrants begin their new lives abroad with lower-than-average incomes, but the extra drive and ambition that persuaded them to migrate usually help them to catch up to comparable native-born persons within ten to fifteen years. This catch-up pattern has become less common with recent immigrants to Canada, such that in 2000, 38 percent of the immigrants who had been in Canada less than five years had incomes below the poverty line. Some research suggests that structural changes in labor markets are making it harder for newcomers to climb the job and earnings ladder and, if the declining economic success of immigrants persists, there may be a reduction in the immigration target of 1 percent a year (Beach et al., 2003).

U.S. Policy

The United States is a nation of immigrants with the motto "e pluribus unum"—from many, one—a reminder that Americans share the experience of having left another country to begin anew in the United States, or of having forebears who did so.[14] Most Americans believe that immigration is in the national interest, and this belief did not change after the September 11, 2001, terrorism attacks, as political leaders consistently drew a distinction between immigrants and terrorists. During the 1990s, more than twelve million newcomers—legal and illegal—settled in the United States, a number that exceeded the ten million who arrived during the first decade of the twentieth century (Martin and Midgley, 2003).

Immigration has economic costs as well as benefits, and these costs have become the focus of often contentious debates, symbolized by Proposition 187 in California, a voter-approved proposal in 1994 to develop a state-funded system to attempt to prevent unauthorized foreigners from receiving state-funded services. Even though Proposition 187 was never implemented, it set the stage for federal restrictions on the access of immigrants to welfare benefits in 1996 (Smith and Edmonston, 1997).[15] During the economic boom of the late 1990s, immigration faded from the headlines, and the access of some legal immigrants to welfare assistance was restored.

The 1990s economic boom and changes in federal policies led to a short-lived tripling of the number of foreign professionals admitted to the United States with so-called H-1B visas and encouraged employers of less-skilled and often unauthorized foreign workers also to demand easier access to what they termed "essential workers." During the spring and summer of 2001, frequent meetings between Mexican President Vicente Fox and U.S. President George Bush kept migration issues in the headlines, and there were expectations as late as September 10, 2001, that Bush would propose new legalization and guest worker programs. Bush announced principles that were to guide negotiations for new ways of managing Mexico-U.S. migration: "The huge majority of

Mexicans among us are hard-working people who contribute to our communities and economy, and simply want the best for their families. . . . Mexico wants to make migration a positive contributor to its development, a source of prosperity for Mexican families, new skills and fresh entrepreneurial spirit. We want Mexico to succeed. It is in our national interest for Mexico to succeed."[16]

The September 11, 2001, attacks stalled Mexico-U.S. migration discussions and set the stage instead for new laws to record the entries and exits of foreigners and to track those who arrived to study in the United States. There was little enthusiasm in Congress for a new legalization program, but President Bush in January 2004 proposed that unauthorized immigrants with U.S. employers be allowed to become guest workers for up to six years. However, no legislation was introduced, and skeptics said that Bush was attempting to curry favor with Hispanic voters before November 2004 elections. Democrats endorsed plans that would allow unauthorized foreigners who have been in the United States at least five years and who are employed and have paid taxes to become legal immigrants.

In his February 2005 state of the union address, Bush reopened the discussion of what to do about ten million unauthorized foreigners, 60 percent Mexican: "America's immigration system is also outdated—unsuited to the needs of our economy and to the values of our country. We should not be content with laws that punish hard-working people who want only to provide for their families, and deny businesses willing workers, and invite chaos at our border. It is time for an immigration policy that permits temporary guest workers to fill jobs Americans will not take, that rejects amnesty, that tells us who is entering and leaving our country, and that closes the border to drug dealers and terrorists."

FRONT, SIDE, AND BACK DOORS

Immigrant-receiving countries such as the United States categorize newcomers by their entry door and status, and the United States has three major doors: the front door for legal immigrants, the side door for nonimmigrants in the country for a specific time and purpose, such as tourism or study, and the back door for unauthorized foreigners. Most immigrants do not arrive via the front door from abroad; instead, most are in the United States via the side door and adjust their status—from, for example, student to immigrant.

There are four major types of immigrants. The largest group includes relatives of U.S. residents, and 675,000, or 63 percent, of immigrants admitted in fiscal year (FY) 2001 had family members in the United States who petitioned the U.S. government to admit them. The second-largest category are employ-

Table 2.3. Persons Entering the United States, Fiscal Year 2001

Category	Number of Persons
Immigrants	1,064,318
Immediate relatives of U.S. citizens	443,035
Other family-sponsored immigrants	232,143
Employment-based	179,195
Refugees and aslyees	108,506
Diversity immigrants	42,015
Other immigrants	59,424
Nonimmigrants	32,824,088
Visitors for pleasure/business	29,419,601
Foreign students	688,970
Temporary foreign workers	990,708
Illegal immigration	
Apprehensions	1,387,486
Deportations	176,984
Estimated illegal population (2000)	7,000,000
Additional illegal settlers per year (1990–2000)	350,000

Source: Immigration and Naturalization Service, 2001 Statistical Yearbook. www.ins.usdoj.gov/graphics/aboutins/statistics/2000ExecSumm.pdf

ment-based immigrants, 179,000 foreigners and their families in FY 2001. U.S. employers requested them because they were outstanding scientists and professionals, or they were admitted because they made investments in the United States that created or preserved jobs. The third group includes refugees and asylum seekers, 108,000 in 2001, and the fourth includes diversity immigrants and others (see Table 2.3).[17]

Side-door nonimmigrants come to the United States to visit, work, or study. The number of nonimmigrants tripled in the past twenty years, primarily because of the growing number of tourists and business visitors, but nonimmigrants also include foreigners who are working temporarily in the United States. There were almost one million admissions of temporary foreign workers in FY2001, and 40 percent were professionals with at least a college degree who were admitted with H-1B visas, which allow up to six years in the United States and permit adjustment from worker to immigrant status.

Half of the H-1B visa holders are from India, and many are computer programmers, a circumstance that prompted a debate over whether U.S. employers preferred Indian computer workers because they were nonimmigrants subject to removal from the United States if they lost their jobs. Employers argued that U.S. colleges and universities do not produce sufficient scientists and engineers, and that employers need easy access to the "best and brightest" of the world's talent to be globally competitive. Critics counter that there is no shortage of Americans interested in computer jobs, only a shortage of Americans willing to work long hours for relatively low wages and short careers in the fast-changing computer industry. Almost all students graduating from U.S. universities with bachelor's degrees in science and math are U.S. citizens, but most do not pursue advanced degrees because they do not find the resulting extra earnings and opportunities sufficient to warrant the trouble and expense. Foreigners with advanced degrees, by contrast, sometimes see the H-1B visa as the first step toward an immigrant visa (Teitelbaum, 2003).

Another important category of nonimmigrants comprises foreign students, whose number has increased faster than total enrollment, so that foreign students now make up about 5 percent of the U.S. college and university student population. The number of foreign students rose slightly to 586,000 in the year after the September 11, 2001, terrorist attacks, while the total number of students in U.S. higher education fell slightly to almost 13 million with the improving economy (see Table 2.4).[18] The share of foreign students is highest in graduate programs, about 13 percent, and foreign students receive between 25 and 50 percent of the doctorates awarded in engineering and the physical and life sciences.

The September 11 attacks slowed the growth of foreign student enrollment and shifted the origins of foreign students, increasing the number from India, China, and South Korea and reducing the number from Muslim nations, although it should be emphasized that there were well-publicized difficulties encountered by foreign students seeking student visas in countries outside the Middle East.[19] At least fifteen of the nineteen hijackers entered the United States with student visas, and several did not enroll in the U.S. schools to which they were admitted. In a major embarrassment, a Florida flight school received a notice six months after the attacks that two of the hijackers' applications for student visas had been approved—they had requested a change in status from business/tourist visitor to student a month before the attacks.[20]

A new computer-based foreign-student tracking program, known as the Student and Exchange Visitor Information System (SEVIS), became operational in 2003. Most foreign students must now pay a $100 fee to apply for an immigrant visa, and another $100 to be tracked during their stay in the United States, with the institutions where they are enrolled updating their information in the Web-based system. SEVIS is designed to allow the U.S. government to

Table 2.4. Foreign College and University Students in the United States, 1954/55–2002/03

School Year	Students	Foreign (%)
1954/55	2,499,800	34,232 (1%)
1959/60	3,402,300	48,486 (1%)
1964/65	5,320,000	82,045 (2%)
1969/70	7,978,400	134,959 (2%)
1974/75	10,321,500	154,580 (1%)
1979/80	11,707,000	286,343 (2%)
1984/85	12,467,700	342,113 (3%)
1985/86	12,387,700	343,777 (3%)
1986/87	12,410,500	349,609 (3%)
1987/88	12,808,487	356,187 (3%)
1988/89	13,322,576	366,354 (3%)
1989/90	13,824,592	386,851 (3%)
1990/91	13,975,408	407,529 (3%)
1991/92	14,360,965	419,585 (3%)
1992/93	14,422,975	438,618 (3%)
1993/94	14,473,106	449,749 (3%)
1994/95	14,554,016	452,653 (3%)
1995/96	14,419,252	453,787 (3%)
1996/97	14,286,478	457,984 (3%)
1997/98	13,294,221	481,280 (4%)
1998/99	13,391,401	490,933 (4%)
1999/00	13,584,998	514,723 (4%)
2000/01	14,046,659	547,867 (4%)
2001/02	13,511,149	582,996 (4%)
2002/03	12,853,627	586,323 (5%)

Source: IIE, http://opendoors.iienetwork.org/?p=35931

quickly learn about those who do not follow their study plans, but it does not track those who graduate and shift to another status, such as worker.

The final category of U.S. entrants includes unauthorized foreigners, those who arrive without inspection at ports of entry as well as those who arrive legally, as tourists or students, and then violate the terms of their visas by overstaying or going to work. An estimated 350,000 to 500,000 unauthorized foreigners settle in the United States each year, and many more enter or stay illegally but leave the same year they entered. The Immigration and Naturalization Service (INS) apprehended 1.4 million unauthorized foreigners in FY2001; almost all were Mexicans caught just inside the U.S. border.[21] The number of unauthorized foreigners in the United States is believed to have tripled in the 1990s to between 9 and 10 million by 2003.

WHITHER POLICY?

Despite living in a "land of immigrants," most Americans favor less legal immigration and more government efforts to reduce unauthorized migration. However, there is a sharp difference between elite and mass opinion, with support for immigration rising with an individual's income and education. In a 2002 poll, for example, 55 percent of the public said legal immigration should be reduced, compared with 18 percent of opinion leaders.[22]

Many politicians dismiss public concerns about immigration by pointing out that U.S. history is replete with fears that particular groups of immigrants would not be integrated. Benjamin Franklin, for example, worried that German immigrants arriving in the then-British colonies in the 1700s could not be assimilated. Why, he asked, should "Pennsylvania, founded by the English, become a colony of aliens, who will shortly be so numerous as to Germanize us, instead of our Anglifying them?" (quoted in Degler, 1970, 50). Franklin was right to predict that the Germans would not become English; instead, they became American. The English also changed: they too became American, emphasizing that the United States is constantly shaped and reshaped by immigration.

Past immigration flows to the United States resemble waves, with the number of immigrants increasing to peak levels and then falling into troughs. The fourth wave of U.S. immigration, which began in 1965, has been climbing since the early 1980s, and early in the twenty-first century a million immigrants a year are being admitted, with no end in sight. Many Americans want the federal government to take steps to reduce immigration, so that in historical perspective the current period would be the peak of the fourth wave. Others are comfortable with current levels of immigration.

Research on the economic, social, and political effects of immigration does not provide clear guidelines for policy. Overall, immigrants have minor effects—for better or worse—in the huge American economy and labor market. Most immigrants are better off financially in America than they were at home, but many arrive with minimal education and skill levels and find it hard to advance to better jobs in the American labor market. State and local governments, meanwhile, point out that the taxes paid by immigrants go mostly to the federal government, while state and local governments bear the brunt of the costs of providing services to immigrants.

For the foreseeable future, the United States will remain the world's major destination for immigrants. History suggests that within a few decades, most of today's immigrants will be an integral part of the American community, albeit a changed community. But past success does not guarantee that history will repeat itself. There are concerns about the size and nature of today's immigrant population, especially about arrivals through the side and back doors. As the United States searches for an immigration policy for the twenty-first century, the country—and the immigrants who are on their way to it—are on a journey to an uncertain destination.

ASIA

Asia has almost 60 percent of the world's residents and is a major source and destination of migrants. Migration patterns in Asia are unique for several reasons. First, the numbers are large and rising—the Philippines is second only to Mexico as a labor exporter, and Middle Eastern nations have some of the highest shares of migrants in their workforces, often more than 50 percent. Second, the majority of migrants leaving countries such as the Philippines and Sri Lanka are women, most of whom are going abroad to work in private homes as domestic helpers, making them especially vulnerable to abuse and exploitation. Third, migration patterns in Asia are in flux, with most receiving countries officially opposed to becoming destinations for migrants, but nonetheless receiving more migrants who are staying longer.

Canada and the United States restricted immigration from Asian countries from the 1880s until the mid-1960s. When immigration from Asia resumed, most migrants who left for industrial countries were professionals, and they often achieved higher-than-average incomes within fifteen years after arrival, the so-called Asian model immigrant. In the late 1970s and 1980s Asian immigrants in industrial countries became more diverse and included a million Southeast Asians resettled as refugees, many of whom had little education. Asian immigrants in Canada and the United States today are diverse—they continue to include highly educated professionals, but they also include persons with very little education, such as the Hmong moving from the highlands of Laos and Cambodia to the United States in mid-2004.

After oil prices rose in the 1970s, there was a new opportunity to work abroad temporarily, and many Asians migrated to the Gulf oil exporters to work on construction projects. As economic growth accelerated during the Asian economic miracle in the 1980s and 1990s, more Asian migrants remained closer to home, moving from the Philippines to Malaysia or Japan. Simultaneously, the world's largest rural-urban migration got under way in China, as millions of migrants have left their rural homes for jobs in urban areas, and some have spilled over China's borders to become international migrants.[23]

Most Asian migrants are less-skilled temporary workers who move from one Asian country to another or to the Middle East. The Middle East attracted a million Asian migrants in the early 1980s to help build infrastructure, but after the demand for construction workers in nations such as Saudi Arabia fell, migrants were expected to be Arab-speakers from countries such as Egypt. However, Asian migrants have continued to dominate labor flows, partly because Middle Easterners seemed to prefer Asian women to fill service jobs, including as domestic helpers in often large households. Simultaneously, more Asians migrated to nearby nations: Filipinos went to Hong Kong and Singapore as domestic helpers, Chinese migrated to South Korea and Japan as "trainees." (Trainees work on assembly lines but are not considered workers entitled to minimum wages because they are supposed to be receiving training in modern production practices.) During the 1990s Asian migration patterns became more complex, as countries such as Thailand simultaneously imported and exported workers, with Thais traveling to Taiwan, Israel, and other countries to work, while Burmese, Laotians, and Cambodians arrived to fill jobs in Thailand.

East Asia includes some of the world's most rapidly aging nations, such as Japan, and more youthful nations that are major countries of emigration, such as the Philippines, so migration could match labor demand in one country with labor supply in another. However, with the exception of Singapore's bid for professionals, no Asian nation is open to immigrants in the sense that it announces open doors for those looking to start anew. Instead, most Asian nations assert that they are not countries of immigration, and they do not welcome foreigners who want to settle, integrate, and naturalize. Thus guest worker rotation is the desired policy in most Asian nations that aim to keep foreigners entering and leaving rather than settling.

Japan and South Korea

Japan has east Asia's largest economy. Government policy favored exporting capital rather than importing workers, so employers who requested migrants in the 1970s were encouraged to invest abroad instead, which they did. However, some jobs could not easily be exported, such as those in construction and services, and as younger Japanese workers rejected these 3-D jobs (dirty, dangerous, and difficult), employers turned to unskilled and often unauthorized foreigners to fill them. Many of these foreigners arrived as tourists or students, and an industry soon developed to facilitate this migration, such as Chinese tour agencies that arrange group tours from which there are regular defections. Some Japanese language schools have more students working than watching the lessons on television monitors, although the government has tried to crack down on both types of abuse.

Japan liberalized rules for the entry and employment of foreign professionals in 1990 but continues to bar the entry of most unskilled foreign workers.[24] An exception is made for the 220,000 Nikkeijin, descendants of Japanese emigrants to Brazil and Peru early in the twentieth century, who were allowed to return to Japan as guest workers. Some of the Nikkeijin have been in Japan for more than a decade and speak Japanese, but many complain that despite their Japanese heritage they are not accepted as Japanese. Problems integrating the Nikkeijin are often cited as a reason why Japan appears incapable of absorbing large numbers of unskilled migrants.

The major entry door for nonethnic Japanese workers is the trainee door. Beginning in the 1950s Japan allowed its manufacturing firms to bring young people from China and other Asian countries to learn about Japanese manufacturing techniques; some of these trainees later became managers of Japanese factories in their home countries. As the trainee program grew, it turned into a low-cost guest worker program, since trainees are not considered workers under Japanese labor law and thus are not entitled to minimum wage. Many trainees thus "run away" from the Japanese firms to which they are assigned, since they can earn more as unauthorized workers than as legal trainees.

Runaway trainees, tourists, and students who overstay, and a few foreigners who slip into Japan on boats, make up most of the unauthorized foreigners in Japan. The government launched a major enforcement effort in 2004 against unauthorized foreigners, especially Chinese who arrived as students but worked more than the twenty-eight hours a week that their student status permits. Japanese junior colleges that are attracting fewer local students because of low birth rates have welcomed the Chinese, but many of the foreign students soon learn that the high cost of living in Japan requires them to work. The Japanese government, which estimates that half of the irregular workers in Japan arrived with student visas, has sharply curbed the number of visas issued to Japanese-language students in China, Myanmar, Bangladesh, and Mongolia.[25]

South Korea, which has had a similar problem with runaway trainees paid less than the minimum wage, developed a guest worker program in response. Trainees are brought to South Korea under the auspices of the Korea Federation of Small and Medium Business (KFSB), which initially opposed a guest worker program because it feared higher labor costs from paying the minimum wage to which guest workers are entitled. However, by 2002, 80 percent of the foreign workers in South Korea, some 290,000, were unauthorized, and the government approved a guest worker program that began operating in August 2004. The Korean Labor Ministry signed memorandums of understanding with the Philippines, Mongolia, Thailand, Vietnam, Indonesia, and Sri Lanka to permit the sending country to select several workers for each job, so that South Korean employers can choose between several candidates. The guest workers may work in Korea for up to four years, and then are expected to depart.

South Korea began to receive foreign workers in the buildup to the summer Olympics in 1988 and imported its first "industrial trainees" in November 1993 for manufacturing firms with fewer than 300 employees. The number of trainees rose steadily—there were 30,000 in 1994, 80,000 in 1996, 85,000 in 2000, and 146,000 in 2002—making the South Korean trainee program the largest in the world. In November 2001 a guest worker system was introduced for ethnic Koreans outside the country, most of whom live in northeastern China, that permitted persons at least forty years old with relatives in South Korea to work in service industries such as restaurants and housekeeping for up to three years and be considered workers, entitled to minimum wages and labor law protections.

In opening themselves to immigration, Japan and South Korea have begun with "ethnics," descendants of past emigrants who have cultural similarities even if they have lost the language of their parents and grandparents. The second source of settlers is likely to be foreign students who enter, learn the language, and are hired after graduation by local employers.

Philippines and China

The Philippines is the major labor exporter in Asia: the government estimates seventy-seven million Filipinos at home and seven million abroad. Migration affects every aspect of Filipino society: more than half of Filipinos have been abroad or have a relative who is or was abroad, and the experiences of migrants are reported daily in the press, depicted in novels, and dramatized in movies. Migrants remit $8 billion a year, equivalent to 10 percent of Filipino GDP, and in recognition of the importance of migration and remittances, the Filipino president usually welcomes some returning migrants at Christmas in a "Pamaskong Handog sa OFWs" (welcome home overseas foreign workers) ceremony.

The importance of migrants to the Philippines was illustrated by the capture of a Filipino truck driver in Iraq. The kidnappers of Angelo de la Cruz threatened to kill him in July 2004 unless the government pulled its troops out of Iraq. The government complied to protect, it said, the 1.5 million Filipinos working in the Middle East, and de la Cruz, the "Filipino Everyman," returned to a hero's welcome. Filipinos in Iraq earn $500 to $1,000 a month, compared with $100 to $140 a month at home, and when the government barred the deployment of additional migrants to Iraq, there were protests in Manila from potential migrants. Many migrants got around the ban on working in Iraq by going first to Kuwait, and from there to Iraq.

Filipino migrants are especially prominent on the world's ships as seamen, in hospitals in many countries as nurses, and in private homes as domestic helpers. The government actively "markets" its workers abroad, and Labor Secretary Patricia A. Sto. Tomas in 2001 said that the "government will be taking on an even more active role in pushing overseas employment as a strategy to boost economic growth and bring about full employment."[26] The Philippines may become ever more dependent on sending workers abroad, as socioeconomic changes make it ever easier for young people to leave but harder to achieve upward mobility at home (Abella, Martin, and Midgley, 2004).

China is home to more than 20 percent of the world's residents, and rural-urban differences have produced the world's largest Great Migration off the land. Estimates vary of the number of internal migrant workers, most of whom move from rural areas of inland provinces to cities in coastal provinces, but China's State Statistical Bureau estimated 114 million migrant workers in 2003, making migrants a sixth of the Chinese labor force of 744 million.[27]

Migrants move from rural to urban areas of China for the same reasons that migrant workers cross national borders: to earn higher wages and to enjoy increased opportunity for upward mobility. However, China has a household registration system that makes it difficult to obtain housing, medical care, or schooling except at the place in which a person is registered, so internal Chinese migrants may be "unauthorized" in the areas to which they moved, making them vulnerable to exploitation by employers and abuse by police. The Chinese government has relaxed the household registration system, but migrants remain vulnerable to authorities away from the place in which they are registered.

Chinese migrants moving from west to east typically travel by train, with men often employed on construction sites and women in factories that produce toys, clothing, and other consumer goods for export. Migrants earn $2 to

$3 a day, far more than they could earn at home, but less than what local workers earn. Migrants can buy residence permits to live in the cities to which they have moved, but such permits can cost $5,000 or more for migrants who earn less than $1,000 a year. This is too much for most migrants, who maintain links to their villages in part for fear that they may be forced back to the countryside. Internal Chinese migrants remit 370 billion yuan ($45 billion) a year to their villages of origin, sustaining life in places whose populations have disproportionately high numbers of the very young and very old.

During the 1990s there were several well-publicized examples of Chinese workers being smuggled into Canada, the United States, and the United Kingdom. Most Chinese who emigrate illegally are from the richest Chinese coastal provinces, such as Fujian and Guangdong. Residents of these provinces have a history of emigration, and there are well-developed smuggling networks that can move them long distances, as was dramatically clear when the ship *Golden Venture* ran aground in New York City in 1993 with several hundred migrants on board. The migrants, most of whom later applied for asylum in the United States, paid $50,000 or more each to be smuggled into the country, and most wound up staying. Canada received four ships with 590 migrants on its west coast in summer 1999 but soon reached an agreement with China that stopped this smuggling. Some 58 Chinese migrants were found dead in a Dutch-registered truck carrying tomatoes to the United Kingdom in June 2000, and 23 Chinese migrants drowned in February 2004 when a fast-moving tide in northwest England caught them while they were picking cockles to be exported.[28]

Senders and Receivers

Malaysia and Thailand exemplify a third type of participant in the labor migration system—they are countries that both send and receive migrant workers and are struggling to develop policies toward migrants. Many Chinese Malays migrate to Taiwan for jobs, while Indonesians and Filipinos migrate to Malaysia to work. Far more migrants move to Malaysia than leave, giving the country one of the highest percentages of foreigners in its workforce—more than one million in a labor force of ten million. The Malaysian government has said that "the use of foreign labor should not be regarded as a permanent solution to overcome the tight labor market situation" but has done little to prevent the spread of migrants from construction and agriculture to manufacturing, services, and private households. Some Malaysian officials fear that the country will be overwhelmed by migrants from its much larger neighbors, and the policy of periodic crackdowns has not stemmed the gradual upward trend in migrant worker numbers. The Malaysian government postponed a planned crackdown on perhaps 800,000 unauthorized foreigners after Indonesia asked it not to return migrants to areas ravaged by the December 26, 2004, tsunami.

Thailand has had a similar experience, attracting migrants from poorer neighbors as economic growth enabled Thais to find better jobs. Beginning in border provinces in agriculture and construction, migrants soon spread to Bangkok and construction and manufacturing, and the number of migrants who were registered more than doubled between 2001 and 2004. The Thai government sees migrants as a short-term bridge to a future without migrants but has not yet developed a strategy to avoid ever more dependence on migrants. Simultaneously, more than 200,000 Thais work abroad, and the government has promised to promote labor exports to Japan, Taiwan, Israel, and other destinations.

There are many other migrant labor flows in Asia. In south Asia, the creation of India and Pakistan, and later Bangladesh, was associated with massive migration, which is why India and Pakistan remain among the top countries hosting migrants half a century after partition. India receives migrants from Bangladesh and Nepal, sends skilled and unskilled migrants to the oil-exporting Gulf nations, and is well-known for sending professionals such as computer programmers and doctors and nurses to industrial countries. Pakistan has similar migration patterns, receiving migrants from Afghanistan and sending unskilled migrants to the Gulf states and professionals abroad. Like the Philippines, Sri Lanka is a major source of female migrants, many of whom go abroad to be domestic helpers.

MIDDLE EAST: OIL AND ISRAEL

The Middle East, which stretches from western Asia to North Africa, has witnessed some of the world's largest population and labor flows in the past quarter-century, measured in per capita terms. After oil prices rose in the 1970s, millions of foreign workers entered the oil-exporting countries to fill the jobs created as higher oil revenues were spent to construct modern infrastructure. The Middle East also includes the world's largest group of refugees from one country—Afghanis—and a long-term refugee-like population, the 3 million Palestinians in Gaza and the West Bank.[29]

Oil price hikes in 1973 and 1979 dramatically increased government revenues in Saudi Arabia and other oil exporters and set off a spending boom that attracted foreign firms and workers to build airports, hospitals, and roads. These foreign workers included Arabs from Palestine, Egypt, and Jordan, and Asians from nearby Pakistan and India, as well as Asians from further abroad, the Philippines and Indonesia. Although most of the oil exporters planned to reduce their dependence on migrant workers after construction projects were completed in the 1970s, this did not happen, and with birthrates high, growth in oil revenues slowing, and native youths shunning local private sector jobs, a foreign worker dilemma has arisen.

This dilemma is neatly illustrated in Saudi Arabia, where foreigners make up 70 percent of the labor force of ten million. Restrictions on the activities of women have led to a population growing by 3.4 percent a year, so that half of all Saudis are under eighteen. The government traditionally guaranteed jobs to Saudis, and many Saudis became accustomed to middle-class salaries and little work. However, as oil prices stabilized and labor force growth increased, guaranteed jobs ended, and unemployment rates among young Saudis rose above 30 percent.

The Saudi government's response has been to "renationalize" the workforce by making it harder for employers to hire foreign workers and easier to hire local workers.[30] For example, the government increased the fees that employers must pay to hire foreign workers and restricted some occupations to Saudis, using well-publicized raids to highlight the fact that foreigners were no longer allowed to work in travel agencies and jewelry stores. Renationalization has so far failed to reduce dependence on foreign workers, in part because many Saudi youth still shun private-sector jobs in which the availability of foreign workers has held down wages for a quarter-century. Most private-sector employers prefer to hire foreign workers, who lose their right to be in Saudi Arabia if they are fired.

Other oil exporters face similar problems: fast-growing populations due in part to restrictions on women working, a tradition of providing "no-work" government jobs for natives at higher-than-average wages, and guest worker admissions systems that require each foreigner to have a local sponsor, such that acting as a sponsor (rather than an employer) can enrich local residents. After the 1990–1991 Gulf war, the Kuwaiti government vowed never again to become dependent on foreign workers, but within a decade foreigners once again made up 40 percent of Kuwait's residents and a majority of its workers.

Israel's law of return welcomes Jews from around the world. Between 1948 and 2000, some 3 million immigrants arrived, although 20 percent later emigrated. Immigration to Israel increased rapidly after 1989, and some 200,000 immigrants arrived in 1990, when Israel had 5 million residents, meaning that immigration increased the Israeli population by 4 percent in one year. Between 1989 and 2000, Israel received a million immigrants; the population increased to more than 6 million as well-educated engineers from the former Soviet Union arrived and helped to turn Israel into a high-tech center.

Israel occupied the West Bank and Gaza after a 1967 war and allowed Palestinian residents there to commute to jobs in Israel. Two decades after the war, some 110,000 Palestinians commuted daily to Israel, but intifadas in the 1990s prompted the Israeli government to reduce the number of Palestinian commuter workers to curb terrorist incidents. Israel turned to Romania, Thailand, and other countries for migrant workers to replace Palestinians, and by 2003 there were about 15,000 Palestinian commuters and 300,000 other foreign workers in Israel, including 200,000 unauthorized foreign workers. Many foreign workers abandoned the contracts that had brought them to Israel to work in agriculture, construction, or care giving because many migrants paid fees to recruitment agents at home, so they arrived in Israel in debt. Some were asked to sign new contracts in Israel that offered lower than promised wages, and they had three choices: sign and earn less than expected, return to face their debts, or become unauthorized workers.

With the unemployment rate in Israel over 11 percent in 2003, a special immigration police force was created to arrest and deport unauthorized foreigners. Police were often accused of abusing the rights of migrants by entering private homes, and fear of the police prompted an estimated 100,000 unauthorized foreigners to leave by July 2004. Critics say that the Israeli enforcement drive has made exploitation of migrants worse, as Israeli recruitment agencies report migrants to police, and then make more fees from new recruits. The Hotline for Migrant Workers says that Israel spends more on removing illegal foreigners than any other country on a per capita basis, yet continues to import 100,000 legal migrants a year.[31]

Many sub-Saharan Africans try to migrate to Europe by transiting Algeria, Libya, Morocco, and Tunisia, using small boats operated by smugglers to cross the Mediterranean. Most do not want to work in the Maghreb states, and there were reports in summer 2004 that 5,000 sub-Saharan Africans were camped on the outskirts of Tangiers, waiting for an opportunity to board boats for southern Spain. In August 2004 several hundred Africans attempting to migrate to Europe broke through the fence at Melilla, a Spanish enclave on the Moroccan coast, in order to travel to Spain via ferry. Other migrants attempt to make the one-hundred-mile crossing from Morocco to Spain's Canary Islands, a less-policed route, and 3,300 were caught in the first seven months of 2004.

Libya is a special case in North African migration. The Libyan leader Col. Muammar el-Qaddafi proposed a United States of Africa in 1998, after African countries defied U.N. sanctions and resumed flights to and business with the country.[32] Africans were invited to come to Libya and work, and perhaps a million did, including some who used Libya as a way station to travel to Europe. The Africans waiting to migrate provide cheap labor for Libyans, most of whom worked for the government. In September–October 2000, there were widespread attacks on the migrants, resulting in the deaths of at least five hundred migrants and flight from the country by thousands more.[33]

In 2003 sanctions were lifted, and Libya began to crack down on migrants. In 2004 the country announced that it would host a conference on ways to combat illegal migration to Europe. Morocco, Algeria, and Tunisia have already, under EU prodding, cracked down on sub-Saharan migrants headed to Europe, and Libya has agreed to an Italian request to establish "reception centers" for migrants seeking to go to Europe via Libya.[34]

AFRICA

Africa is often associated with long lines of refugees fleeing civil wars, such as in Rwanda and Burundi in the mid-1990s. Africa has an eighth of the world's people, a fourth of the world's nation-states, and a third of the world's refugees. Many national borders in Africa were drawn by colonial powers, leading to large-scale "international migration" when nomadic tribes continued traditional migration patterns. The tribal structure of many African societies means that neighboring African countries sometimes host refugees from each other, as those out of favor with the government flee over national borders. For example, there are Mauritanian refugees in Mali, and Malian refugees in Mauritania.

Africa in April 1994 witnessed one of the largest mass movements of refugees ever recorded—2 million Rwandans left the densely populated country in the Great Lakes region of Africa in a matter of weeks. Some 500,000 to 800,000 mostly ethnic Tutsi residents were killed in a genocide organized by the Hutu-led government, and after the Tutsi-led rebel army defeated the government's military forces, Hutu leaders encouraged Hutus to flee with them to the Congo to avoid retaliation. Today there are hopeful signs that the number of African refugees may shrink. For example, Mozambique produced 1.3 million refugees in the early 1990s, according to UNHCR, and none in 1998–1999. Liberia was the source of 800,000 refugees in the mid-1990s, but of fewer than 300,000 in the late 1990s.

Refugee movements are often mixed with economically motivated migration in Africa, and labor migration patterns often reflect the colonial economy, when natural resources and plantations drew workers from what later became independent countries.[35] Many migrants move from poorer inland countries to richer coastal ones, as when the Ivory Coast attracted migrants from poorer neighbors such as Burkina Faso and Mali. By 2000 about 40 percent of the 16 million Ivory Coast residents were foreigners, but conditions for many of the migrant workers, some of whom were under fifteen years old, were often poor. Recruiters travel to villages in Burkina Faso and Mali and offer parents $50 to $100 in exchange for "work and training" for their children, who are then "sold" to plantation owners and expected to work for several years. The ILO, which defines a slave as someone "forced to work under physical or mental threat, and where the owner or employer controls the person completely," estimates there may be "tens of thousands" of migrants under eighteen employed in slavelike conditions on the Ivory Coast's cocoa plantations.[36] However, conditions were so bad at home that some of those "rescued" from Ivory Coast willingly went with recruiters for another stint. In 2002–2003, the Ivory Coast was in turmoil, in part because of clashes between the mostly Muslim immigrant north and west and the Christian south.

A major destination for African migrants is South Africa, a country of 46 million that is far richer than its neighbors. South African mine owners, with their operations in remote places, recruited migrants from nearby countries who were housed in barracks near the mines: the goal was to discourage the growth of cities around the mines that could lead to protests. Some 170,000 migrants were recruited in Lesotho, Swaziland, and Mozambique to work in South African mines for $200 a month in the early 1990s. After apartheid ended in 1994, there were high expectations among Blacks that they would be hired to fill relatively high-wage mining jobs, since the new government discouraged the recruitment of foreign miners. However, relatively few South Africans went to work in the mines—instead, there was a wave of mechanization.

There are 3 to 4 million foreigners in South Africa, and most arrived since the mid-1990s. Unemployment among South African Blacks is very high, as is resentment against some of the foreigners from neighboring countries and countries as far away as Nigeria. South Africa's political leaders are reluctant to crack down on illegal migration because many of the migrants' countries of origin sheltered them during the struggle to end apartheid, but many South Africans, Black and White, blame foreigners for rising crime. Many of the migrants report being stopped by police and being called *makwerekwere,* a derogatory term for foreigners, and opinion polls suggest that 80 percent of South Africans want a total ban on immigration (Crush and Williams, 1999).

South Africa attracts migrants from neighboring countries but is also suffering from a brain drain as a million skilled workers, managers, and other professionals have emigrated since 1994, many to the United Kingdom and Australia. Some South African employers want to recruit workers in eastern Europe and elsewhere to replace the emigrants, but the government is resisting, believing that employers should train local Blacks for jobs rather than seek immigrants. The Immigration Act of 2002 requires employers to pay a fee if they want to employ foreign professionals, and there were more than 500,000 vacant jobs for professionals in 2003. Many of those emigrating are doctors and nurses trained at government expense. The South African government says that it has spent $1 billion educating health workers who emigrated—the equivalent of a third of all development aid it received from 1994 to 2000.[37]

Another migration-related drama playing out in Africa involves farmland. In South Africa some fifty thousand White farmers own 87 percent of the farmland. The Restitution of Land Rights Act of 2004 allows the Ministry of Agriculture to appropriate land, with compensation, that was taken forcibly from Blacks under apartheid, and give it to Blacks who today often work as farm workers. The hope is that if some Blacks become farmers, rural-urban migration may be slowed. The government hopes that Black farmers will have 30 percent of South African land by 2015, but White farmers complain that 90 percent of the farms already transferred to Blacks have gone bankrupt.

In neighboring Zimbabwe, the government in June 2004 announced a plan to take control of all farmland, abolishing deeds, and allocating cropland to farmers under ninety-nine-year leases (twenty-five-year leases on wildlife conservancies). The government has already confiscated more than forty-two thousand square miles of formerly white commercial farmland and game reserves, and only about five hundred of the original five thousand or so white farmers still own farmland. Land confiscations that began in 2000 ruined the farm economy. The government agrees that farm production and exports are down, but says that blacks resettled on previously white owned land failed because they could not get loans without title to their land. Critics counter that the government's goal was to eliminate white farmers who supported opposition parties regardless of the economic consequences. Many of the white Zimbabwe farmers moved to Mozambique and are farming there.[38]

LATIN AMERICA

Most Latin American countries send more people abroad than they receive as immigrants. Mexico is the major emigration country in Latin America, and most Mexican migrants "go north for opportunity," following networks that are rooted in the recruitment of rural Mexicans to work on U.S. farms during World Wars I and II. The networks established during these bracero (strong arm) programs permitted Mexican workers and U.S. employers to develop a mutual dependence that encouraged migration to continue illegally after government-approved recruitment stopped. Today, most legal Mexican immigrants "admitted" to the United States as immigrants are unauthorized foreigners already in the country, and half of the ten million Mexican-born U.S. residents in 2004 are believed to be unauthorized.

During the 1990s, Mexico alone and in conjunction with Canada and the United States took steps expected to reduce future Mexican-U.S. emigration. The major instrument was the North American Free Trade Agreement (NAFTA), which lowered trade and investment barriers between the three countries beginning January 1, 1994. NAFTA was expected to speed up economic and job growth in all three countries, but especially in Mexico, and thus reduce economically motivated emigration as export-led growth created jobs. The result was expected to be less Mexican-U.S. migration; in the words of Mexican President Salinas: "We want to export goods, not people."[39]

Freer investment and trade are likely to reduce Mexican emigration in the long run, but in the short term closer economic integration can lead to a migration hump—temporarily more migration—as Mexican industries that were previously protected from competition must restructure to compete with imports (Martin, 1993). Until foreign and domestic investment creates jobs for displaced Mexican workers, as well as for a million new labor force entrants each year, wages in Mexico are likely to remain low, encouraging emigration to a U.S. economy that offers plenty of entry-level jobs. In this sense, it is not surprising that NAFTA has been associated with more Mexican-U.S. migration because freer trade and investment accelerated structural changes that displaced workers in Mexico and created jobs in the United States.

The changes in Mexico increasing Mexican-U.S. migration are especially visible in the countryside. Many farmers, who constituted about 30 percent of Mexican workers in the early 1990s, saw their incomes fall as corn imports rose. Corn production accounted for about half of the days worked in Mexican agriculture in the early 1990s, but U.S. farmers can produce corn much more cheaply than can Mexican farmers (Martin, 1993). Mexican corn farmers and their children found few new local jobs created by NAFTA where they lived, and the jobs most associated with NAFTA in border-area maquiladoras went primarily to young women who had finished secondary school, not to farmers and their children, who tend to have six years of education or less. With NAFTA signaling that there was no future in the countryside, many rural Mexicans headed for the United States.

Vicente Fox, elected president of Mexico in 2000 and ending seventy years of same-party rule, made protecting Mexicans in the United States one of his government's priorities. Fox called Mexican migrants "heroes" for remittances that reached $16 billion in 2004, and the Fox government launched several programs to lower the cost of remitting money and to match migrant remittances invested in the migrants' areas of origin in order to improve infrastructure and create jobs. Fox also asked the U.S. government to legalize unauthorized Mexicans, to provide them with "as many rights as possible, for as many Mexican immigrants as possible, as soon as possible . . . [to] turn migration from a source of friction into shared responsibility that is mutually beneficial."[40]

The Mexican push for legalization, which seemed on the verge of success in 2001, was revived in January 2004, when President Bush laid out "principles" that would allow U.S. employers to legalize their unauthorized workers and to easily obtain additional foreign workers. The Mexican government welcomed Bush's Fair and Secure Immigration Reform proposal, which Bush said would "match willing foreign workers with willing U.S. employers when no American can be found to fill those jobs." However, Democrats in Congress complained that the Bush plan would offer unauthorized workers only six-year work permits, not a path to immigrant status. On the other hand, many congressional Republicans complained that the Bush plan would "reward lawbreakers." Skeptics said that Bush's goal was not to exert leadership in an area fraught with political danger but rather to reestablish his credentials as a compassionate conservative, particularly with Hispanic and swing voters, ahead of November 2004 elections.

The seven countries of Central America, with forty million residents, were not integrated into the global migration system until civil wars broke out in the 1980s, killing thousands and displacing millions. To escape the fighting, many residents fled El Salvador (seven million residents), Guatemala (twelve million), Honduras (seven million), and Nicaragua (five million), with some going to neighboring Costa Rica and Mexico and others migrating to the United States and Canada. Many Central Americans applied for asylum in the United

States, and foreign policy concerns in the 1980s influenced decisions on whether to grant asylum. Most Nicaraguans fleeing a government the U.S. government opposed got asylum if they made it to the United States, but not so Salvadorans fleeing a government the U.S. government supported. Lawsuits against the U.S. government for this pattern of asylum decisions allowed most Central Americans to remain and eventually become immigrants.

In the meantime, remittances from Central Americans abroad became very important to local economies. After natural disasters in 1998 and 2001, Central American government leaders told U.S. officials that temporary protected status (TPS) for their citizens in the United States was more important than aid for the recovery—the leaders wanted their unauthorized nationals to be able to work legally in the United States so that they could send home more remittances, and the U.S. government obliged. The United States has promoted a NAFTA-style trade-in-place-of-migration strategy with the Central American Free Trade Agreement, which aims to ease trade and investment barriers and promote economic and job growth that reduces migration pressures; CAFTA was pending in Congress in April 2005.

Many Central American countries are grappling with tough U.S. policies that lead to the return of their citizens convicted of crimes in the United States. When returned to countries such as El Salvador, such citizens can overwhelm local police forces. In response, police in El Salvador in 2004 were arresting gang members deported from the United States even if they had committed no crimes in El Salvador. Many so-called *maras,* named after *marabuntas,* a species of swarming ants, have terrorized Central America's cities since large-scale removals from the United States began in the mid-1990s.

The fifteen independent Caribbean nations, plus several dependencies, have some of the world's highest emigration rates.[41] Cuba, the Dominican Republic, Haiti, and Jamaica account for about 75 percent of the 39 million Caribbean residents, and each sends immigrants to the United States. There are 900,000 Cuban immigrants in the United States—almost 10 percent of living persons born in Cuba—with most settling in southern Florida, where they have been extraordinarily successful in business and politics.

More than 800,000 Dominicans have immigrated to the United States, most since 1985 and many moving to New York City. According to a 1997 poll, half of the residents of the Dominican Republic have relatives in the United States, and two-thirds would move there if they could. Some 570,000 Jamaicans have emigrated to the United States in one of the oldest migrations from the Caribbean. Jamaicans were recruited to work in U.S. agriculture beginning in 1943, and 10,000 to 12,000 a year arrived to cut sugarcane in Florida and pick apples on the East Coast until the mid-1990s, when the sugarcane harvest was mechanized and U.S. farmers turned to Mexico for apple pickers.

About 400,000 Haitians have migrated to the United States, including a third who arrived in the 1990s. Beginning in the late 1970s, some Haitians began to make the 720-mile trip by boat to Florida, and 25,000 arrived in summer 1980. In 1991 the elected president of Haiti, Jean-Bertrand Aristide, was overthrown by the military, and large numbers of Haitians began leaving for the United States in small boats. In part to forestall this migration, the United States restored Aristide to power in 1994, but economic conditions failed to improve, and Haitians set out in small boats for the Bahamas en route to Florida. In February 2004, under U.S. pressure, Aristide resigned as Haiti's president, but there is still no strategy in place that promises stay-at-home development. An estimated 500,000 Haitians are in the Dominican Republic, which shares the island of Hispaniola with Haiti; many were recruited to work on Dominican sugar plantations that offered poor working conditions but nonetheless represented better employment than any available in Haiti.

If there were no barriers to migration between Caribbean islands and the United States and Canada, how many island residents would emigrate? One indicator may come from Puerto Rico. Puerto Ricans have been U.S. citizens since 1917, and in 1998 there were about 2.7 million residents of Puerto Rican origin on the U.S. mainland, and 3.8 million in Puerto Rico—about 42 percent of "Puerto Ricans" had emigrated. Migration between the island and the mainland responds to changing economic conditions, especially in New York and Chicago, but a narrowing of the mainland-island wage gap as well as the availability of food stamps and other assistance has produced an apparent migration equilibrium.[42]

South America was a destination for immigrants, especially from southern Europe and Japan, in the nineteenth and early twentieth centuries. However, economic problems in the 1990s, as well as higher wages in their parents' countries of origin, encouraged some of the immigrants' descendants to return to their countries of heritage. The first to return were ethnic Japanese from Brazil and Peru—1.3 million people of Japanese ancestry live in Brazil, the largest such population outside Japan, and in 1990 Brazilians of Japanese descent and their spouses were allowed to move to Japan on temporary work visas; 250,000 had done so by 2000.

Ethnic Italians and Spaniards in Argentina also applied for immigration visas to Italy and Spain amid economic crises in the past decade—an estimated

10 million of the 36 million Argentines are at least half Italian, and Italy allows them to claim Italian citizenship and move to Italy. Meanwhile, Argentina's economic woes slowed immigration from poorer countries, including Bolivia, Peru, and Paraguay, whose migrants often fill service and construction jobs. Colombia, wracked by civil war and economic problems, has experienced the emigration of more than 1 million persons since 1997 from a population of 44 million, with Colombians first moving to Venezuela and Ecuador, and more recently to Spain and the United States. Ecuador is also a major country of emigration, sending migrants to the United States and Spain.

OCEANIA AND THE PACIFIC ISLANDS

Oceania is the world's least populous region, with 32 million people, two-thirds in Australia. Australia and New Zealand welcome immigrants from around the world, about 75,000 and 35,000 a year, respectively, and they also permit freedom of movement between them under the Trans-Tasman Travel Agreement.

Australia was originally a place to which the United Kingdom shipped criminals: beginning in 1788, some 160,000 convicts were transported to Australia. Free British and European immigrants also arrived, and immigration peaked during the gold rush between 1851 and 1860, when 50,000 immigrants a year arrived. Until 1971 Australia had a White Australian policy that favored the immigration of Europeans.

Most of the immigrants to Australia and New Zealand are selected on the basis of a system that awards individuals points for personal characteristics and contacts that are associated with economic success. For example, Australia requires immigrants to receive at least 110 points under a system whose awards include a maximum of 60 points for a college degree and three years' experience, a maximum of 30 points for being eighteen to twenty-nine years old, 20 points for knowledge of English, and 15 points for having an Australian sponsor. New Zealand has a similar selection and immigration system, and the countries have parallel family unification and refugee resettlement systems.

A major migration issue in Australia is what to do about foreigners arriving in boats seeking asylum; most of the boats leave from Indonesia and land on Australia's north coast. Since 1994 Australia has detained foreigners who arrive without documents or on small boats, and the migrants placed in often remote detention camps have rioted on numerous occasions. Then–Australian Immigration Minister Philip Ruddock defended the detention policy: "Detention is not a punitive policy. . . . It is there to ensure people can be detained in order to process claims (for refugee status). It gives the system integrity, and it ensures that those people who are found not to be refugees are deported."[43]

The migrant boat issue reached a climax in August 2001, just before national elections, when an Indonesian ferry with 433 Afghans and Sri Lankans aboard sank near Christmas Island, Australia. The migrants were rescued by a Norwegian cargo ship, but the conservative government in power in Australia refused to allow the Norwegian ship to discharge the migrants there, a decision popular with voters but condemned by refugee groups. The rescued migrants were taken to Pacific island nations such as Nauru, where UNHCR screened them for refugee status, with Australia footing the bill.

Australia and New Zealand have active anti-immigrant movements, but so far they have been short lived. A newly elected member of the Australian Parliament, Pauline Hanson, in 1997 asserted that Australia was "in danger of being swamped by Asians . . . [who] have their own culture and religion, form ghettoes and do not assimilate." Hanson's One Nation party had 10 percent support in opinion polls in 1997, but a series of scandals reduced its support, and Hanson eventually went to prison for election fraud. The New Zealand First party, led by Winston Peters, also opposes Asian immigration, ostensibly to protect the 500,000 indigenous Maori.

Most Pacific island nations have relatively few residents, often 200,000 to 400,000, and many face unusual migration issues. The Commonwealth of the Northern Mariana Islands (CNMI), a U.S. territory since 1976 with its own immigration policies, includes 28,000 CNMI natives and 42,000 foreign guest workers. This mix of local residents and guest workers reflects a deliberate policy choice: the CNMI government permits Chinese and other firms to establish garment shops on the island, import women to sew clothes, and then send the clothes to the United States bearing "Made in the USA" labels. Conditions in the Saipan garment factories are often poor, and class-action suits were filed in the United States accusing U.S. retailers of knowing that their garments were being manufactured in violation of Saipan's $3.05 an hour minimum wage. In 2002 such major U.S. retailers as Gap, Inc., and J. C. Penney agreed to pay $20 million to monitor working conditions in Saipan and to compensate migrants who had been underpaid.

Global warming that causes ocean levels to rise might lead to emigration from many Pacific islands, including Kiribati, the Marshall Islands, and Tuvalu. Few of these governments have made plans to evacuate their citizens if the islands are flooded, but some have found a way to make money on immigration. Many Pacific island governments offer "economic citizenship" to foreigners who make local investments of at least $50,000, a practice that came under sharp attack by the U.S. government after the September 11, 2001, terrorist attacks.[44] The USA Patriot Act prohibits U.S. banks from dealing with banks in countries supporting terrorism—the so-called economic nuclear bomb—and the U.S. government threatened to apply this provision of the Patriot Act to Nauru. Nauru, an island of eight square miles with 12,000 residents that has run out of the phosphate it used to export, offers economic citizenship for as little as $15,000 and has attracted offshore banks that the U.S. government accuses of money laundering.

Global warming may prompt emigration from Pacific islands as well as from coastal areas around the world. Half of the world's six billion people live within one hundred miles of coastlines, and the Intergovernmental Panel on Climate Change projects that a billion people could be forced to move before 2100 by rising waters. Areas that may have to be evacuated range from the west coast of Africa to the Chinese coast and coastal areas of India and Bangladesh. Most of these environmental migrants would probably remain within their countries, but the prospect that coastal areas of many countries could be flooded opens the possibility of a new type of large-scale migration.

Part II Professional and Unskilled Migrants

Most foreign worker programs are designed to add temporary workers to the labor force without adding permanent residents to the population. The terminology—temporary, migrant, or guest worker—emphasizes the rotation principle at the heart of guest worker programs: migrants are expected to work one or more years abroad and then return to their countries of origin. If the demand for migrant workers persists, replacements may be admitted, but the theory of migrant worker programs is that the employment-migrant ratio in the host country should remain near 100 percent, meaning that all foreigners related to the program are employed.

All guest worker programs fail, in the sense that some of the migrants settle in destination countries. The employment-migrant ratio falls as the demand for guest workers persists, leading to the aphorism that "there is nothing more permanent than temporary workers." However, the fact that some migrant workers settle does not prove that guest worker programs are "bad." In some cases, migrants are permitted or even encouraged to settle: European guest worker programs allowed migrants whose employers requested their continued presence to have their families join them, and industrial countries from Australia to Spain encourage highly skilled migrants to settle. However, guest worker programs generally aim to rotate foreigners in and out of a country's labor market, and the entry and exit of migrants affect sending and receiving country workers and societies.

Guest workers tend to be concentrated at the extremes of the job ladder, with more or less education than the average worker in the destination country. In Chapter 3 we examine guest worker programs that admit foreign professionals for employment in health care and high-tech and similar industries and occupations. In Chapter 4 we turn to unskilled workers, and review program developments since World War II, comparing large-scale guest worker schemes of the 1950s and 1960s that led to settlement with seasonal and other programs of the 1990s that are designed to improve the rotation of workers. In Chapter 5 we show how economic instruments can align the rights and obligations of employers and migrants to keep guest worker programs truer to their purpose.

3 Highly Skilled Guest Workers

Professional, technical, and kindred or related (PTK) workers are those with at least a college or university degree or equivalent work experience.[1] A key characteristic of professionals is that they have education and training that takes time to acquire, so their number cannot be increased quickly unless trained workers who are not employed in their field of training—nurses who are not working as nurses, for example—are induced to rejoin the workforce. Alternatively, PTK workers can be imported from abroad to quickly increase the supply. During the 1990s most industrial countries made it easier for foreign professionals to enter and work temporarily or permanently in response to the Internet-related economic boom.

The world's workforce is 3 billion strong, but reliable data do not exist on how many workers have professional credentials, nor how many of those with professional credentials are migrants. The United Nations estimated that 105 million of the world's 175 million migrants in 2000 were in the more-developed countries.[2] Since half of the residents of more-developed countries are in the labor force, and migrants tend to have labor force participation rates similar to native-born workers, this suggests that 52 million migrants are in the labor forces of more-developed countries.[3] Migrants come from developing as well as developed countries; the best estimates are that 75 percent or 40 million are from developing countries.

How many of the 40 million migrants from developing countries have professional credentials? The general rule is that the more difficult it is to migrate from one country to another, the higher the percentage of professionals among the migrants from that country. About 20 percent of workers in developed countries have professional credentials, a bachelor's degree or more, suggesting that 94 million of the 470 million developed-country workers are professional workers. If professionals constitute 20 percent of the migrants from developing countries, there are 8 million professional migrants from developing countries in more developed countries, meaning that migrants account for 9 percent of developed country professional workers.

There are no estimates of the stock of professional workers among the 2.5 billion workers in developing countries.[4] If professionals make up 4 percent of developing-country workforces, there is a total of 101 million, and professional migrants represent 9 percent of the stock of professionals born in developing countries. Alternatively, if developing countries have fewer professionals, if they are only 2 percent of developing-country workforces, as other estimates suggest, developing countries have a total of 50 million professionals, and professional migrants represent 16 percent of developing-country professionals (see Table 3.1). Both estimates suggest that there is a far higher share of developing-country professionals in industrial countries than of ordinary workers.

Table 3.1. Global Labor Force: 1980, 2001, 2010

	Population 15–64 (millions)		Labor Force (millions)			Average Annual Growth Rate	
	1980	2001	1980	2001	2010	1980–2001	2001–2010
World	2,600	3,882	2,036	2,983	3,377	1.8	1.4
Developing countries	2,071	3,240	1,662	2,517	2,894	2	1.6
PTK=4%			66	101	116		
PTK=2%			33	50	58		
High-income countries	529	642	373	467	483	1.1	0.4
PTK=20%			75	93	97		

Note: For PTK estimates, see text.

Source: World Bank. 2003. World Development Indicators, 44.

The difficulty of estimating migrant stocks and flows by skill level is highlighted in a pioneering study that divided foreign-born U.S. residents in the 1990 census who were twenty-five and older, and thus had presumably finished their schooling, into three groups based on their years of education: less than nine years, nine to twelve years, and thirteen or more years.[5] William Carrington and Enrica Detragiache (1998) considered those with thirteen or more years of schooling to be skilled or highly skilled and compared them with adults living in the sixty-one developing countries from which they came.[6] Half of the foreigners in the Organization for Economic and Cooperative Development (OECD) countries in 1990 were in the United States, and this study assumed that the characteristics of foreign-born U.S. residents were the same in other OECD countries, such that the educational distribution of South African–born U.S. residents was assumed to apply to South African–born U.K. residents as well.[7]

SELECTIVITY AND LOSS

Carrington and Detragiache measured educational selectivity among immigrants and cumulative loss to countries of origin from emigration. Educational selectivity, a measure of the share of migrants from a country who have professional credentials, varies widely from country to country for immigrants in the United States. For example, 75 percent of adult Indian-born U.S. residents in 1990 had thirteen or more years of schooling, as did 60 percent of the Egyptian-, Ghanaian-, and South African–born U.S. residents, 40 percent of Jamaican-born U.S. residents, and 13 percent of Mexican-born U.S. residents.

Cumulative loss is the share of migrants with thirteen or more years of schooling from a particular country who are abroad, and was highest for Jamaica, Guyana, and Trinidad and Tobago; these countries had more professionals abroad than at home. By region, Africa had the highest cumulative loss—a third of African-born professionals are believed to be abroad (World Bank 2000, 39; IOM, 2001). Carrington and Detragiache included as "tertiary educated" all persons with a postsecondary education (a high school diploma) or more, and they excluded professionals who moved between developing countries, as from India or the Philippines to the Gulf states, which may explain why they found that only 7 percent of Filipino professionals were abroad.[8]

A different approach was taken by Jean-Baptiste Meyer and Mercy Brown (1999), who estimated that there were 170,000 foreign-born scientists and engineers in the United States from developing countries in the mid-1990s.[9] They concluded that half of the foreign-born scientists and engineers employed in industrial-country research-and-development activities are in the United States; that conclusion was the basis of their estimate that there are 331,000 foreign-born scientists and engineers from developing countries in industrial countries.

There are sharp differences in the educational levels of foreign-born U.S. residents by region of birth. The percentage of foreign-born and U.S.-born adults with college degrees or more is similar, about 27–28 percent, but a far higher percentage of the foreign born have less than a high school diploma, producing an hourglass shape in data on immigrants when arrayed by level of education. Immigrants from Asia and Europe are most likely to have advanced degrees, while immigrants from Latin America are least likely to have high levels of education (see Table 3.2).

Most economists believe that attracting immigrant professionals is good for destination countries because such immigrants raise incomes and growth rates in three major ways. First, professional migrants can fill vacant jobs until more local workers are trained in such boom sectors as information technology, helping to minimize production losses. Second, professional migrants can increase productivity in strategic sectors by increasing the diversity of work teams, which may boost the rate of innovation as people with different backgrounds and perspectives work together to solve problems. Third, foreign professionals can add to the labor supply in particular sectors, helping to hold down wage increases and reduce the cost of providing such labor-intensive services as medical care and education.

BRAIN DRAIN FEARS

Migrants and the countries to which they move generally benefit from migration, and the major concern of the global community has focused on the effects of a brain drain on developing countries. In neoclassical economic-growth models, the outflow of any labor, unskilled or skilled, can slow economic growth. More recent economic-growth models emphasize that, with human capital scarce, professional emigration can transfer human capital from poorer to richer countries and slow economic growth in emigration countries, as when African professionals who have emigrated are replaced in part by 100,000 foreigners who range from Peace Corps volunteers to private and public experts trying to promote development (Straubhaar, 2000). Studies confirm that lower

Table 3.2. Education of Foreign-born U.S. Residents, Age Twenty-five and Older, March 2002

Percentage	All Foreign-Born	Europe	Asia	Latin America	Other	U.S.-born
Less than HS diploma	33	16	13	51	18	13
HS diploma, some college	41	49	38	38	49	60
Bachelor's degree or more	27	35	49	11	34	27
Master's degree or more	10	16	18	3	12	9
Number (millions)	25.790	3.969	6.879	12.835	2.107	156.352

Source: http://www.census.gov/population/socdemo/foreign/ppl-162/tab02-05.xls

levels of education are associated with slower productivity and economic growth for many reasons, including the fact that the temporary or permanent loss of human capital can make a country less attractive to local and foreign investors and because emigration can lead to less dynamism, innovation, and creativity.[10]

It is hard to hold other factors constant and isolate the effects of professional immigration or emigration, which explains why brain drain studies often revert to overall evaluations of migration. David Ellerman (2003) distinguishes between "internationalists," who assert that because voluntary migration from poorer to richer places leads to higher incomes for migrants and more economic output, migration is good even if migrant countries of origin are worse off (that is, the global gains from moving people from lower- to higher-income areas should minimize fears of a brain drain), and "nationalists," who treat countries as the fundamental unit of analysis and worry that economic growth may sometimes be faster if professionals are not allowed to emigrate or if those abroad are encouraged to return in order to set in motion virtuous circles of growth and development (7).

During the nineteenth century, the transatlantic migration of largely unskilled workers from Europe to the Americas had an equalizing or convergence effect on jobs and wages in sending and receiving areas, so that European–North American migration stopped "naturally." The arrival of migrants in the land-abundant and labor-short Americas put downward pressure on wages, while emigration put upward pressure on wages in a land-scarce and labor-abundant Europe. The result was a convergence in factor prices and a "natural end" to emigration pressures as "wage gaps shrank and living standards began to converge" (Hatton and Williamson, 1998, 252).

The question today is whether current developing-to-developed migration will produce a similar convergence, especially if contemporary migration flows include a significant number of PTKs.[11] Neoclassical economics treats convergence between emigration and immigration areas as the natural or normal outcome, but professional migration from developing countries could put some developing countries in a low-level equilibrium, analogous to residents of desert regions sustaining a low-level existence with remittances (Ellerman, 2003, 10). The significant number of programs aimed at encouraging the return of professionals suggests that many countries and organizations worry that some areas could slip into such a remittance-fueled low-level equilibrium, a possibility that has attracted little study or attention.

There has been a burgeoning economic literature that argues, counterintuitively, that the emigration of skilled workers can *accelerate* economic growth in their countries of origin. The so-called new economics of the brain gain imagines a developing country that first prohibits emigration and later opens its borders to allow professionals to leave and earn five or ten times more abroad. By allowing emigration, this theory argues, a developing country realizes educational improvement for all its citizens, migrants and nonmigrants considered together, which should induce more people to get more schooling. Not all of the newly educated will emigrate, which explains the paradox of a brain drain leading to a brain gain: more precisely, there is an "optimal level of brain drain": low enough to avoid a vicious downward spiral from too few educated residents but high enough to encourage more residents to get more schooling (Mountford, 1997).

In empirical studies brain gain effects of a brain drain are hard to measure, in part because there has been an increase in the movement of professionals over borders as education levels rise in most countries. Efforts to isolate "brain gain" effects from emigration must make heroic assumptions. For example, one study assumed that the 1994 level of education in a developing country was a function of the average number of migrants from that country who left for OECD countries between 1988 and 1994 and concluded that "emigration prospects seem to play a significant role in education decisions" (Beine, Docquier, and Rapoport, 2001, 288). Perhaps the strongest conclusion from this literature is that if developing countries face a choice between prohibiting the emigration of professionals and allowing some emigration, they should allow some.

Emigration that increases the return to schooling and the stock of human capital in a country may not accelerate economic growth if it is not appropriate to the country's development needs. After the 1998 financial crisis in Russia, student enrollment in science and engineering courses increased sharply, in part because many Russian students thought that science and technology credentials would improve their opportunities to emigrate (Ellerman, 2003, 31). Not all of the newly trained scientists and engineers emigrated, and Russia wound up with more scientists and engineers, which increased pressure on the government to create jobs at government-financed research institutes for what some called "second-class" talent—those who could not get job offers from abroad. Similarly, there was a significant emigration of health care workers and engineers from South Africa in the 1990s, but the big surge in enrollment in South African universities was in the humanities, not medicine or engineering.[12]

PROFESSIONALS: IMPACTS ABROAD

The OECD and the International Labor Organization (ILO) assessed the effects of the migration of professionals on sending and receiving countries and concluded that current migration patterns risk deepening inequality between developing and developed countries. The OECD examined data on the migration of professionals and on their impacts in host countries, and called for policies that could make such migration mutually beneficial (OECD, 2002). The ILO commissioned country studies that examined the impacts of professional migration on selected countries, and warned that, without changes, inequality between developing and industrial countries could increase.[13]

Definitions and Trends

There is no broadly accepted definition of "skilled migrant." The OECD recommends the use of standard definitions, such as those developed in the so-called Canberra Manual that includes definitions of professionals to facilitate international comparisons (OECD, 1995). For example, the Canberra Manual defines human resources in science and technology (HRST) in both supply and demand terms. Supply measures the number of persons with at least a postsecondary (college) degree in a science or technology field, while the demand approach includes all persons employed in science or technology occupations, even if they lack a degree in a science or technology field (OECD, 2002, 13). There were an estimated sixty-five million HRST workers in the EU in 1997, but only a third satisfied both education and employment criteria, suggesting that many persons with science and technology degrees are not employed in science or technology occupations, and many people in those occupations do not have science or technology degrees.[14]

The number of HRST migrants has been rising, but "because of data problems, it is not possible . . . to quantify movements in comparative or global terms" (OECD, 2002, 29). Most employers in OECD countries do not engage in long-distance labor recruitment, so one way for developing country nationals to get hired in industrial countries is to study in the country to which the migrant wants to move, which enables the student to learn the language of the host country and increase the chance of coming to the attention of local employers. In the United States, for example, a quarter of those getting H-1B visas in the late 1990s previously held U.S. student visas, suggesting that study abroad can be part of a plan to work abroad.

The number of foreign students in the OECD countries doubled between

1980 and 2000 to almost 1.8 million, and their number is projected to quadruple to 7 million by 2025.[15] The traditional reasons for fostering student mobility over borders—cultural exchange and foreign aid—have been joined by two others: generating revenues for universities by attracting fee-paying students and attracting highly skilled workers and immigrants to work and settle. Universities thus play a potentially important gatekeeping role in the movement of human capital between nation-states, including from developing to developed countries. Foreign students usually prefer to acquire easily transferable skills—pursuing, for example, science and engineering degrees rather than law degrees—so that they can get jobs elsewhere if they are not allowed to stay. The OECD has concluded that student mobility "deserves encouragement" but that "greater coordination and cooperation . . . would lead to a fairer sharing of the advantages linked to international student mobility" (OECD, 2002, 64).

The number of professionals from developing countries in developed countries is expected to continue rising for several reasons. First, developed countries have aging populations, which increases the demand for health care, a labor-intensive service paid for at least in part by governments that want to hold down health care costs. It is relatively easy to recruit doctors and nurses in developing nations, since by migrating they earn higher wages, often have better working conditions, and usually have more opportunities for career advancement. Second, continued globalization encourages multinationals to form diverse teams comprising nationals of the various countries in which the firm operates to develop global strategies, while increased trade and investment lead to additional migration as sales people and investors cross borders.

Third, rigidities in host-country labor markets may also lead to increased migration, as when salary ladders for nurses do not encourage them to remain in or return to nursing or discourage experienced nurses from working in inner-city hospitals, at night and on weekends, or in private homes. Instead of salaries rising with experience, climbing the job ladder in nursing is more often associated with "better working conditions," which means working during the day in suburban hospitals (Weinberg and Gordon, 2003). Hospitals often find it cheaper and easier to recruit foreign nurses and leave the salary structure and career ladder unchanged rather than taking the steps that would be needed to induce more local nurses to accept less-desirable jobs.

Health care is a special industry and occupation, with governments affecting both patient demand for services, via health insurance and tax policies, and the supply of doctors and nurses, via training and immigration policies. Research and development is a similar special industry for which government policies affect the demand for and supply of scientists. Most students in U.S. science and engineering doctoral programs are foreign born, which leads to the argument that the U.S. government should make it easy for foreigners to enter and fill classrooms and labs, and encourage graduates to stay and work. However, research laboratories funded by government grants depend on low-cost research assistants and postdoctoral fellows, and the dominance of foreigners in such jobs may be explained by the fact that most Americans do not want to prolong their education for the low wages paid to postdocs. One study found that bioscientists could expect to earn $1 million less in their lifetimes than masters in business administration graduating from the same university, $2 million less if stock options are taken into account, which helps to explain the very different immigrant shares of students in MBA programs and graduate science programs (Teitelbaum, 2003).

Migration often begets more migration, as migrants tell their friends and relatives about opportunities abroad, and an infrastructure of middlemen and brokers evolves to move migrants over borders. Most of the literature on the migration infrastructure focuses on people-to-people networks that provide information to make the migration of unskilled workers ever easier if people have a reason to move (Massey et al., 1998). Professionals are often moved over borders with the help of multinational employers, some of whom hire workers in one country and move them to another. Over the past two decades, more labor brokers have emerged to recruit IT specialists, nurses, and teachers in one country for jobs in another, and their activities promise to make professional migration ever easier.

Are Professional Migrants Needed?

Do industrial countries "need" professional migrants? *Need* is a word not found in most economic texts; instead, the operative phrase is "supply and demand," two factors that interact to determine an equilibrium price and quantity that clears markets, eliminating shortages and surpluses. Professional migrants normally enter an industrial country in response to employer requests, and employers "need" migrants because they cannot find local workers to fill vacant jobs. As with hospitals seeking nurses in inner cities, or labs seeking postdoctoral researchers, there are alternatives to foreign professionals, including higher wages, which tend to reduce the demand for and increase the supply of workers. Most governments require employers seeking foreign workers to satisfy an "economic needs test" to demonstrate that they truly "need" migrants, but this test does not include determining what wage would equate supply and demand without migrants.

Economic needs tests assume that employers can usually find local workers to fill jobs. There are two basic types of economic needs tests: certification and attestation. Under certification, the border gate stays shut until a government agency agrees that local workers are unavailable despite employer efforts to recruit local workers.[16] Under attestation, a declaration by employers that they have tried and failed to find local workers is sufficient to open the border gate. Government oversight or enforcement waits until the migrants are in the country and at work.

Most economic needs tests for professionals involve attestation, and checks are often perfunctory under the theory that the local workers with whom foreign professionals compete are able to look out for themselves. The U.S. H-1B program, named for the part of immigration law that authorizes it, uses this trust-the-employer approach "to meet urgent, short-term demand for highly skilled, unique individuals who are not available" in the United States. The admissions procedure uses attestation, with most employers filing a labor condition application that names the foreigner with a university degree who is in or coming to the United States to fill a job that requires a university degree or more. As long as the employer certifies that the prevailing wage is being paid and that the job is not vacant because of a strike, the U.S. Department of Labor must approve it.

During the 1990s the H-1B program became the world's largest channel for professional migrants. Approved in the Immigration Act of 1990, during the post–Cold War recession, it went undiscovered for several years before employers, brokers, and migrants became aware of the program and began to use it. However, by the mid-1990s the number of requests for H-1B workers was bumping up against the annual ceiling of 65,000 a year, and computer-related firms in particular pressed Congress to raise the ceiling. Congress did so, making the limit 115,000 and later 195,000 a year before restoring it to 65,000 a year in FY2004 (see Table 3.3).[17]

The rise and fall of H-1B numbers highlight several lessons about professional migration. First, most H-1B workers from developing countries want immigrant visas, not the six-year work permits that H-1B visas provide, and easy entry as a temporary worker soon bumps up against a much tougher certification process for the smaller number of immigrant visas available to U.S. employers. H-1B migrants have an incentive to find an employer who promises to

Table 3.3. Employment-based Immigration and H-1Bs, 1992–2004

	1992	1993	1994	1995	1996	1997	1998	1999	2000	2001	2002	2003
Employment-based ceiling	140,000	140,000	140,000	140,000	140,000	140,000	140,000	140,000	140,000	140,000	140,000	140,000
Employment based immigration	116,198	147,012	123,291	85,336	117,499	90,607	77,517	56,817	107,024	179,195	174,968	82,137
Employment-waiting list	140,000	161,207	143,213	146,503	140,000	140,000	160,898	142,299	194,074	142,632	NA	NA
H-1B visa ceiling	65,000	65,000	65,000	65,000	65,000	65,000	65,000	115,000	115,000	195,000	195,000	195,000
H-1B admissions (double count)	110,223	92,795	105,899	117,574	114,458	200,000	240,947	302,326	355,605	384,191	370,490	360,498

Notes: Employment-based immigration can exceed the 140,000 ceiling if visas were not fully used in previous years. 1997 admissions are estimated; the INS has no data.

Source: Department of Homeland Security. Office of Immigration Statistics. Yearbook of Immigration Statistics, various years.

sponsor them for this lengthy and cumbersome certification process, which means that they work hard to please their employers.

The contrast between the easy attestation process to get an H-1B visa and the much harder certification process is the source of considerable frustration. Getting certified for an employment-based immigration visa usually requires physical presence in the United States—in recent years 85 percent of the immigrant visas issued for employment reasons went to foreigners who were already in the country. This means that in most cases U.S. employers requesting immigrant visas for "needed workers" already employ them; a Department of Labor audit of employer requests for 24,000 immigrant visas in 1993 found that 99 percent of the foreigners being sponsored for employment-based immigrant visas were working for the employers who requested them, including 4,000 who were not authorized to work in the United States. Labor certification requires employers to advertise for U.S. workers, and this required advertising produced 165,000 applicants. But in virtually every case, the employer found the U.S. worker applicant unqualified, and the foreign applicant eventually received an immigrant visa, clear evidence that the employers involved did not want to hire U.S. workers for the jobs already filled by foreigners.[18]

Most foreigners receiving employment-related immigrant visas get them only after the U.S. Department of Labor certifies that they are uniquely qualified to fill vacant jobs. However, many of the foreigners receiving immigrant visas between 1988 and 1996 had doubtful "unique qualifications." During these years, some 40,000 housekeepers received immigrant visas, 5,000 cooks and chefs, 3,000 auto repair workers, 252 fast-food workers, 199 poultry dressers, 173 choral directors, 156 landscape laborers, 122 short-order cooks, 77 plumbers, 68 doughnut makers, 53 baker's helpers, and 38 hospital janitors.[19]

Second, the premise that professional U.S. workers can look out for themselves has been tested by events. There are few checks before the H-1B workers arrive: "Labor can certify that an employer's application form for H-1B workers is error free, but it has no authority to verify the information on the form. Labor cannot take enforcement action even if it believes that employers are violating the law," unless it receives a complaint of violations, as from a competitor or a U.S. worker (GAO, 2000). Indeed the H-1B program allows most U.S. employers to hire H-1B workers, have U.S. workers train them, and then lay off the U.S. workers, and examples of employers doing just this abound.[20] American International Group in September 1994 laid off 130 U.S. programmers and outsourced its computer work to Syntel, an Indian-American firm that provides computer services in both countries, prompting the laid-off U.S. programmers to protest that they were told to train some of the workers who replaced them in India and the United States.

Third, the U.S. experience demonstrates the importance of intermediaries or body brokers in moving professional migrants over borders. The interests of brokers are generally to maximize fees and migrants, and broker interests may be quite different from the interests of migrants, employers, and the governments of sending and receiving countries.[21] In an extreme case, Atlanta-based Deep Sai Consulting Inc. in November 1999 was charged with harboring illegal migrants after it brought forty-three Indian programmers to the United States for jobs that did not materialize. Only twelve of the H-1B workers got jobs, and the others disappeared, prompting the INS to call the scheme "white-collar alien smuggling."[22]

Complaints against brokers rose with the number of H-1B workers, and the *Wall Street Journal* profiled a typical complaint involving an Indian who arrived in November 2000 to work for Indian-owned ChristAm. The company never found him a U.S. job, paid him no wages, and went out of business after collecting his recruitment fees.[23] Most body brokers require H-1B workers to sign contracts that include significant penalties if the worker finds a "regular" U.S. employer, as occurs if an H-1B worker assigned to IBM is offered a job there. However, a California court in April 2001 ruled that a $25,000 penalty clause in a contract between Compubahn and an H-1B worker was unlawful and ordered Compubahn to pay the affected Indian $215,050 in legal fees and other expenses.

After the information technology bubble burst in 2000, complaints by U.S. workers about H-1B workers rose, and a new migration-related issue arose: the use of L-1 visas to bring foreign professionals into the United States to work. L-1 visas allow multinationals to transfer managers and workers with "specialized knowledge" from foreign to U.S. operations, the only requirement being that the employee was employed at least one year in the foreign operation. There is no requirement that the employer pay the worker the prevailing wage, as under the H-1B program. There are relatively few restrictions on L-1 visas, since it was presumed that multinationals would police themselves and not transfer large numbers of workers to the high-cost United States. However, a Siemens subsidiary in Florida in 2002 subcontracted its software maintenance work to Tata, which brought Indian workers to the United States on L-1 visas. Siemens had its U.S. workers train the migrants and then laid off the U.S. workers; Tata then sent some of Siemens's software work to India and left other Tata workers with L-1 visas at Siemens to handle ongoing work.

There was disagreement within the U.S. government over whether this arrangement was lawful. The U.S. Bureau of Citizenship and Immigration Services said: "If an L-1 comes into the United States to work, they're coming to work for their specific company that petitioned for them, not for another company that they're being contracted out to," suggesting that L-1 workers cannot be farmed out to other companies. However, the U.S. State Department said: "The fact that someone is on the site of [a client] does not make them ineligible for an L-1 as long as . . . the company they actually work for is truly functioning as their employer in terms of how they're paid and who has the right to fire them." The L-1 Visa and H-1B Visa Reform Act of 2004 requires that any instructions must flow from Siemens to Tata supervisors to the Tata L-1 workers—that is, Siemens may not deal directly with the Tata L-1 workers.

The U.S. experience raises questions about how easy a government should make importing skills compared with allowing rising wages to induce changes in student preferences and employer decisions. The information technology and economic booms in the United States in the late 1990s convinced many that new guest workers in the new economy could avoid both distortion, which occurs if some employers assume that migrants will continue to be available, and dependence, which occurs when migrants and their families need foreign jobs and earnings, encouraging illegal migration after guest worker recruitment ends.

Return or Stay?

Do professionals who move from developing countries stay abroad or return to their countries of origin, and what are the implications of high and low return rates? If the migrant rate of return is high, the appropriate term may be *brain circulation, brain exchange,* or *professional transience,* emphasizing the temporary nature of professional migrants abroad. If the rate of return is low, the appropriate terms may be *brain drain* from sending countries and *brain gain* in receiving countries. Studies of foreign students who completed advanced degrees in science and engineering in the United States suggest that half eventually return to their developing countries of origin (Johnson and Rogers, 1998), and case studies in South Africa also suggest a 50 percent return rate.

There is no agreement on whether a 50 percent return rate is high or low, or whether government policies should be crafted to raise or lower the return rate of professionals who study or work abroad. B. Lindsay Lowell and Alan M. Findlay (2002) have urged developed countries to promote returns by enforcing rules that require returns, citing as a best practice the U.S. cultural exchange

(J-1) program, which requires a two-year return to the migrant's country of origin after a "cultural exchange" visit in the United States that can involve employment. However, the J-1 program shows that it is very hard to enforce return rules. Foreign doctors who enter the United States for paid medical residency training with J-1 visas have been allowed to stay despite the return rule because of pressure from hospitals in rural areas, and these J-1 visitors get immigrant visas if they stay several years in medically underserved areas of the United States.

EMIGRATION IMPACTS

There are several types of responses to the brain drain. Countries such as South Africa and Jamaica decry the brain drain and demand compensation from developed countries for the loss of their professionals, while India and the Philippines have governmental marketing agencies that seek out foreign opportunities for nurses, teachers, and other professionals. Who is right—should the emigration of professionals lead to compensation, or should developing countries try to market their professionals abroad?

The impacts of professional emigrants on their countries of origin depend on the three R's that are the major channels for assessing the impacts of emigration: recruitment, remittances, and returns. Recruitment is shaped by receiving-country employers and policies, but individuals in developing countries decide whether to emigrate, how much to remit, and whether to return. The spectrum of impacts from professional migrants can be framed by two extremes: Indian information technology (IT) workers and African health care workers. In the case of IT professionals from India, emigration seems to have set in motion virtuous circles that led to new industries and jobs and improved the quality of IT services throughout India, suggesting that nonmigrants benefited from this emigration. However, the emigration of African doctors and nurses often leads to worse health care in rural areas, threatening to put the health care system in a downward spiral, with remaining workers forced to assume more responsibilities, the quality of care declining, and more health care workers considering emigration to escape.

What determines whether the emigration of professionals from developing countries leads to virtuous or vicious circles? Virtuous circles are most likely if migrants are abroad for only a short time, send back remittances, and return with new skills and links to industrial countries that lead to increased trade and investment. Vicious circles can be the outcome if migrants flee what they believe to be a sinking ship and cut ties to their countries of origin.

Recruitment

Most governments subsidize higher education, so the emigration of graduates can represent a "loss" of subsidized human capital to developing countries. Efforts to prevent the emigration of professionals are rarely effective, since professionals can leave as tourists or conference participants and simply stay abroad. The most common control policy is to withhold the final license for a doctor or nurse until she has completed a period of service, usually in a medically underserved area, a policy that can postpone but not prevent emigration. For example, South Africa graduates about thirteen hundred doctors and twenty-five hundred nurses a year, and surveys suggest that 40 percent of medical graduates want to emigrate. Graduates who received government support for their education must serve two years in rural areas before receiving their license to practice, but enforced duty in rural areas with poorly equipped clinics often reinforces the desire to leave.

The South African government, unwilling to recruit doctors from poorer neighboring countries to replace those who emigrate, has turned to Cuban doctors—80 percent of the doctors in rural South Africa are Cubans (Martineau et al., 2002). It should be emphasized that, especially in nursing, there can be both unfilled nursing vacancies and unemployed nurses, so stopping emigration or getting all nurses abroad to return could be less effective than persuading South Africans to return to nursing. In 2000 there were about thirty-two thousand unfilled nursing jobs in South Africa and seven thousand South African nurses abroad, but there were thirty-five thousand nurses in South Africa not working as nurses.

In Malawi, where public sector registered nurses earn $1,900 a year, almost two-thirds of the nursing jobs in the public health system are vacant, in part because of emigration but also because many nurses staying in the country have switched to private hospitals and foreign-financed nonprofit groups, an extreme example of the brain drain. With the demand for health care in Africa growing because of AIDS and recent initiatives to provide funds for immunization against common diseases, African countries at the annual assembly of the World Health Organization in May 2004 urged developed nations to compensate them for their lost investment in training nurses, and won a pledge from the organization to study ways to reduce the damage from the emigration of nurses.

Much of the controversy over nurses is due to the expansion of the British National Health Service (NHS) in the past decade, with the NHS recruiting nurses in English-speaking former colonies that train them to British standards. In response to complaints from African countries, the United Kingdom's Code of Conduct for Recruitment of Health Professionals, developed in 2001 but applicable only to the National Health Service, asserts that "international recruitment is sound and legitimate" but advises the NHS not to "target developing countries for recruitment of health care personnel unless the government of that country formally agrees" (Buchan, 2002, 19).[24] Physicians for Human Rights (PHR), winner of the Nobel Peace Prize in 1997 for its work to ban land mines, issued a report in July 2004 that called on industrial nations to reimburse African countries for the loss of health professionals educated at African expense but also emphasized that there is a trade-off between the rights of African health professionals to seek a better life and the rights of people in their home countries to decent health care.[25]

Countries worried about the emigration of their health care professionals could do more to retain them, including making health care institutions more employee friendly, improving working conditions, increasing respect for nurses, and developing career ladders with transparent criteria for advancement. Money is important, but most studies conclude that money is not the only factor prompting emigration. Just as the return of overseas nurses would not fill as many vacancies as could be filled by persuading local nurses to return to nursing, so higher salaries alone are not likely to fix systemic problems in human resources management in health care and other sectors that are losing professionals to jobs abroad.

Countries such as the Philippines and India seek to "market" their health care professionals abroad. In both countries, many health care workers are trained in private, tuition-charging schools; students take out loans to get their education, and private recruitment firms find jobs abroad for graduates. Recruitment firms compete to attract professionals interested in going abroad by finding foreign employers who will offer better wages and working conditions, but the real prize for many migrants is an immigrant visa.[26] The Philippine government regulates the activities of labor recruiters, and has labor attachés abroad to whom migrants with problems can turn (Abella, 1997).[27]

The United States is a major destination for migrant nurses, including Filipinos. Most U.S. hospitals require foreign nurses to speak English, have a degree in nursing, and to have worked at a hospital with at least 150 beds for two or more years. Filipino nurses often satisfy these requirements, since they receive a four-year degree and are educated in English, and the private schools training nurses often use U.S. materials and tests; partly as a result, 75 percent of the seventeen thousand foreign nurses who took the U.S. certification exam in 2001 were Filipinos. Filipino migrants earn far more in the United States than at home: pay for Filipino nurses abroad was reported to be $3,000 to $4,000 a month in 2003, versus $170 a month in urban areas of the Philippines, $75–95 a month in rural areas.

Sending Indian IT workers abroad accelerated the establishment of modern IT services in India. India in 2002 had about $10 billion in revenues from exports of computer-related products, including services provided to foreign firms in India (outsourcing), a result of exporting IT workers and gradually transforming itself from an exporter only of labor to an exporter also of computer services. The benefits of this emigration-led growth included a sharp jump in enrollment in science and engineering courses and the provision of world-class IT services to foreign firms, as well as to government agencies and private firms in India.

These spillover effects of what began as an island of 7,000 IT specialists in the mid-1980s were not preordained. The Indian government initially opposed IT, fearing job losses, but multinationals in India recognized their talented employees and moved Indians to their operations outside India. Indian firms such as Tata evolved to move IT specialists overseas, and they soon saw the virtues of returning some of the computer work to India, where labor costs were lower. The Indian government bolstered the budding IT industry by reducing barriers to imports of computers, helped to assure a reliable communications infrastructure, and allowed the state-supported Indian Institutes of Technologies to set quality benchmarks for education. India in 2003 had about 700,000 IT workers and sees itself dominating the low-cost, high-quality square of the cost-quality matrix, though China and the Philippines are rapidly catching up.

Jamaica represents an extreme case of professional emigration—an estimated 75 percent of Jamaicans with higher education have emigrated, and "migration fever" is common among graduates (Thomas-Hope, 2002). Jamaican Minister of Foreign Trade Anthony Hylton has said that he would not try to prevent the emigration of teachers to the United States and nurses to the United Kingdom; he proposed instead "bilateral and multilateral arrangements with countries like England and the United States so that they pay at least a part of the training cost to the government for recruiting people that we have trained and will not necessarily benefit from their service."[28] However, many Jamaican graduates cannot find jobs or refuse to accept jobs in rural areas, where health care worker shortages are severe, prompting the government to recruit Cubans to replace some those who emigrated.

Remittances

Most migrants remit some of their earnings to family and friends, and during the 1990s, when remittances to developing countries doubled, many governments and institutions became aware of the significance of remittances to cover balance-of-payments deficits. Most developing countries took steps to increase remittances by making it easy and cheap to send money home, but studies demonstrate convincingly that the best way to maximize remittances is to have an appropriate exchange rate and economic policies that promise sustained economic growth (Ratha, 2003). Otherwise, migrants remit to help their families but not to invest, and lack of investment can prompt more emigration and discourage the return of successful migrants.

Professionals with higher earnings can be important sources of investment capital for their countries of origin, investing their own savings and steering others' investments to their countries of origin. In the subsequent virtuous circle, these investments can be accompanied by technology transfers that lead to new industries, as in Taiwan, Korea, and India. Many governments have recognized the potential of migrants abroad and have begun to hold meetings that acknowledge their potential to accelerate development. The Indian government, for example, held its first meeting for the twenty million people of Indian origin abroad in 2003 in a bid to increase investments by Indians abroad.[29] Indians abroad remit $14 billion a year, but overseas Indians have invested relatively little in India, $500 million, compared with the $60 billion invested in China by overseas Chinese.

The spending of remittances can generate jobs. Most studies suggest that each $1 in remittances generates a $2 to $3 increase in GDP, as recipients buy goods or invest in housing, education, or health care, improving the lives of nonmigrants via the multiplier effects of remittance spending. Research suggests that the exit of men in the prime of their working lives initially leads to reduced output in local economies, but that the arrival of remittances can lead to adjustments that maintain output. For example, migrant families can shift farming operations from more labor-intensive crops to less labor-intensive livestock, hire labor to produce crops, or rent cropland to other farmers, enabling them to achieve economies of scale.

In addition to remittances, migrants can steer foreigners' investments to their countries of origin and persuade their foreign employers to buy products from their countries of origin. Having migrants abroad increases travel and tourism between countries, as well as trade in ethnic foods and other home-country items. Migrants abroad may undertake other activities, including organizing themselves to provide funds for political parties and candidates and collecting funds via hometown associations to improve the infrastructure in their areas of origin, since many plan to return.

Returns

The third R in the migration and development equation is returns. Ideally, migrants who have been abroad provide the energy, ideas, and entrepreneurial vigor needed to start or expand businesses at home. Migrants are generally drawn from the ranks of the risk takers at home, and if their new capital is combined with risk-taking behavior, the result can be a new impetus for economic development. On the other hand, if migrants settle abroad and cut ties to their countries of origin, or if they return only to rest and retire, there may be few development impacts of returning migrants. There is also the possibility of back-and-forth circulation, which can under some conditions contribute to economic growth in both countries.

There are several cases of diaspora-led development, sometimes fostered by government programs and policies that planted the seeds that led to the return of migrants and investment and job creation at home.[30] For example, Taiwan invested most of its educational resources in primary and secondary education in the 1970s, so Taiwanese seeking higher education often went abroad for study, and more than 90 percent of those migrants remained overseas despite rapid economic growth in Taiwan.[31] During the 1980s, even before the end of martial law, more Taiwanese graduates began to return, while others maintained "homes" in North America and spent so much time commuting via air that they were called "astronauts."

The Taiwanese government made a major effort to attract professional migrants home, establishing the Hinschu Science–based Industrial Park in 1980 with the goal of creating a concentration of creative expertise to rival Silicon Valley in California. The government provided financial incentives for high-tech businesses to locate in Hinschu, including subsidized Western-style housing (Luo and Wang, 2002). By 2000 the park was a major success, employing more than 100,000 workers in three hundred companies that had sales of $28 billion, with 40 percent of the companies headed by returned overseas migrants. Ten percent of the 4,100 returned migrants employed in the park had doctoral degrees.

The Taiwanese experience suggests that investing heavily in the type of education appropriate to the stage of economic development, and then tapping the "brain reserves overseas" when the country's economy demands more brainpower, can be a successful development strategy. Then–Chinese Premier Zhao Ziyang seemed to embrace such a strategy when he called Chinese abroad "stored brainpower overseas" and encouraged Chinese cities to offer financial subsidies to attract them home, prompting the creation of Returning Student Entrepreneur Buildings.[32] However, most Chinese who study abroad continue to stay abroad: 580,000 have gone abroad since 1979, but only 25 percent had returned by 2002.

The poorest countries pose the largest return challenges. The International Organization for Migration (IOM) operates a return-of-talent program for African professionals abroad, providing them with travel and housing assistance and wage subsidies if they sign two-year contracts that require them to work in the public sector in their countries of origin. The United Nations Development Program has a similar Transfer of Knowledge Through Expatriate Nationals (TOKTEN) program that subsidizes the return of teachers and researchers. However, most professionals who return home under these programs have an immigrant or long-term secure status abroad and are in their countries of origin only while receiving the subsidy. Since subsidizing the return of African professionals is expensive and leads only to short-term stays, Sussex University's Richard Black calls return-of-talent programs "expensive failures."[33]

Many countries have made new commitments to maintain links with their migrants, and one popular way to do so is to encourage dual nationality or dual citizenship. The number of countries approving dual nationality increased sharply in the past twenty years, and immigration countries such as the United States do not ask whether a foreigner naturalizing has relinquished his original citizenship. Jagdish Bhagwati (2003) urges emigration governments to embrace dual nationality to achieve what he calls "a Diaspora model, which integrates past and present citizens into a web of rights and obligations in the extended community defined with the home country as the center."

GATS AND MIGRANTS

Will increased trade in services make the migration of professionals over borders even easier? The General Agreement on Trade in Services (GATS), a World Trade Organization document that entered into force in January 1995, is a cen-

Table 3.4. Global Trade in Services by Mode, 2000

Mode	Trade (in millions of dollars)	Distribution
Cross-border supply	1,000	28%
Consumption abroad	500	14%
Commercial presence	2,000	56%
Migration-compensation	50	1%
Total	3,550	

Source: WTO Statistics, March 14–15, 2002.

tral focus of the current Doha round of negotiations aimed at liberalizing flows of goods and services over borders in ways that benefit developing countries. Services are usually defined as items that are produced and consumed simultaneously, and usually change the consumer, as with medical services.

Table 3.4 summarizes the four major modes or ways to move services over borders—cross-border supply; consumption abroad; Foreign Direct Investment (FDI) or commercial presence; and migration, which GATS refers to as the "temporary movement of natural persons."[34] About 85 percent of world trade in services occurs as cross-border supply and FDI, but many developing countries have made liberalization of service migration their "litmus test" for judging whether the Doha round of trade negotiations, scheduled to conclude in 2005, truly helps to ensure that freer trade accelerates development. GATS does not apply to "measures affecting natural persons seeking access to the employment market" and does not apply to "measures regarding citizenship, residence, or employment on a permanent basis," which suggests that the movement of service providers could be slowed by immigration restrictions.

Migration

GATS has twenty-nine articles covering four major modes of providing services:

Mode 1. *Cross-border supply* is a service provided from the territory of one country to another, such as telephone calls that cross borders to call centers. Mode 1 service supply is most analogous to trade in goods, since services but not producers or consumers cross borders.

Mode 2. *Consumption abroad* is a service provided within one country to consumers from other countries, such as tourism or educational and health services; consumers cross borders to reach the provider and receive the service.

Mode 3. *FDI or commercial presence* is a service provided abroad via a subsidiary of a bank, insurance company, or other firm established in the country where the service is provided. Mode 3 services are often accompanied by some migration, as with intracompany transfers of staff from one of the firm's locations to another.

Mode 4. *Temporary movement of natural persons* involves services provided by individuals abroad. These migrants can be foreign workers, as when Indian IT workers are employed abroad, or self-employed migrants, as with architects or consultants who cross borders to provide services to clients.

Liberalization of trade in services has been achieved primarily via the most-favored-nation (MFN) principle: if a country allows foreign firms to enter a sector such as banking, GATS generally requires the country to treat all banks from WTO member countries equally. However, unlike reciprocal trade liberalization in goods, as when the United States and Mexico simultaneously reduce tariffs on auto imports, GATS negotiations are often not reciprocal, as when the United States allows foreigners to enter to teach in public schools but other countries do not allow Americans to teach in their public schools. Once a GATS liberalization commitment is made, there is to be no backtracking—for example, the United States committed to sixty-five thousand H-1B visas a year in the first round of GATS negotiations and is thus obliged not to reduce the ceiling below sixty-five thousand a year.

The second GATS liberalization principle is national treatment—equal treatment for foreigners (or foreign firms) and nationals (or national firms). Under trade in goods, national treatment means that there should be no additional taxes on foreign-made cars or subsidies for U.S.-made cars. However, many services are provided by governments, and GATS allows exemptions for national treatment in service provision. For example, GATS allows governments to permit only citizens to provide government-provided or -funded services such as education.[35] Finally, GATS is about trade and not migration, so it explicitly allows countries to cite national immigration policies as a reason not to open a particular sector to the temporary movement of natural persons and to deny entry to particular individuals.

Services account for 70–80 percent of output and employment in the world's high-income economies, and the service sector tends to expand with economic development, as when women work outside the home, generating a demand for day care and restaurant meals. The demand for services is income elastic, which means that if incomes rise 10 percent, the demand for tourism or health care services rises more than 10 percent. Finally, many services that were once considered to be immobile have become mobile with falling telecommunications costs, including back-office jobs processing bank and medical records. They first moved from inner cities to suburbs within industrial countries and are now increasingly outsourced to lower-wage workers abroad.

Labor typically constitutes the largest share of the cost of supplying services, accounting for 70–80 percent of production costs, compared with 20 percent for manufactured goods. Lower wages give developing countries a "comparative advantage" in providing many services, especially as technologies and training in computer-related occupations becomes standardized around the world. Industrial country firms have begun to aggressively outsource some computer-intensive services, as exemplified by call-center operations in India and coupon-redemption centers in the Caribbean, enlarging trade in cross-border supply services. Multinationals that establish subsidiaries abroad and then move managers and specialists there for a few years help to expand FDI-related trade in services.

GATS Demands of Developing Countries

Industrial countries, led by the United States and the EU, have pushed for liberalization of FDI trade in services so that their banks, insurance companies, and other service providers could more easily establish subsidiaries and sell services to consumers in developing countries. Developing countries, led by India, have advocated liberalization of temporary migration. Developing countries have made demands in four major areas to facilitate cross-border movements: elimination or reduction of economic needs tests, easing of visa and work permit issuance, expedited recognition of an individual's credentials, and elimination of the requirement that service-providing migrants pay social security and related taxes.

Economic needs tests (ENTs) require employers seeking permission to hire foreign service providers to satisfy their governments that local workers are not available. There are two major types of tests, preadmission and postadmission.[36] Preadmission tests require employers to demonstrate that they have tried to find local workers while offering at least prevailing or government-set wages. Employers place ads seeking local workers and keep logs that record why applicants were not hired, and the border gate remains closed until the employer satisfies the government that foreign service providers are truly needed. The alternative is employer attestation, a trust-the-employer approach: the employer attests or asserts that the foreigner is needed and, in the application to hire foreigners, makes such assurances as promising to pay at least the prevailing wage. On the basis of this attestation, the government agency approves the foreigner's admission, and there is generally no enforcement unless the government receives complaints. Under postadmission attestation, the employer opens the border gate, which is why most employers prefer postadmission to preadmission economic needs tests.

Developing countries would prefer few or no economic needs tests and more transparency in procedures used by government agencies to determine prevailing wages and other factors used in both preadmission and postadmission systems. Their long-term goal is a WTO-issued GATS visa that would allow professionals from architects to zoologists initially, and later less-skilled workers, to move freely between GATS signatory nations, either as employees or as self-employed persons.[37] One model often cited is the Asian-Pacific Economic Co-operation (APEC) Business Travel Card, a three-year multiple-entry visa issued by national authorities to facilitate business travel among APEC countries. The card expedites entries for two- to three-month stays in other APEC countries but does not allow its holders to work for wages as local workers (Nielson, 2002).

Visa and work permit procedures comprise the steps required to obtain permission to enter another country and work as a service provider. After an employer receives permission to hire a foreign service provider, the foreigner must normally be interviewed by a government agency, such as consular staff in the migrant's country of origin, to determine whether she is eligible for a residence and work visa. In some countries, separate agencies issue work and residence visas, and there can be conflicts between them over whether a visa should be issued, which increases costs and uncertainties. Developing countries would like GATS to call for countries receiving service-providing migrants to develop "one-stop shops" that would issue multiple entry visas and work permits and give sending countries the right to file trade complaints if interagency conflicts in the host country slow visa issuance or renewal.

Most industrial countries make it easiest for professionals to enter, and a major demand of developing countries in the GATS negotiations is recognition of a migrant's qualifications. Professional migration is facilitated if credentials are recognized outside the country in which they were issued. Within some regions, such as the European Union, mutual recognition agreements (MRAs) facilitate migration, and a similar process inside a country such as the United States facilitates the migration of doctors, nurses, and lawyers across states. Mutual recognition means that states or countries that issue licenses to professionals acknowledge the validity of licenses issued by other states or countries on a reciprocal basis, and MRAs are most common when educational systems are similar, such as within the EU, and between previous mother countries and colonies, as in the British Commonwealth. Efforts to develop MRAs among more diverse countries have been limited largely to accounting and actuarial sciences, perhaps the most global occupation, although there is discussion of standardizing medical education around the world as well.

Many developing countries would like a global MRA administered by the WTO, so that if the WTO certified a person as a doctor, all member countries would be obliged to recognize her credentials. The WTO is unlikely to issue global credentials soon, and even if it did, a global credential or more MRAs might not lead to an upsurge in migration. For example, within the EU relatively few professionals such as doctors move from one country to another despite significant salary differences, highlighting the importance of such factors as recruitment to persuade people to move and language as an obstacle to employment abroad.[38] As a second-level demand, developing countries would prefer employer assessments of qualifications to government checks of credentials so that only an employer's word is necessary to deem a foreigner qualified. This sometimes happens in high-tech fields, where there are few government-established credential-vetting systems.

The fourth developing country demand centers on social security–related issues. Payroll taxes add 20–40 percent to wages in most industrial countries, and developing countries complain that migrant service providers are often required to pay such taxes, even though they may have limited access to the benefits these taxes finance. If the comparative advantage of developing countries is lower labor cost, requiring migrants to pay social security taxes erodes their comparative advantage, according to developing countries. On the other hand, many migrants find ways to stay abroad, so excluding them from social security systems might leave them with fewer benefits than other workers if they settle, raising equity issues.

Can GATS Liberalize Migration?

Industrial countries say that it is hard for them to liberalize the migration of service providers in 2005 because of high unemployment rates in information technology, the sector that accounted for much of the growth in migration over the past decade. In addition, security concerns and fears of illegal migration make most industrial countries reluctant to embrace the liberalization desired by developing countries that could lead to more migration. These concerns help to explain why there are few liberalization offers in the Doha round. One exception is an offer to allow multinationals to transfer university graduates freely to EU subsidiaries for one year of training.

There may be an alternative to migration in FDI, which currently offers the easiest way to move temporary workers over borders. If a firm is multinational, it can move managers and specialists to the foreign subsidiary with relative ease—there are generally no economic needs tests, no numerical limits, and no prevailing-wage or other salary requirements for such migrants. Many developing countries complain that their firms are unable to establish subsidiaries abroad, but Indian IT firms have demonstrated that developing-country multinationals can use intracompany transfers to move IT workers over borders.[39]

What about independent service providers, such as architects and translators, who often work in a nonemployee relationship with their client-consumers? Most industrial countries require self-employed migrants to provide the service for which they are entering to a final consumer, but few developing-country service providers have the contacts to find consumers abroad in advance of their presence. Developing countries would like industrial countries to allow their professionals to enter and work as employees for such service providers as architecture firms, movements that are currently considered labor migration and subject to guest worker rules. Many developing countries emphasize that they want only temporary access for their service providers abroad. In practice, it is hard to separate temporary and permanent migration; professionals are among those most likely to settle abroad.

If the goal of developing countries is to increase the employment of their citizens abroad, the easiest current path is via transfers between subsidiaries, followed by adjustment of status, as when foreigners arrive as students, find local employers, and adjust to become temporary workers. Most industrial countries have made it easier for foreign students to enter and stay, but there is no consensus on whether such a side-door student migration route helps or hurts developing countries of origin. Some countries complain that the exit of health care workers leads to a vicious downward spiral, while others find that the exit of IT specialists sets in motion a positive virtuous development process. Developing countries hoping that the GATS negotiations make it easier for their nationals to cross borders may want to be careful what they wish for—they could find more of their highly skilled workers leaving under a liberalized migrant-service-provider regime.

4 Guest Worker Programs

Guest worker programs are designed to add workers temporarily to the labor force, not settlers to the population; workers are admitted with the understanding that they will not become immigrants and naturalized citizens. In most cases, guest workers fill year-round or permanent jobs, meaning that individuals should rotate in and out of the labor market and country in a revolving-door fashion. Most foreigners admitted under guest worker programs are unskilled workers who fill so-called 3-D jobs: dirty, dangerous, and difficult.

In this chapter we review the shift from large-scale guest worker programs, in which admissions varied with the overall unemployment rate, to current small-scale programs, which are distinguished by the lack of a relationship between admissions and general economic indicators. We then turn to guest worker programs that admit temporary workers for temporary (often seasonal) jobs; these are the programs most likely to succeed in rotating migrants.

UNINTENDED CONSEQUENCES

During the heyday of guest worker programs in the 1950s and 1960s, hundreds of thousands of migrants were recruited to work in economic sectors that included construction, agriculture, and manufacturing, but migrants were rarely recruited for service-sector jobs. Most countries had only one major guest worker program, and overall labor market indicators were used to determine the number of migrants to be admitted, so that admissions fluctuated with macroeconomic indicators such as the unemployment rate. In countries such as Germany in the 1960s, changes in unemployment almost perfectly explained changes in guest worker admissions.

Recruitment under European large-scale guest worker programs was halted in 1973–1974, when there was still a close relationship between migrant employment and the total number of foreigners in a country. For example, the number of foreigners employed as wage and salary workers was about two-thirds of foreign residents in Germany in 1972–1973, but then the number of foreign residents rose as migrants were joined by their families, and rose further in the 1980s and 1990s with more family unification, plus asylum seekers, and the arrival of other foreigners. Meanwhile, the number of foreigners employed as wage and salary workers fell, reaching a low of 1.5 million in the mid-1980s. The growing gap between employed foreign workers and total foreign residents became a powerful argument against more immigration, since more immigration did not necessarily lead to more employment.

The German experience—where foreigners were first associated with employment and hard work, and later with unemployment and welfare—is typical in Europe. Non-EU foreigners have low employment and high unemployment rates in many European countries, which is one reason why arguments that European countries "need" immigrants for demographic and economic reasons are often countered by assertions that more immigration could simply add to unemployment. In 2000 adding one hundred men between twenty-five and thirty-nine years old from outside the EU increased employment by seventy-three, while adding one hundred EU nationals increased employment by eighty-six, or 20 percent more. The employment gap was even larger for women, and the unemployment rate for young men and women from outside the EU countries was about twice as high as for young EU nationals (see Table 4.1).

Lagging employment-population ratios among foreigners helped to set the stage for the new guest worker programs of the 1990s, each aimed at filling jobs

Table 4.1. Non-EU Foreigners in the EU: Employment and Unemployment, 2000

	Men	Women
Percentage Employed, Ages 25–39		
Non-EU Foreigners	73	44
Nationals	86	68
Ratio of non-EU/nationals	0.8	0.6
Percentage Unemployed, Ages 25–39		
Non-EU foreigners	15	19
Nationals	6.5	10
Ratio of non-EU/nationals	2.3	1.9

Source: Thorogood and Winqvist, 2003, 6.

in particular industries or occupations in "rifle fashion." The role of sending countries also changed: most programs are unilateral, meaning that employers decide where and how to recruit migrants, while in other programs sending-country governments recruit and screen migrants for foreign employers. Finally, the right of migrants to adjust their status and remain abroad as longer-term workers or immigrants varies by type of worker and country of employment, with professionals in the United Kingdom having the easiest path to settlement. Macroeconomic policies have far less impact on the demand for migrants in today's narrowly focused guest worker programs, and in deregulated labor markets government labor agencies have less detailed information on whether migrants are needed. As a result, employers have gained more power over the operation of the border gate.

Guest worker programs tend to become larger than originally planned and to last longer than anticipated because of "distortion" and "dependence." *Distortion* refers to assumptions by employers: Labor markets are flexible, so jobs can be structured in a manner that assumes the presence or absence of migrants. However, once businesses begin to make investment decisions that assume migrants will (continue to) be available, employers resist policy changes that would curb the influx of foreign workers; that is, their assumptions about labor supply are distorted because they assume they can reach over borders for additional workers. *Dependence* refers to the fact that migrants, as well as their families, communities, and home country governments, often depend on earnings from foreign jobs, so they too resist policy changes that might reduce emigration opportunities, which is why irregular migration often follows recruitment stops.

Another unintended consequence of guest worker programs is the emergence of "immigrant sectors" in the host economy that can grow, increasing an economy's need for migrants. There can also be various forms of exploitation in the recruitment and employment of migrant workers (Ruhs, 2003). Governments' declared policies of controlling migration may be undermined by unexpected settlements as well as the inflow of irregular foreign workers. The bottom line is clear: despite the proliferation of guest worker programs, there are more migrants from developing countries employed outside official programs than inside them, which means that many foreign workers are not protected effectively by labor laws.

LARGE-SCALE GUEST WORKER PROGRAMS

The United States and western European nations began guest worker programs during and after World War II in response to employer requests for foreign workers (Congressional Research Service, 1980; Böhning, 1972). The timing was important, since it helps to explain why policies that were to have profound socioeconomic effects were not debated extensively before migrants arrived to fill jobs. Perhaps the single most important assumption of large-scale guest worker programs was that migrants could be rotated in and out of host-country jobs, as laid out in program rules, acting as a buffer labor force, recruited when unemployment was low and sent home when unemployment rose, thus keeping the unemployment rate low for native workers.

Most migrants rotated in and out of host-country labor markets as expected. For example, during the twenty-two years of Mexican-U.S. guest worker or bracero programs, most braceros returned at the end of their seasonal farm jobs, and a combination of tougher enforcement and easier employer access to braceros in the mid-1950s explains the shift from mostly illegal to more legal bracero workers. However, apprehensions of Mexicans unauthorized to stay and work in the United States were higher in the late 1950s than before bracero programs began in 1942, and Mexican immigration increased as some braceros found ways to adjust their status from worker to immigrant. Over the twenty-two years of bracero programs, there were more apprehensions, 4.9 million, than bracero worker admissions, 4.6 million (see Table 4.2; both apprehensions and admissions double-count individuals who are caught or who were admitted several times).

Similarly, most European guest workers rotated in and out of jobs as anticipated. Between 1960 and 1973, 75 percent of the 18.5 million foreigners who ar-

Table 4.2. Bracero Admissions, Apprehensions, and Immigrants, 1942–1964

Year	Mexican Braceros	Mexicans Apprehended	Mexican Immigrants
1942	4,203		2,378
1943	52,098	8,189	4,172
1944	62,170	26,689	6,598
1945	49,454	63,602	6,702
1946	32,043	91,456	7,146
1947	19,632	182,986	7,558
1948	35,345	179,385	8,384
1949	107,000	278,538	8,803
1950	67,500	458,215	6,744
1951	192,000	500,000	6,153
1952	197,100	543,538	9,079
1953	201,380	865,318	17,183
1954	309,033	1,075,168	30,645
1955	398,650	242,608	43,702
1956	445,197	72,442	61,320
1957	436,049	44,451	49,321
1958	432,857	37,242	26,721
1959	437,643	30,196	22,909
1960	315,846	29,651	32,708
1961	291,420	29,817	41,476
1962	194,978	30,272	55,805
1963	186,865	39,124	55,986
1964	177,736	43,844	34,448
Total	4,646,199	4,872,731	545,941

Source: INS Statistical yearbook, various years.

rived in Germany left as expected (Hönekopp, 1997, 1). However, Germans who assumed that the rotation principle would be honored strictly were not prepared for the settlement of 25 percent of the guest workers. This settlement, as well as continued immigration via family unification, led to the perception that guest worker programs failed because they opened immigration doors in declared "nonimmigrant" countries such as Germany. By 2000, 60 percent of the 7.3 million foreigners in Germany had arrived after 1985—that is, twelve years after guest worker recruitment stopped.

Because of the conditions existing when the guest worker programs were started, there was very little discussion of alternatives to recruiting migrant workers. For example, instead of importing migrants, governments could have raised wages directly by raising minimum wages, or simply allowed wages to rise by limiting immigration, which should have reduced the supply of labor and increased the demand. Employers argued that market forces should not be allowed to close the labor demand-supply gap because in the U.S. case that could lead to more expensive food during wartime, and in the European case could risk a fragile economic recovery in the postwar period. There were also foreign policy reasons for importing migrants: the U.S. offer of jobs helped to win Mexican support for the Allies in World War II, while the European Economic Community's four freedoms included freedom of movement, so that migration from labor-surplus to labor-shortage areas was expected and encouraged to reduce economic differences within the Common Market.

Europe's Guest Workers

Many European countries had guest worker programs, but we focus on Germany, France, and Switzerland, the countries that recruited more than half of all guest workers during the 1950s and 1960s. Their experiences illustrate the labor market, social, and political impacts of foreign workers in western Europe.

GERMANY

Although Germany remains the number-one source of recorded immigrants to the United States, it also has a long history of using migrant workers, including hiring Poles and Italians to work in Ruhr-area mines and factories in the nineteenth century and using foreign workers in German factories during World War II.[1] The wartime experience with foreign workers is credited by some for encouraging German employers to ask again for migrants during the 1950s and 1960s.

Germany's large-scale guest worker programs began in 1955 with a labor recruitment agreement that permitted German farmers to hire Italian workers to harvest their crops. However, the growing demand for labor was in German factories, mines, and construction sites, and these nonfarm employers received permission to hire migrants under a series of bilateral agreements that eventually included seven non-EC "recruitment countries": Greece, Morocco, Portugal, Spain, Tunisia, Turkey, and Yugoslavia.[2] There was no significant discussion of alternatives to guest workers for four major reasons. First, the German labor force was shrinking for demographic and social reasons, including a delayed baby boom that led many to believe that female labor force participation could not be raised, increased educational opportunities that kept more youth in school, and better pensions that prompted earlier retirements.

Second, there was a reluctance to risk what was perceived to be a fragile economic recovery on the likely alternatives to foreign workers: mechanization and rationalization (Kindleberger, 1967; Martin, 1998). Unions did not oppose importing foreign workers, especially after securing a promise that foreigners would be treated equally and thus not undercut German workers.

Third, unifying Europe was based on freedom of movement, meaning that after January 1, 1968, an EEC/EU worker could leave his country and enter any other EEC/EU country for up to three months in search of a job; if he found a job, the host country had to issue any needed work and residence permits (Böhning, 1972). By recruiting guest workers in the early 1960s, Germany simply fast-forwarded a process, many argued, that would soon happen in any event.

Fourth, the early 1960s provided western Europe with a peculiar international economic environment. Germany and other European nations had undervalued currencies in a world of fixed exchange rates, which made Europe a center for investment and exports because $1 bought DM5 when it "should have" bought DM4. Local and foreign capital was invested to build and expand factories that produced goods for domestic and export markets, and a French writer looked with alarm at U.S. investments and warned of *The American Challenge* to Europe (Servan-Schreiber, 1967).[3]

Guest worker recruitment expanded sharply. In 1960 there were 329,000 foreign workers in Germany, and their number topped 1 million in 1964. After a dip in 1966–1967 due to recession, the number of guest workers climbed to a peak 2.6 million in 1973, when migrants made up 12 percent of employed wage and salary workers. Most guest workers were ex-farmers between eighteen and thirty-five years old, although a significant number of semiskilled construction workers, miners, and schoolteachers became guest workers.[4]

Guest workers were admitted legally only after the German Employment Service (ES) made a preadmission certification that migrants were needed; that is, employers requested workers, and if local workers were not available, the employer or a joint German-Turkish or German-Yugoslav office recruited workers. However, employers could also request workers by name, which gave Turks and Yugoslavs an incentive to go to Germany as tourists and find an employer to request them, thus avoiding long queues of migrants waiting to go abroad (Miller and Martin, 1982).

Rotation rules and return "myths" discouraged planning for the settlement and integration of guest workers and their families. When guest worker recruitment started, employers, unions, and governments agreed that migrants would stay abroad at most two or three years and then depart with their savings and newfound skills to accelerate development in their home countries. Many migrants soon learned that they could not, as they had imagined, earn German wages while living in German cities at rural Turkish costs. Employers, on the other hand, often encouraged migrants to stay rather than to return, since rotation meant that new migrants had to be recruited and trained. Even though the incentives of many employers and migrants favored settlement, social scientists interviewing migrants reported that migrants wanted to return to familiar languages and cultures, citing factors ranging from the cold weather and strange food to racism and discrimination in the intention of most guest workers to return.

The belief that migrants were truly guests planning to return prevented the development of policies that might have slowed the explosive growth in migrant numbers, such as levies or fees charged to employers that might have reduced their demand for migrants. Eventually, noneconomic arguments were largely responsible for stopping additional recruitment. Fringe politicians made a rallying cry of "Foreigners out! Germany is for the Germans," prompting mainstream parties to assert repeatedly that "Germany is not a country of immigration," implying that the guest workers would eventually leave. However, wildcat strikes involving migrants in summer 1973 reinforced the sense that migration was "out of control," and the October 1973 oil embargo threatened a recession and higher unemployment. On November 23, 1973, the German government stopped the recruitment of non-EC workers for more than ninety days of work, and this "recruitment stop" remains in place today—the 1990s guest worker programs are exceptions to the general recruitment stop.[5]

FRANCE

France traditionally has had a two-pronged approach to immigration: on the one hand, foreign workers were to fill labor market gaps; on the other, migrants were to compensate for demographic deficits. This meant that there were two separate policies: rotate guest workers when they were no longer needed but also encourage the settlement and integration of foreigners.

France began its large-scale recruitment of guest workers shortly after the creation, in November 1945, of a new type of public entity, the National Immigration Office (Office national d'immigration, ONI). ONI was given a monopoly on introducing foreign workers and those from France's overseas territories into France, as well as powers over the recruitment of French nationals wishing to work abroad.[6] The postwar tripartite French government wanted to empower the state to regulate migration because of abuses of foreign workers during the interwar years, when French employer cartels enjoyed great freedom in migration matters (Plewa and Miller, 2004, 8).

A first bilateral agreement was concluded with Italy in 1947 and allowed for both anonymous and nominative recruitment. In practice, many French employers bypassed the official recruitment system by hiring Italians already in France. This practice was technically illegal but allowed by the government, which routinely legalized such hiring, thus undercutting its bilateral agreement with Italy and similar agreements concluded with Spain (1956), Morocco (1963), Portugal (1964), Yugoslavia (1965), Tunisia, Turkey, and Algeria.[7] Almost two-thirds of all foreign workers recorded in French statistics as legally admitted between 1945 and 1975 were in fact legalized after they were in France and found employers to hire them (Miller, 2002).

By 1948 the tripartite French government had collapsed, the French Communist Party had gone into opposition, and migration had become a minor issue as successive conservative French governments engaged in "benign neglect," even though "migration-related social problems festered, especially as migration from North Africa grew" (Plewa and Miller, 2004, 9).[8] A key turning point came in 1968, when foreign workers participated in strikes and protests started by students in May, and hundreds were expelled. The extreme left tried to mobilize migrants to participate in struggles over housing conditions, while the extreme right denounced out-of-control migration. Migration policy became problematic, and by 1972 the French government declared its intent to end routine legalizations. "Mastering migration" became the stated aim of the French governments, prompting the decision to stop the recruitment of non-EC foreign workers, with the exception of seasonal labor, in 1974.

Algeria in 1973 unilaterally suspended the recruitment of its nationals to work in France after attacks in France on Algerians and other North Africans. Relations between Algeria and France further deteriorated when French President Valéry Giscard d'Estaing (1974–1981) tried to repatriate hundreds of thousands of Algerians. French efforts to induce voluntary returns by offering cash bonuses to departing foreigners largely failed (Plewa and Miller, 2004, 12).

SWITZERLAND

With a booming economy that escaped destruction during World War II, Switzerland was one of the first European countries to engage in guest worker recruitment after 1945 and, in contrast to France and Germany, never stopped labor recruitment. Instead, Switzerland began to gradually control immigration first by introducing a ceiling on the number of foreign workers per enterprise in 1963, then by putting an upper limit on the number of entries in 1970.[9] Switzerland left the recruitment of foreign workers to the country's employers; it did not have public recruitment agencies such as those in France and Germany.

Switzerland believed in the rotation model: import foreign workers when needed, and send them home when not. Foreign workers thus served as a *Konjunkturpuffer* (cyclical buffer), much like other macroeconomic policies aimed at maximizing growth and minimizing unemployment. Swiss immigration policy was based on the ideas laid out by the governing Federal Council in 1924, when what became the 1931 Foreigners Law was first discussed: "There is nothing to object to the influx of foreigners as long as they do not think of establishing themselves." The first bilateral agreement was made with Italy in 1948, and it reflected these views by requiring Italians to live in Switzerland at least ten years before they could receive long-term residence permits (Piguet and Mahnig, 2000, 4).

The Swiss preference for seasonal foreign workers was motivated by a desire to avoid settlement. In the years that followed, the Swiss-Italian agreement, about half of the migrants were seasonal, required to return home each year and allowed to stay a maximum of nine months in Switzerland (permit A). The other half had renewable annual work permits (permit B) or permanent residence permits (permit C).

In the early 1960s Switzerland was forced to renegotiate its agreement with Italy. With other European countries recruiting guest workers, Italy wanted better conditions for its migrants in Switzerland and forced a new agreement in 1964 that facilitated permanent residency and family reunion, and the improved rights granted to Italian migrants were eventually extended to non-Italian migrants, including those from Spain, Portugal, and Yugoslavia.

However, anti-immigrant groups mounted campaigns to reduce immigration, prompting the Swiss government to develop a complex quota system to regulate foreign labor. The overall quota on migrants introduced in 1970—after two anti-immigration popular initiatives designed to change the constitution were narrowly defeated in referenda—was a compromise between employers demanding more foreign labor and anti-immigrant forces (Piguet and Mahnig, 2000, 13). The quota reduced the number of foreign workers, and their number fell further with the 1973–1974 recession. Switzerland did not have mandatory unemployment insurance, and many of the foreigners who lost their jobs and had no benefits returned to their countries of origin. In this way, the foreign workers fulfilled their desired role as "cyclical buffer": the Swiss labor force fell 8 percent after 1973, but the unemployment rate stayed below 1 percent (Liebig, 2003, 9).

However, the right of settled migrants to unify their families, as well as the birth of foreign children, increased the foreign population, and asylum seekers also trickled into Switzerland. Today, a third of Swiss residents are immigrants or the descendants of an immigrant—some two million people. The most common names of newborn children are no longer Karin or Christoph but Laura and Luca, and almost half of the Swiss national soccer team has foreign roots. A quarter of all Swiss work is done by foreign nationals, and migrants make up half of those employed in hotels and restaurants (IMES, 2004). As in other European countries, the unemployment rate for foreigners is higher than for Swiss: 4.2 percent for male foreigners and 4.9 percent for female foreigners, compared with 1.7 percent for male and female Swiss (*Statistisches Bundesamt,* 2004).

Switzerland became a country in which migrants settled despite the effort to rotate foreign workers, and migrants today face greater labor market challenges than Swiss nationals. There is still an active anti-immigrant campaign in some parts of the country that ignores the largely successful integration of two million foreigners. The confusion between immigration and integration was demonstrated in a September 26, 2004, referendum in which a majority of the voters and the cantons refused to grant easier access to Swiss citizenship to second- and third-generation foreigners.

LESSONS

There are four important lessons from these different European experiences with large-scale guest worker programs. First, distortion and dependence are real phenomena that allow guest worker programs to grow larger and last longer than anticipated. Second, rule-based programs with no economic incentives or with incentives that are not aligned with program rules face pressure from migrants and employers for exemptions and eventually undergo rule changes. Rotation and return rules are difficult to implement while protecting the human rights of migrants, a fact underscored by the Swiss writer Max Frisch in 1965: "We asked for workers and people came."[10] Third, the three Rs of recruitment, remittances, and returns do not guarantee that guest worker migration will turn emigration areas into stay-at-home areas in a short time, and instead may set in motion forces that increase migration in the short run. Fourth, guest worker programs may strain foreign relations instead of producing the expected benefits for both the host and the origin country in the form of increased trade or other exchanges.

Mexican Braceros in the United States

One industry, agriculture, and one occupation, farm worker, have taken the lead in the recruitment of unskilled temporary foreign workers in the United States (Martin et al., 1995). The reasons are rooted in history. Agriculture in the western United States required large farms for extensive cattle grazing and grain farming, and when lower transportation costs linked the West with the rest of the United States in the late nineteenth century and irrigation justified a shift to labor-intensive fruits and vegetables, large farms were expected to be broken into family-sized units to obtain the necessary seasonal workers. However, waves of immigrants with no other U.S. job options—Chinese, Japanese, Filipinos, Punjabi Sikhs, and Mexicans—were available as seasonal workers.

Because these newcomers were shut out of urban labor markets by discrimination and other factors, farm employers could pay seasonal workers a minimum wage and assume that they would be available when needed. These low labor costs were soon capitalized or incorporated into land prices, pushing them up, which gave landowners and their bankers incentives to keep the door open for migrants. The internal migration of small midwestern farmers to California during the 1930s exposed this farm labor market and, with John Steinbeck's 1939 novel *The Grapes of Wrath* giving an emotional push for major policy changes, many reformers assumed that federal water, labor, and land policies would finally break factories in the fields (Martin, 2003). However, World War II allowed large-farm employers instead to sign a bilateral agreement with Mexico allowing the admission of bracero (strong arms) guest workers.

The availability of braceros aggravated distortion and dependence. U.S. farmers planted additional crops in remote areas, and since such plantings would not have been profitable if the influx of migrants were reduced, farmers exerted political pressure to continue bracero admissions. Many Mexicans became dependent on U.S. jobs, and to increase their chance of being selected under a program that required U.S. employers to pay the cost of transportation from the workers' homes to the U.S. jobs, many braceros moved with their families to the Mexican-U.S. border. This reduced farmers' transportation costs but provided no employment alternatives in Mexico when the program was eventually ended unilaterally by the U.S. government. President John F. Kennedy, announcing in 1963 that the program would soon end, said that braceros were "adversely affecting the wages, working conditions, and employment opportunities of our own agricultural workers" (Craig, 1971, 172–173). Bracero recruitment ended December 31, 1964.

There were several long-term effects of the bracero program. First, farm worker earnings did not rise as fast as nonfarm worker earnings during the booming 1950s. Average farm worker earnings in California rose 41 percent in the 1950s, while average factory worker earnings rose 63 percent. Second, Mexican-Americans, who lived mostly in rural and agricultural areas before the bracero program began, migrated to cities such as San Jose and Los Angeles to escape competition from braceros. Third, in order to create jobs for braceros and their families in Mexican border cities, the Mexican and U.S. governments allowed the establishment of *maquiladoras,* assembly plants that imported parts from the United States, assembled them in Mexico, and paid duties only on the value added by Mexican workers. Maquiladora employment rose very slowly and employed young women rather than experienced braceros.

The bracero program demonstrates the truth of the proposition that the best way to begin a flow of immigrants from a country is to recruit guest workers there. After the bracero program ended, some ex-braceros became immigrants by having U.S. farmers offer them employment—even an offer of a seasonal job was sufficient in the 1960s to obtain an immigrant visa. These immigrant visas, printed on green paper, allowed thousands of Mexicans to become "green card commuters," living in Mexico and commuting to seasonal U.S. jobs, as they had under the bracero program. As green card commuters aged, their sons and relatives replaced them, often illegally; others became farm labor contractors whose binational experience made them efficient recruiters, smugglers, and employers of Mexican migrants in the United States.

SMALL-SCALE GUEST WORKER PROGRAMS

In the 1990s new small-scale guest worker programs were launched in North America and western Europe. Each program had its own admissions criteria, unique rules governing length of stay and adjustment of status options, and a wide range of provisions aimed at avoiding long-term dependence on migrants and migrant settlement. In most small-scale programs, employers have more power over admissions and employment than they did in the large-scale programs of the 1960s, so there can be farm labor "shortages" today despite double-digit unemployment rates. The detailed rules of small-scale programs tend to stifle debate, since only those truly interested in the programs have taken the time to learn about adverse-effect wage rates in U.S. agriculture or which provisions of German construction union contracts apply to project-tied workers.

Classifying Programs

Small-scale guest worker programs can be compared along several dimensions, but two of the most important are (1) the requirements employers must satisfy to obtain guest workers and (2) the rights of migrants. These criteria are summarized for U.S. programs below, starting with what an employer must do to get migrants.

Under most programs, employers must satisfy preadmission certification criteria, which means that employers must advertise for local workers and offer at least a government-set wage in ads that are reviewed by the Department of Labor; offer housing to workers in some cases; and satisfy other job-related requirements. Under postadmission attestation, government checks of employers occur only in response to complaints after migrants are at work.

Worker rights are a second comparative dimension of small-scale guest worker programs, and the major distinction between programs is whether a migrant has a contract that ties him to a particular employer or whether the migrant is a free agent in the labor market, able to change employers. (Migrants who can change employers are sometimes restricted to a particular economic sector.) The largest U.S. program is the H-1B program, a postadmission attestation that allows U.S. employers to obtain foreigners with a bachelor's degree or more to fill U.S. jobs that require that level of education. The U.S. employer asserts that the H-1B recipient is being offered the prevailing wage, and H-1B visa holders sign contracts that generally tie them to one U.S. employer. The two major U.S. programs that admit unskilled workers, H-2A and H-2B, require preadmission certification (see Table 4.3); in these programs the job offer that the employer provides to the Department of Labor and uses to recruit local workers becomes a contract between the employer and the migrant. Migrants can, but rarely do, sue U.S. employers for violations of the "job orders" that employers provide to the Department of Labor.[11]

Employers do not have to satisfy any labor market tests to transfer managers and specialists from their foreign operations to their U.S. subsidiaries, provided that the migrants have been employed in the firm's foreign operations for at least one year. Once in the United States, these L-1 visa holders are restricted to the employer who sponsored them. Similarly, there are no preadmission tests

Table 4.3. Employer Requirements and Worker Rights, U.S. Programs

Employer Requirements	Worker Rights	
	Contractual Worker	Free-Agent Worker
Preadmission certification	H-2A/B unskilled	
Postadmission attestation	H-1B professionals	F-1 students
No employer tests	L-1 intra-company transfers; J-1 exchange visitors	NAFTA professionals

Source: Martin, 2005.

on employers who want to hire J-1 exchange visitors who enter the United States for cultural exchanges that include employment.

Since the principal rationale of guest worker programs is to fill vacant jobs, few programs allow guest workers to be free agents in the labor market. NAFTA's provisions for professionals come very close to allowing Mexicans and Canadians in sixty-seven occupations that generally require at least a college degree to be free agents in the U.S. labor market. A professional from Canada and Mexico may, under NAFTA's chapter 16, enter the United States with proof of her qualifications and a U.S. job offer and receive a TN visa that can be renewed indefinitely, and while in the United States, she may change employers.[12] Similarly, the U.S. program allowing a foreign student to find a job as an adjunct to his studies does not restrict him to any particular employer.[13]

Rationales for Small-scale Programs

While labor shortages remain the principal rationale for today's new guest worker programs, there are also other justifications. For example, foreign policy considerations loomed large in several programs, such as German programs with eastern European nations after 1989 that admitted seasonal workers, project-tied workers, and trainees (Hönekopp, 1997). The German government believed that it had obligations to states whose citizens previously had found work in the former East Germany, while Poland made employment of its workers an issue during negotiations on the recognition of the German-Polish border (Kuptsch, 1994, 3). Similarly, Italy and Spain developed programs to admit legal migrant workers from Albania and Morocco in part to encourage cooperation with those governments in the fight against illegal migration.[14]

In some cases, borders divide "natural" labor markets, so commuter guest programs allow workers to live in one country and work in another. Most governments facilitate such cross-border commuting, as with the special commuter lanes along the Mexican-U.S. border for trusted travelers; border inspections for commuters in many European countries are cursory at best.

An additional rationale for guest worker programs is to promote cultural exchange or development in sending countries. Typically, young people are invited to cross national borders to work while learning the language and culture under cultural exchange and working holidaymaker programs. Trainee programs are designed to provide foreigners with skills in workplace settings, and they vary from programs that are mostly education to programs that are mostly work, as in Korea and Japan.

Other arguments for guest worker programs include the assertion that workers should be freer to cross borders to increase trade in services; that multinational firms should be allowed to assemble diverse workforces to remain competitive; and that allowing migrants to circulate between developing and developed countries lets them act as economic bridges.

Germany: New Programs

The year 1989 was a major turning point in world history, especially for (West) Germany, which received one million newcomers in 1989, half from Poland, increasing the population by 1.7 percent. To deal with the influx from the east, Germany and other European countries developed new and usually bilateral guest worker programs. These small-scale guest worker programs were designed to deal with seemingly inevitable east-west migration, but they were also structured to avoid what was seen as the major failure of the 1960s large-scale programs, settlement and family unification.

Germany admitted 260,000 migrants in its peak year, 1996. Elmar Hönekopp (1997) has noted that, even though some unauthorized workers became legal guest workers under the programs, there were still "perhaps as many illegal workers as legal workers" (11).[15]

The most controversial program is for project-tied or posted workers. It allows a German firm to subcontract part of a construction project to foreign firms that provide primarily labor. The foreign firms then post migrants to Germany for up to two years, and the German firm is to ensure that its Polish, say, subcontractor is paying the prevailing (German) wage to the migrants. However, the migrants are considered employees of the Polish rather than the German firm, so their payroll taxes are far lower than would be the case if they were considered German workers. After abuses in the early 1990s, the admissions ceiling was lowered from 95,000 to 56,000 a year. In 2004 Germany had bilateral agreements on project-tied migration with twelve eastern European states and Turkey.

The trainee program allows up to 11,050 young (eighteen- to forty-year-old) eastern Europeans to work and learn in Germany for up to eighteen months and allows young Germans to work and learn in eastern European nations.[16] German employers submit work-and-learn offers to local employment service offices that, without testing the German labor market, transmit them to a foreign employment service office. For each foreign trainee, the participating enterprise must have at least four German-speaking permanent staff, an effort to ensure that there is cultural and language training for trainees. There is a ceiling for each participating country—2,000 each for Russia and Hungary, for example—but only 44 percent of the available slots were filled in 2002. Poland, which has a ceiling of 1,000 trainee slots, fills 60 to 80 percent, but Hönekopp (1997, 10) notes that many Poles seem to prefer to earn higher wages harvesting apples under the seasonal program rather than taking lower trainee wages.

The border commuter program allows Czech and Polish workers living within fifty kilometers of the German border to commute from their homes to German jobs if the German labor ministry certifies that local workers are not available. The emphasis is on daily commuting, but border commuters are allowed to stay in Germany up to two days a week. This program involved 6,000 Czechs and 1,500 Poles in 1996 but will disappear with EU expansion and freedom of movement.

Among the newest German small-scale programs is one bringing nursing and care personnel from Croatia and Slovenia to Germany, based on memoranda of understanding between the German Employment Service and its foreign counterparts. In contrast to the other programs, the nurses fill permanent jobs. Before recruitment, interviews are conducted in the country of origin, and nurses wanting to go to Germany must have their qualifications recognized under the German Nursing Care Law within a year of arrival or leave. Until they pass the test, nurses and caregivers may be employed as "assistants" at lower wages, and employers must pay a fee of EUR250 per nurse or caregiver; private households do not qualify as employers (ZAV, 2004).

The German green card program, launched in August 2000, made up to twenty thousand five-year work permits available to non-EU nationals coming to Germany to work as computer specialists.[17] In a first for Germany, the admissions process was simplified: foreigners can register their qualifications on

Table 4.4. German Green Cards Issued, August 2000–June 2003

	Total	From Abroad	University Degree	% of Total
India	3,771	3,574	2,771	26%
Ex-USSR	1,851	1,680	1,697	13%
Romania	1,033	971	954	7%
Czech/Slovakia	974	935	809	7%
Ex-Yugoslavia	746	632	647	5%
Hungary	503	467	425	3%
North Africa	430	150	404	3%
Bulgaria	419	351	378	3%
S America	384	314	298	3%
Pakistan	207	169	185	1%
Others	4,248	3,109	3,514	29%
Total	14,566	12,352	12,082	100%

Source: German Labor Ministry.

the Internet, and German employers can search there for needed workers or name the specific individuals they want to hire. Fewer green cards were issued than expected—fewer than fifteen thousand in the first three years of the program. About 85 percent went to non-EU foreigners who were abroad (rather than to foreign students graduating from German institutions), and 83 percent of the green card holders were admitted on the basis of having a university degree in computer science. Lacking an information technology (IT) degree, non-EU foreigners could be admitted if their German employers pay them at least EUR51,000 a year. About a fourth of those admitted were from India, another quarter from eastern Europe, and an eighth from the former Soviet Union (see Table 4.4).

The green card program arose from the failed effort of the Social Democratic Party (SPD)–Green government elected in September 1998 to change German naturalization policy from one of the most restrictive in Europe to one of the most liberal. Under the government's original plan, foreigners who became naturalized Germans could have routinely retained their original nationality. The opposition Christian Democratic Union–Christian Social Union (CDU-CSU) parties in February 1999 won a state election in Hesse by opposing routine dual nationality (they argued it would give dual or double benefits for foreigners), and the naturalization compromise eventually adopted allowed children born to legal foreign residents of Germany to be considered dual nationals until age twenty-three, when they normally lose German citizenship unless they give up their old citizenship.

When the IT industry asked for non-EU foreign professionals, the SPD-Green government saw a way to refocus the immigration debate on the benefits of immigration. There was some opposition to the green card program within the government.[18] The opposition CDU based its May 2000 campaign in a state election in North Rhine–Westphalia on opposition to the green card proposal, using the slogan "Kinder statt Inder" (children instead of Indians) to argue that Germans should have more children and train them instead of importing workers from India. This campaign failed, and the green card program went into effect, but did not lead to a comprehensive immigration law.

The IT boom and the green card program led many German leaders to argue that, to be successful economically, Germany would have to become an immigration country. A commission was appointed to make recommendations for Germany's first planned immigration system, and it delivered a report in July 2001 that recommended an immigration policy in which migrants could be admitted after they scored sufficient points on a test involving age, education, language, and other salient factors.[19] The resulting immigration bill was approved by the lower house of the German Parliament in March 2002, but was not approved properly in the upper house. The bill was reintroduced in 2003 and was again approved by the lower house, but it took until July 2004 and lengthy nationwide debates before the government and the opposition found a compromise that allowed the bill to pass the upper house, where the opposition had a majority. The idea of a point system disappeared in the process, and the law that became effective in 2005 has more provisions on national security than the initial bill.

Major changes in comparison to the "old immigration system" include a reduction in the previous five titles of legal residence to two, a short-term residence permit *(befristete Aufenthaltserlaubnis),* and a settlement permit *(unbefristete Niederlassungserlaubnis).* Highly qualified migrants will be admitted with a settlement permit or permanent status. Foreigners investing at least EUR1 million or creating at least ten jobs will be entitled to permanent status, but the recruitment stop will continue for low- and semiskilled persons. Foreign students may stay up to one year after their graduation in Germany to find a job, rather than leaving within ninety days of graduation. Integration is an explicit policy goal, with language training and integration courses mandatory for some new arrivals and current foreign residents, under threat of nonrenewal of residence permits or reductions in social benefits.

Evaluations of German small-scale guest worker programs suggest that they have succeeded in turning some otherwise unauthorized migrants into legal guest workers and hastened the conversion of seasonal farm jobs into "foreigners' jobs." The major disputes were in construction, which expanded rapidly with German unification in 1990 but was plagued by overcapacity and high unemployment after the mid-1990s, a result of self-employed EU nationals exercising their freedom to provide services and the presence of unauthorized and guest workers.[20] There was little debate about the usefulness of importing Polish workers to work on German farms despite high unemployment in Polish agriculture due to significant trade barriers; Germany at least implicitly endorsed migration for farm work as a substitute for trade in farm commodities. The opportunity for eastern Europeans to work in Germany and other countries generated significant remittances, which were about equal to FDI in 1995 in Poland (Hönekopp, 1997, 20).[21]

However, the creation of transnational networks and semilegal migration also led to distortion and dependence. The short-term movements between Poland and Germany in the domestic helper and caregiving sectors dominated by Polish women imply rotation, but wages and working conditions may have deteriorated and Germany may have avoided having to reorganize its own labor markets to provide assistance in private households (Hillmann, 2003). Without foreign IT workers, Germany's IT sector would probably have engaged in more training and retraining of local workers and may have moved some IT jobs abroad.

U.K. Programs: Top and Bottom

Unlike France, Germany, or Switzerland, the United Kingdom after World War II imported workers from former colonies under systems in place since the end of World War I rather than launching new guest worker programs. In 1919–1920, the United Kingdom began to regulate the employment of non-Commonwealth foreigners, and such labor immigration was first controlled in 1962 when the Commonwealth Immigration Act was introduced. (Immigration from Ireland has never been controlled.) Migration to the United Kingdom was largely characterized by postcolonial flows from countries such as India, Pakistan, Hong Kong, and the Caribbean islands.

Until the late 1960s there was an upward trend in inflows, with most migrants unskilled and semiskilled workers. The 1971 Immigration Act tightened controls, barring unskilled and semiskilled foreign workers after January 1, 1972, and requiring foreigners to have a job offer and a needed skill or qualification. Commonwealth nationals were treated like other non-EEC foreigners, and the number of work permits issued to foreigners declined throughout the 1980s (Clarke and Salt, 2003, 563, 564).

Like other countries, the United Kingdom moved from one large-scale guest worker system to several small-scale schemes. The main scheme changed in October 1991, when a two-tier system simplified admissions for senior management positions and to fill vacant jobs in sectors facing skills shortages in Britain, and new schemes were introduced to admit both highly skilled and unskilled foreign workers.

Applications under the main scheme tripled between 1995 and 2002, reflecting the IT boom and shortages of doctors and nurses. In analyzing work permits by nationality and occupation, James Clarke and John Salt found that migrants from the Philippines, Zimbabwe, and Nigeria were mostly health care workers, those from India were engineers and computer specialists, and those from Japan and the United States filled managerial and administrative positions.

The United Kingdom's Highly Skilled Migrant Programme was launched in January 2002 to attract foreigners who were among the top 10 percent of the global workforce, with applicants selected on the basis of their educational qualifications; work experience; past earnings; and achievement in a given field. A foreigner accepted under the program may initially come for one year to accept job offers, be self-employed, or seek work as a free agent in the labor market; if she finds a job, she can receive permission to stay another three years, after which she can expect permanent residence rights.

The U.K. government launched a Science and Engineering Graduate Scheme (SEGS) in October 2004 to encourage non–European Economic Area science and engineering graduates of U.K. universities to pursue careers in the United Kingdom.[22] Foreign graduates may remain and work for one year after completing their studies.[23] In addition, to address shortages of teachers, foreign nationals may come to the United Kingdom to work in schools during their "gap year," between high school and college if they have written offers of employment in a teaching or teaching assistant capacity; acceptance in a college to begin immediately after their stay in the United Kingdom; and the means to pay for their return or onward journey.[24]

The Sector Based Scheme (SBS) admits low- and semiskilled workers in food processing and hotels and catering, with an annual quota initially set at ten thousand for food manufacturing and ten thousand for hospitality. But the number of permits was reduced on June 1, 2004, to six thousand for food processing and nine thousand for hotel and catering jobs, and no nationality can have more than 20 percent of the total SBS work permits in a particular sector, which stopped the entrance of Bangladeshis to fill hotel jobs.[25]

The lowering of the SBS quota reflected the expansion of the EU to eastern Europe. The United Kingdom, Ireland, and Sweden were the only EU-15 countries that did not impose restrictions on migrant workers from the eight eastern European countries that joined the EU on May 1, 2004, so Poles and Czechs could come and work in those countries. However, to work in the United Kingdom, Poles and Czechs had to register under the Workers Registration Scheme (WRS), and 90,950 did between May and September 2004. Most of the migrants registering were young: 84 percent were twenty-four to thirty-four, and 80 percent earned between £4.50 and £5.99 an hour. The leading countries of origin of the registrants were Poland (56 percent), Lithuania (17 percent), Slovakia (10 percent), and Latvia and the Czech Republic (7 percent each).

It is not clear how many of those registering were already in the United Kingdom on May 1, 2004, and how many were new arrivals. The government says that most were in the United Kingdom already and that registration brought migrants out of the informal economy; it estimated that registered migrants paid £20 million in tax and national insurance between May and September 2004. Critics said that because the United Kingdom did not impose restrictions on freedom of movement as other old EU countries did, it was becoming a magnet for unskilled migrants.

The United Kingdom also has a Working Holidaymakers Scheme (WHMS) targeted at people from the Commonwealth aged between seventeen and thirty. Working holidaymakers can work in nonprofessional jobs for one of the maximum two years they can stay in the United Kingdom if their work is "incidental to a holiday" in Britain. Working holidaymakers must show that they have an onward ticket and that they can support themselves without public assistance while in the United Kingdom, and nearly forty thousand youth are admitted as working holidaymakers each year.

In September 2004 the Home Office's Web site had information on twenty-one ways that foreigners could enter the United Kingdom to work. The goal is to attract needed skills while curbing irregular migration and unfounded asylum claims—that is, testing the theory that opening legal channels for migrants can reduce illegal migration, a position articulated by Home Office Minister Lord Rooker in May 2002:

> The expansion of these schemes will help us meet recruitment gaps and demand for seasonal workers. . . . Properly managed legal migration also helps us tackle illegal working, which fuels the black economy, often involves dangerous and clandestine

> entry and leaves workers vulnerable to dangerous conditions, poor pay and exploitation from unscrupulous employers and criminal trafficking gangs. It also helps deal with abuse of the asylum system. . . . By opening up the routes for people to come and work here legally—in ways that help our economy—we can help reduce unfounded asylum claims. Workpermit.com, 2004a

The United Kingdom is struggling to ensure that opening legal channels for workers does not contribute to unauthorized migration. In May 2004 the government announced that the number of migrants allowed to work as seasonal agricultural workers and under the Sector Based Scheme would be restricted from countries whose governments did not cooperate with the return of their citizens found to have overstayed their visas. In July 2004 rules were tightened to stop temporary migrants from switching from temporary to permanent employment.[26] It is not yet possible to determine whether opening legal channels for migrants has reduced illegal migration and dubious asylum claims.

United States: 1990s Guest Worker Programs

The United States has more than twenty nonimmigrant programs that permit foreigners to enter and work. These programs are often referred to by the type of visa issued to the foreigner, such as E for treaty traders and investors, H for workers, and L for intracompany transfers. The three major worker visas are H-1B for specialty workers, H-2A for agricultural workers, and H-2B for nonfarm workers.

The best-known U.S. guest worker program is the H-1B program, included in the Immigration Act of 1990 to deal with late-1980s shortages of scientists and engineers that appeared when there was a buildup of defense efforts (Star Wars) at the same time that the computer industry was increasing employment. Employers got easy access to H-1B workers in exchange for a cap on the annual number of visas, 65,000 a year. Admissions, which double-count individuals who enter and leave the United States within one year, were initially low, due to the end of the Cold War and the economic recession of the early 1990s, as well as lack of employer familiarity with the program. Admissions began rising sharply after 1995 and doubled between 1995 and 1998. The annual ceiling was raised to 115,000 in 1998 and to 195,000 in 2000 before reverting to 65,000 in 2004.

As the program expanded, there were changes. First, most employers had to pay a $500 and later $1,000 fee per H-1B visa application to generate funds to encourage U.S. students to study science and engineering. These fees have since expired. Second, in response to complaints of abuses by so-called "body shops," which brought H-1B workers to the United States even if they did not have jobs for them, beginning in 1998 employers with 15 percent or more H-1B workers had to certify that they had not laid off U.S. workers to open jobs for the H-1B workers.[27] Third, universities and nonprofit research institutions were made exempt from the annual ceiling and the fee.

Two U.S. programs admit unskilled workers to fill temporary jobs: H-2A visas are offered to farm workers, and H-2B visas to nonfarm workers. Unlike the H-1B visa, employers must have their need for H-2A and H-2B foreign workers certified before the workers arrive. If recruitment fails to find U.S. workers, the employer is certified to recruit foreign workers in any country and under any procedure that the source country allows.

The H-2A program erects more hurdles in front of employers than does the H-2B program, including the requirement that employers offer out-of-area workers free and approved housing and pay the workers' inbound transportation costs. H-2A admissions rose to a peak in 2000 and then fell sharply (see Table 4.5). Some forty-two thousand jobs were certified by the U.S. Department of Labor to be filled with H-2A workers in 2002, and most were tobacco-harvesting jobs filled by Mexicans in the southeastern states. Many U.S. farmers say that they would like to obtain guest workers under the H-2A program but do not because of litigation. SAMCO, a custom harvester of citrus, brought thirty-eight H-2A Mexican workers to California to harvest lemons in March–April 2002 in what it said was a humanitarian act to save Mexicans from attempting to enter the United States via Arizona deserts illegally. SAMCO was sued by worker advocates for failing to pay overtime wages to the H-2A workers, not providing rest periods and lunch breaks, and not reimbursing some workers fully for expenses they incurred traveling to and from Mexico.

The H-2B program admits foreign workers to fill seasonal jobs for which U.S. workers cannot be recruited at the prevailing wage. Employers of H-2B workers do not have to pay the workers' transportation to the United States or provide them with free housing. In 2001 the Department of Labor certified 121,665 U.S. jobs as needing to be filled by H-2B workers, and immigration statistics reported that 72,387 workers with H-2B visas were admitted.[28] A fourth of the H-2B certifications were for landscape laborers, 10 percent were for forestry workers, 7 percent were for housekeepers in hotels and motels, and 4 percent each were for stable attendants and tree planters.

Admissions of H-2B workers rose almost fivefold between 1992 and 2002, and the program has come under more scrutiny. In Maine in September 2002,

Table 4.5. Admissions Under H-Worker Visas, 1992–2002

	1992–1994 Average	1995	1996	1997	1998	1999	2000	2001	2002
H-1B specialty occupations	105,828	100	111	137	228	286	336	363	350
H-2A ag workers	16,486	80	69	58	166	196	202	168	95
H-2B nonfarm unskilled	18,114	87	78	79	137	198	284	400	480

Note: Figures for 1995–2002 are percentages of the 1992–1994 averages.

Source: Yearbook of Immigration Statistics, www.immigration.gov

fourteen Honduran and Guatemalan H-2B workers died when the van driven by their foreman went off a bridge on a private road. Their workplace was two and a half hours each way from their housing, and the men were charged $84 a week to ride in the van. Their employer was fined the maximum amount for not registering the driver but continued to bring H-2B workers into the United States for reforestry work, much of which is done on public land at government expense. The H-2B program is likely to expand further, especially as more labor brokers advertise the availability of H-2B workers.[29]

There are a number of other guest worker programs, including those admitting foreign nurses, workers with extraordinary ability or achievement, and NAFTA professionals. There was a peak of 7,200 admissions of registered nurses with H-1A visas in 1992. After this program was phased out in 1995, another program for registered nurses, Nursing Relief for Disadvantaged Areas, was launched; there were 111 admissions with H-1C visas in 2002. Admissions of foreign workers with extraordinary ability or achievement (O-1 visas) tripled between 1992 and 2002 to 25,000, while admissions of foreign workers who are internationally recognized athletes or entertainers (P-1 visas) doubled to 41,000 in this period. Workers in religious occupations receive R-1 visas, and admissions tripled between 1995 and 2002 to 19,000.

The number of U.S. admissions of Canadians and Mexicans with TN visas tripled between 1995 and 2002 to 74,000; beginning in 2004, the ten-year anniversary of NAFTA, the annual limit of 5,500 TN visas a year for Mexican professionals ended.[30] NAFTA freedom-of-movement professions, listed in chapter 16 of the treaty, range from accountant to zoologist. Mexicans and Canadians appear at U.S. ports of entry with proof of citizenship and education and a U.S. job offer and receive their TN visas.

Most U.S. guest worker programs place no caps on admissions, permit spouses and children to accompany the visa holder, and allow employers to have foreign workers admitted under fairly simple procedures. The impacts of the migrants admitted under these small-scale programs are hard to assess, in part because data are often unavailable for the particular labor markets affected by the migrants. However, the impacts of foreign workers may be larger than suggested by annual admissions data because many workers stay longer than one year. Foreign workers follow network paths, so the activities of particularly successful recruiters may fairly quickly turn jobs in some industries and occupations—harvesting tobacco or planting trees, for example—into "migrants' jobs," even though migrants are a small fraction of a sectoral or national labor force. Finally, there was a sharp increase in admissions in almost all programs in the second half of the 1990s.

SEASONAL-WORKER PROGRAMS

Programs that admit seasonal workers to fill seasonal jobs constitute the litmus test for the promise of guest worker programs to add workers temporarily to the labor force but not settlers to the population. Many seasonal jobs reflect the biological production process in agriculture, and importing seasonal workers who return home when the season ends helps farmers to minimize their production costs. Seasonal employment is generally not attractive to local workers who can obtain year-round work.

Seasonal foreign worker programs can be compared along dimensions that include (1) caps on the number of admissions, (2) requirements for employers to try to recruit local workers, and (3) housing and transportation requirements. Most countries require farm employers to attempt to recruit local workers before employing foreign workers, but not all require employers to provide guest workers with free housing and transportation. Historically, the argument in favor of requiring employers to "take care of" seasonal farm workers was that, as generally low-skill and low-wage workers in an area only a short time, they could be vulnerable to abuse if employers did not provide services for them.

Seasonal-worker programs are growing in Germany, the United States, and Canada, while shrinking in France and Switzerland, even though labor-intensive fruit, vegetable, and horticultural specialty production, a major employer of seasonal foreign workers, is rising in all these countries. The general trend in program administration is to shift more power over the border gate to employers by giving them more voice in admissions, transportation, and employment (see Table 4.6). Worker representatives are rarely involved in seasonal-worker program design or administration, which leads to extensive litigation in the United States, and to union and advocate criticism of seasonal-worker programs in Canada, the United Kingdom, and France.

Seasonal-worker programs may be ripe for reform because of World Trade Organization talks aimed at freeing up farm trade. Farmers in industrial countries receive almost $1 billion a day in subsidies, an average of $15,000–20,000 per year per farmer. Although many of the farmers receiving direct government payments do not hire large numbers of foreign workers, the fruit and vegetable

Table 4.6. Seasonal-Worker Programs for Agriculture

	Admissions 2002–2003	Ceiling	Labor Market test?	Free Housing?	Free Transport?
United States	45,000	no	yes	yes	yes
Germany	293,000	no	yes	maybe	maybe
Canada	15,000	no	yes	yes	no
United Kingdom	25,000	yes	yes	yes	no
France	15,000	no	yes	yes	maybe
Switzerland	1,000	yes	yes	yes	maybe

Note: In Germany, seasonal workers have contracts that may or may not provide transport, etc.
Source: Martin, 2005.

farmers who hire most of the foreign migrants receive indirect benefits from farm subsidies, since without them, some land now used to grow subsidized crops such as grains and cotton would likely switch to fruits and vegetables, putting downward pressure on prices. If the rationale for farm subsidies changes from food security to agriculture's social amenities, such as providing open space (as is occurring in Europe), there may be an effort to link the payment of subsidies to employers satisfying other conditions as well, such as adequate treatment of migrant and other farm workers.

Canada: A Model?

The Commonwealth Caribbean and Mexican Seasonal Agricultural Workers Program has allowed Canadian farmers to import foreign workers for up to eight months a year from the Caribbean since 1966, and from Mexico since 1974. About 80 percent of the migrants admitted are employed on fruit, vegetable, and tobacco farms in Ontario, where the average stay is four months and migrants fill about 20 percent of seasonal farm jobs (see Table 4.7).

Many Canadian and Mexican officials think the program is a model exemplifying best practices. In March 2003 then–Canadian Prime Minister Jean Chretien told Mexicans: "This program, where your farmers can come and work in Canada, has worked extremely well and now we are exploring [ways] to extend that to other sectors. The bilateral seasonal agricultural workers program has been a model for balancing the flow of temporary foreign workers with the needs of Canadian employers." Carlos Obrador, Mexican vice consul in Toronto, said the program "is a real model for how migration can work in an ordered and legal way."[31] Suggested industries for additional Mexican employment included hospitality, meatpacking, and construction.

Table 4.7. Canadian Guest Worker Employment in Agriculture, 1987–2002

Year	Mexicans (%)	Caribbean[a]	Total
1987	1,547 (25%)	4,655	6,202
1988	2,721 (32%)	5,682	8,403
1989	4,468 (37%)	7,674	12,142
1990	5,149 (41%)	7,302	12,451
1991	5,111 (43%)	6,914	12,025
1992	4,732 (43%)	6,198	10,930
1993	4,710 (45%)	5,691	10,401
1994	4,848 (44%)	6,054	10,902
1995	4,884 (43%)	6,376	11,260
1996	5,194 (45%)	6,379	11,573
1997	5,670 (46%)	6,705	12,375
1998	6,480 (48%)	6,901	13,381
1999	7,528 (50%)	7,532	15,060
2000	9,222 (55%)	7,471	16,693
2001	10,446 (56%)	8,055	18,501
2002	10,778 (58%)	7,826	18,604

[a]From Barbados, Jamaica, and Trinidad and Tobago, http://www.cic.gc.ca/english/pub/facts2002-temp/index.html

Source: Citizenship and Immigration Canada

Mexicans are recruited and employed under the terms of a government-to-government memorandum of understanding (MOU) that makes the Mexican Ministry of Labor responsible for recruiting workers in Mexico and negotiating their Canadian wages with Human Resources Development Canada (HRDC). The admissions process begins with farm employers who apply to local Human Resources Centers (HRCs) for certification at least eight weeks before their anticipated need for workers, and under the Canadians First Policy, farmers must hire qualified Canadian workers. To hire Mexicans, farmers must offer at least 240 hours of work over six weeks, free approved housing and meals or cooking facilities, and the higher of the minimum wage (C$7.15 an hour in Ontario in 2004, projected to rise to C$8 by 2007), prevailing wage, or piece-rate wage paid to Canadians doing the same job.

Approval to hire foreign workers is sent to an organization funded by farmer-paid fees, Foreign Agricultural Resource Management Services (FARMS). Migrants in Mexico are given entry papers, and a FARMS affiliate arranges their transport to Canada and to the employer's farm.[32] Employers advance the cost of transportation to Canada, then deduct 4 percent of worker wages (up to C$575) to recoup transport costs; farmers also deduct payroll taxes and insurance costs from workers' pay. Workers are on probation for two weeks, and farmers provide written evaluations of each worker at the end of the season; these employer evaluations are placed in sealed envelopes and delivered by returning workers to Mexican authorities. Farmers may specify the names of workers they want, which they do more than 70 percent of the time, so that the average worker interviewed in one study had seven years' experience in Canada (Basok, 2002). Farmers face fines of up to C$5,000 and two years in prison for hiring unauthorized workers or lending their guest workers to other farmers, but enforcement of such fines is much rarer than these activities occur, according to local observers.

The southern Ontario greenhouse industry is expanding by using hydroponics and natural gas heat to produce tomatoes and cucumbers that are exported, and the employment of Mexican migrants is rising. Farmers report negative experiences with local workers, recounting stories of workers threatening to break equipment in order to get fired and return to the welfare rolls, or workers "breaking faith" by walking away during busy times even after being hired during slow seasons. In one study, 40 percent of the jobs in 40 vegetable greenhouses were filled by migrants, up from 10 percent a decade ago (Basok, 2002).

Most of the Mexican migrants are married men who leave their families in rural Mexico, travel to Mexico City at their own expense, and pay for required medical exams, so that they arrive in Canada in debt.[33] In Canada the migrants are isolated on farms, where they report spending little money, enabling them to save an average C$1,000 a month from their average C$1,400 pay, earned for working fifty-hour weeks. These savings opportunities may explain why migrants report that they prefer the security of contracts in Canada to the insecurity of unauthorized status in the United States.[34] Mexican consular officials can inspect worker housing and solicit worker grievances, but some migrants say that they are cheated rather than helped by Mexican consular officials. Many Mexicans leave Canada before they get their last paychecks, or have their tax refund checks sent to addresses in Canada. Since 1982 small checks owed to Mexican migrants have been sent to Mexico's Foreign Ministry, which reportedly has not contacted the workers to whom the money was owed.

There have been protests over wage deductions and a strike on April 29, 2001, that led to deportations and complaints made on behalf of the migrants by the United Food and Commercial Workers union (UFCW) and the United

Farmworkers Union. (Ontario farm workers do not have the right to strike.) The UFCW, which operates migrant worker centers in Leamington and Bradford, Ontario, calls the migrant program "Canada's shameful dirty secret" and has filed suits against provincial authorities for excluding farm workers from the Occupational Health and Safety Act and for charging migrants C$11 million a year in unemployment insurance premiums but not allowing them to obtain benefits. (Unemployed migrants must leave Canada.) On the other hand, migrants are eligible for health insurance coverage upon arrival in Canada—the usual three-month wait for coverage under provincial health care programs is waived.

The potential best-practice aspects of the Canadian seasonal farm worker program include the active involvement of farm employers in program design and administration, Mexican government involvement in recruiting and monitoring migrants in Canada, and the health insurance coverage. Worker organizations do not play a role in program design or administration, and their complaints focus on legal restrictions that apply to all farm workers, including guest workers. Researchers emphasize that most migrants arrive in debt, and thus have an incentive to be good employees and follow program rules so that they can return, repay debts, and accumulate savings, as they often do in their second or third year of traveling north.

The United Kingdom: Student Migrants

Most foreign workers on British farms are admitted under the Seasonal Agricultural Workers Scheme, or SAWS, which began in 1945 to provide jobs for displaced persons after World War II. SAWS now permits full-time non-EU agricultural students from eastern Europe and the former Soviet Union to enter the United Kingdom for up to six months to work on farms. Almost half of the students, who must be eighteen to twenty-five, are from Poland and the Ukraine (see Tables 4.8, 4.9), and most are in the United Kingdom between April 1 and November 30 for farm work and an "educational-cultural experience." Some SAWS workers are covered by the Agricultural Wages Orders, which require a minimum wage of £5.15 an hour for an adult standard worker and £4.50 an hour for a manual harvest worker in 2004, while other farm work is covered by the national minimum wage.

Initially seven scheme operators handled recruitment, usually using agents at eastern European universities to find student workers and sending students after their arrival in the United Kingdom to their own farms or other farms.[35] The farm employer must provide housing, and SAWS students are to be em-

Table 4.8. U.K. Seasonal Agricultural Workers Scheme: Ceiling and Admissions

Year	Ceiling	Admissions
1992	5,500	5,019
1993	5,500	5,011
1994	5,500	
1995	5,500	5,052
1996	5,500	6,152
1997	10,000	10,255
1998	10,000	10,394
1999	10,000	10,464
2000	10,000	10,846
2001	15,200	14,870
2002	18,700	19,372
2003	25,000	

Notes: Admissions are cards issued: about 95 percent reported to work in the U.K. No data for 1994, 2003.
Source: Work Permits UK, www.workpermits.gov.uk

ployed only on the farm to which they have been assigned. The students must have visas before arrival, must come without their families, and may not adjust status in the United Kingdom, but an estimated 4–10 percent of SAWS workers overstay. Since 2003 SAWS workers may return to the United Kingdom af-

Table 4.9. U.K. Seasonal Agricultural Workers Scheme, Admissions in 1996 and 2002

Country	1996	2002
Poland	2,338	4,867
Ukraine	554	4,003
Bulgaria	562	2,252
Lithuania	767	2,161
Russia	341	1,089
Latvia	98	1,029
Subtotal	4,660	15,401
%age of total	76%	80%
Total	6,152	19,372

Notes: Admissions are cards issued; about 95 percent reported to work in the U.K.
Source: Work Permits UK, www.workpermits.gov.uk

ter a break of at least three months outside the country, and the ceiling on SAWS admissions has been raised several times as more farm employers participate.[36]

The June 2001 census reported that 64,000 seasonal and casual workers were employed in U.K. agriculture, and they represented a third of the 188,000 total workers, including farmers and unpaid family workers. However, it is hard to obtain an accurate picture of supply and demand in the seasonal farm labor market because most farm workers are organized into crews by labor contractors or gangmasters, who receive payments from farmers that reflect wages paid to workers plus a 25–30 percent commission. These gangmaster crews include EU foreigners, non-EU foreigners, and British citizens, some of whom are working for cash wages while drawing unemployment benefits. Gangmaster crews usually move from south to north harvesting and packing fruits and vegetables, and some gangmasters reportedly underreport their workers to authorities to avoid paying taxes.[37]

The U.K. government believes that expanding guest worker admissions can reduce illegal migration and employment, and a government commission on agriculture has recommended that the SAWS ceiling be raised from twenty-five thousand to fifty thousand a year.[38] Newspapers report that at least fifty thousand illegal workers—unauthorized foreigners and British workers drawing unemployment and welfare benefits while working for cash wages—were employed on British farms and in packinghouses in 2003.[39] However, the ceiling was reduced to 16,250 in 2005 because nationals of the EU-10 countries (those joining the EU on May 1, 2004) may travel to the United Kingdom without visas and work simply by registering.

Germany: Polish Seasonal Workers

The German seasonal-worker program, which operates under memoranda of understanding signed by the German Labor Ministry and labor ministries in source countries, admits migrants for up to ninety days if local workers are not available to fill vacant jobs in agriculture, forestry, the hotel and catering sector, fruit and vegetable processing, and sawmills. Only individual enterprises that grow fruit, vegetable, wine, hops, or tobacco may hire rotating groups of seasonal workers for more than seven months per year.

About 90 percent of the 293,000 seasonal migrants admitted in 2002 were Poles, and 90 percent worked in agriculture. Employers request seasonal foreign workers and submit to local labor offices proposed contracts that spell out wages and working conditions as well as provisions for employer-provided housing, meals, and travel arrangements, if any. The German Employment Service's instructions for employers require employers to provide "adequate housing" to seasonal workers; this provision governs the quality of the housing and any rent charged to workers and mandates that employers specify that rent on the contracts they offer workers (Arbeitsagentur.de, 2004). However, press reports during the asparagus harvest regularly find Polish seasonal workers sleeping in their cars, suggesting the presence of illegal workers, collusion of workers with employers to circumvent housing requirements, or both.

When employers request foreign seasonal workers, the employment service tests the local labor market to ensure that local workers are not available at the prevailing wage. Employers must pay an administrative fee of EUR60 per worker to the employment service, and may not deduct it from migrant wages (Arbeitsagentur.de, 2004). German employers may request foreign workers by name, and they do for about 90 percent of those admitted in recent years. Migrants arrive with copies of the bilingual contracts that were checked by employment services in both Germany and their country of origin, and both German employers and migrants make payroll tax contributions that are about 35 percent of wages.[40]

French Programs

The number of seasonal foreign workers admitted for employment in French agriculture peaked in 1972, when 138,000 seasonal foreign workers were admitted, two-thirds from Spain and two-thirds to harvest grapes (Miller, 1991b). The admissions process began with French farmers having their need for foreign workers certified by local labor offices, and most French farmers requested Spanish migrants by name. The migrants arrived by train in prearranged crews that shifted from employer to employer, receiving housing from their employers. The recruitment of seasonal farm workers was not halted with the recruitment of other foreign workers in July 1974.

Southern French agriculture by the 1980s had become dependent on seasonal migrants, who supplied up to 80 percent of the hours of hired work in labor-intensive agriculture (Berlan, 1984). Some farmers used a series of short-term contracts to employ seasonal workers almost year-round. There were efforts to reform the seasonal foreign-worker program in the mid-1980s that included increasing employer-paid fees, but these efforts had mixed effects, leading Mark Miller (1991b, 864) to conclude that "seasonal foreign workers are addictive. . . . Through time, dependency develops."

As the seasonal-worker program shrank in the 1990s (see Table 4.10), some

Table 4.10. Admissions of Non-EU Seasonal Foreign Farm Workers, France, 1960–2001

Year	Number
1960	109,800
1970	135,000
1980	120,400
1990	58,249
1991	52,241
1992	13,597
1993	11,283
1994	10,339
1995	9,352
1996	8,766
1997	8,210
1998	7,523
1999	7,612
2000	7,929
2001	10,794

Notes: In 1992 Spanish and Portuguese workers got EU freedom-of-movement rights. In 1990 there were 43,000 Spanish and Portuguese workers in France. They were probably still in France in 1992 bur are not recorded in these data.

Sources: Tapinos, 1984, 54; Miller, 1991b, 836.

French officials wanted to expand admissions to reduce illegal migration. France signed agreements with Morocco, Poland, and Tunisia, and admissions, after slipping below 8,000 a year in the late 1990s, rose to almost 11,000 in 2001, when half of the migrants were Moroccans and 43 percent Poles. French officials favoring more admissions noted that settlement can be minimized if workers come without their families and migrant contracts are limited to six months.

The current seasonal program permits non–European Economic Area (EEA) foreigners to enter France under bilateral contracts to fill seasonal farm jobs for up to six months—in exceptional cases up to eight months—provided that their French employer has demonstrated that local workers could not be recruited at government-set wages to fill the jobs in question. Employers must offer housing to workers in France without families and must ensure that the seasonal workers leave France at the end of their contracts. Employers risk fines and disqualification from the program if the migrants they employed do not depart, and both employers and migrants pay taxes.

Activist groups such as CODETRAS (Collectif de défense des travailleurs étrangers dans l'agriculture) point out that southern French agriculture continues to be dependent on foreign workers—in the department of Bouches du Rhone, for example—but that the migrants are not filling "seasonal jobs." Extraordinary extensions of contracts to eight months have become the rule, and many migrants have come to France for decades and are in effect "permanent seasonal workers." CODETRAS says that working and housing conditions are often inadequate, and that employers sometimes violate the terms of migrant contracts and French labor laws—by not paying for all hours worked, for example. However, enforcement is difficult, since most migrants do not fully understand their rights, and permission to remain in France depends on their employer. CODETRAS charges that because seasonal migrants must leave France for at least four months a year, they are prevented from ever getting a *carte de séjour,* or entitlement to bring their families, which requires at least one year of continuous residence in France (CODETRAS, 2004).

Swiss Programs

In Switzerland the gradual extension of settlement rights to seasonal workers eventually led to the abolition of the seasonal-worker program in June 2002. Before the program was abolished, it allowed migrants employed at least thirty-six months in four consecutive years under nine-month A-seasonal permits to "earn" B-annual and eventually C-permanent residence permits.

By the mid-1980s, seasonal-worker adjustment to permanent-resident status had become the major source of new resident aliens in Switzerland (Plewa and Miller, 2004, 13). About 35 percent of all seasonal workers obtained an annual permit, and 60 percent of them eventually settled in Switzerland (Liebig, 2002). The seasonal program "worked" in the sense that it provided workers for truly seasonal industries such as construction, agriculture, and hotels, but most of these jobs were unskilled, so "earned residence via work" was giving Switzerland more unskilled foreigners.[41] The southern Europeans becoming permanent residents had higher than average unemployment rates and often shifted to permanent-resident status when their employment situation in Switzerland became more precarious (de Wild and Sheldon, 2000, 4, 5).

In 2002 the Swiss government changed its migration policies, officially in anticipation of freedom of movement with other European countries by 2007, but also to deal with the settlement of unskilled foreigners, which was also the focus of several referenda aimed at preventing "overforeignization." The government abolished the seasonal-worker program and established four categories of labor immigration permits: cross-border commuter, short-term residence, annual residence, and settlement. Under the new policy, border commuters can more easily obtain one-year renewable work permits, and the new short-term work and residence permit is available for non-EEA foreigners for up to twelve months, although it may be extended to a maximum total of two years.

Annual work and residence permits are for foreigners who intend to be in Switzerland more than one year, and there is an annual ceiling that usually restricts these permits to highly qualified workers. Once issued, annual permits may be renewed indefinitely, and a change in the labor market situation may not be invoked for a denial of prolongation (Liebig, 2003). EEA nationals get five-year permits when they find employment in Switzerland, and receive permanent status after five years' residence, while other foreigners must wait ten years for permanent status.

The new Swiss policy is designed to draw sharper distinctions between temporary and permanent permits and make it harder to adjust from temporary to permanent status. Those foreigners who gain permanent residence status will have more rights. However, there remains considerable skepticism about immigration in Switzerland, as exemplified by voter rejection in September 2004 of an initiative that would have permitted the grandchildren of immigrants to get Swiss citizenship automatically and would have let children in Switzerland from an early age apply for Swiss citizenship quickly.[42] A year earlier, Christoph Blocher, leader of the anti-immigrant Swiss People's Party, won a post in the seven-seat federal cabinet after elections gave his party 27 percent of the vote.

LEARNING FROM EXPERIENCE

Most guest worker programs have flaws linked to the concept of rotation. It is hard to enforce rotation after labor markets are distorted by employer reliance on migrants and after some migrants become dependent on higher-wage foreign jobs. If guest worker programs are considered probationary immigrant programs that allow employers to select and then "test" newcomers to determine whether they should be invited to settle, then the lack of rotation may not be considered a problem. However, such a policy allows a relatively small group of residents in a country, the employers who hire foreign workers, to make immigration decisions that affect everyone.

Guest worker programs do not operate in a vacuum, and they change with economic conditions and in response to employer and migrant requests. Foreign policy and workers' rights considerations can also lead to changes in program rules that facilitate settlement, which is why many governments introduced large-scale programs that strengthened rules aimed at ensuring truly temporary stays. However, economic and political constraints can make it difficult for governments to learn from their country's own experiences with migrant workers or from others. In Germany, for example, the Swiss seasonal-worker policy was considered a model even as it was being phased out (Plewa and Miller, 2004, 13). Italy and Spain had legalization programs in the 1990s reminiscent of French backdoor legalization programs, allowing unauthorized foreigners who found jobs to get work permits, even though the effect of such programs is to encourage more unauthorized immigration in the hope of future legalization. Britain debates the problems associated with the integration of "old" immigrants, and deludes itself into seeing today's "temporary workers" as an entirely new phenomenon.

5 Managing Guest Workers

There was and is a gap between the goals and outcomes of guest worker programs: employer decisions are distorted as some employers look beyond national borders for workers, and some migrants become dependent on foreign jobs and wages, so that guest worker programs tend to get larger and to last longer than originally anticipated. In this chapter we explain how to minimize the distortion and dependence that are inevitable in guest worker programs, how cooperation can ensure that the exodus of highly skilled migrants does not slow development in countries of origin, and how various policies can protect the rights of migrants.

There is a sharp contrast between the red carpet rolled out for some foreign "brains" and the red card often shown to foreign "brawn" when the seasonal jobs end. In many industrial countries, it is relatively easy for foreign students to enroll in higher education institutions. An increasing number of industrial countries are advertising for foreign students and allowing graduates to stay if local employers offer them jobs. The employment of foreign "brawn," on the other hand, can oscillate between irregular status and legal status in small-scale and seasonal guest worker programs designed to ensure that migrants return to their countries of origin. Many of the new guest worker programs include incentives to encourage returns, often by allowing a subsequent legal stay if the migrant departs as scheduled.

However, moving more workers who are at the top and the bottom of the education ladder from developing to developed countries could widen the inequalities between them. In this chapter we tackle an important question: how can guest worker programs be managed so that the inequalities promoting migration narrow over time? Our answers vary with the type of migrant. For highly skilled migrants, we propose that developed nations partially replenish the human capital they have attracted from developing countries by supporting and strengthening primary and secondary schooling systems in migrant countries of origin. For unskilled migrants, we propose taxes and subsidies to align the rights and duties of employers and migrants—such as, on one hand, a rising tax on employers who continue to request migrants to minimize distortion, and, on the other, refunds of social security and other tax contributions to encourage migrants to return to their countries of origin.

Replenishing human capital in countries of origin to minimize the brain drain and levying fees on employers while providing tax refunds to migrants can make guest worker programs operate closer to their long-term goals, but neither strategy is a panacea. It would be hard to design a system to equitably and efficiently replenish brains in countries sending professionals abroad, and the correct level of taxes and refunds that would align employer and migrant behavior with guest worker program rules is likely to vary by industry, occupation, and country. However, there is an urgent need to at least experiment with such policies, because the status quo in labor migration may wind up increasing the inequalities that motivate migration, making migration management a progressively more difficult challenge.

REPLENISHING BRAINS

The fastest growth in labor migration over the past decade has involved the movement of professionals from developing to developed countries to fill jobs that range from computer scientist and engineer to nurse and teacher. Moving 10, 20, or 30 percent of the professionals from a developing to a developed country benefits the employers who hire them, the professionals who move, and generally the society in which they work. However, the migrants' countries of origin may lose important keys to their economic development.

Three policies could help to ensure that the fast-growing professional segment of international migration does not contribute to the inequality that perpetuates international migration.[1] They include having sending countries maintain links to their "stored brainpower" abroad, having receiving countries provide human capital replenishment, and reexamining the content and financing of education in countries of origin. Developing countries need a strong human resource base to achieve an economic takeoff, but it is often hard for graduates in developing countries to find jobs. Since it is difficult to block the emigration of students and professionals, at least some are likely to go abroad, and the question is what governments in developing countries can do to maintain links that encourage them to remit and eventually return. A simple strategy is to maintain links with the diaspora. Governments in Taiwan, South Korea, China, and Ireland have established links to organizations of their nationals abroad, ensuring that migrants know what is happening at home and that they are welcome to return.

Professional migrants obtain most of the benefits of migrating to richer countries in the form of higher wages, and their generally richer host countries are more likely to benefit from their presence than their countries of origin benefit from their absence. In order to avoid widening differences because of professional migration, developed countries receiving professionals could provide human capital replenishment assistance (HCRA) to migrant countries of origin. Two extremes mark the ends of the "compensation" spectrum: link compensation to the number of migrants and their earnings abroad or increase overall foreign aid.

A leading proponent of compensation linked to the number and earnings of migrants is the Indian-born economist Jagdish Bhagwati, whose professional career has been in the United States. Bhagwati recommends that emigration countries tax the "windfall higher earnings" of migrants that reflect the difference between their earnings at home and abroad. Since it is generally hard for emigration countries to tax their citizens abroad, Bhagwati has urged immigration countries to collect normal taxes from migrants and simply divert some to their countries of origin (Bhagwati, 1976). There are few examples of countries successfully taxing their migrants abroad. Eritrea has since 1993 imposed a 2 percent tax on the earnings of nationals abroad, enforcing collection via the moral suasion of asking migrants to help the newly independent country to free itself from Ethiopia as well as by making it hard to buy or retain land in Eritrea or renew passports unless the tax is paid. The United States taxes the worldwide income of residents but exempts the first $80,000 in foreign earnings from U.S.

income taxes, which means that most Americans abroad do not owe taxes to the U.S. government.[2] Having destination countries divert some of the taxes collected from migrants is also problematic, since the constitutions of most countries prevent governments from charging migrants higher taxes than other residents with the same tax obligations. If some of the taxes collected from migrants were diverted to their countries of origin, migrants would be paying less than other residents for such government services as defense, which also violates constitutional guarantees of equality.

Providing more foreign aid could have richer destination countries contributing the recommended 0.7 percent of GDP in Official Development Assistance (ODA), which would enable ODA to rise from $55 billion to $175 billion a year.[3] There is little enthusiasm for increasing ODA, in part because over the past fifty years the industrial countries provided about $1 trillion in development aid, with mixed results. Critics of ODA say that it is naïve to think that the 800 million people in the twenty richest countries that provide most ODA can solve the poverty problem in the seventy-five countries that have 2.5 billion residents living on less than $750 a year.

Targeted human capital replenishment is an alternative to earnings-linked tax compensation and more ODA. Targeting is an increasingly common way to provide foreign assistance, and human capital replenishment has a precedent in the compensation paid by industrial country firms for the renewable resources such as forestry products that they take from developing countries.[4] The best-practice model in such cases is to ensure that the resource is renewed by replanting trees, as well as paying some kind of severance tax, so that the country's long-term productive capacity is maintained.

Treating human capital as a renewable resource raises the question of appropriate payment. One guideline for a "severance tax" is the cost of recruiting a professional, normally 5–10 percent of first-year earnings. Under such a program, a country accepting one thousand nurses or IT engineers, each earning $40,000 a year or a total $40 million, would provide an additional $2–4 million in targeted human capital replenishment assistance. There could be "no additional net cost" replenishment assistance if tax-supported employment services could handle recruitment and job matching, so that public employment services could save migrants and employers the fees that both currently pay to brokers.[5]

We believe that human capital replenishment assistance should be spent in developing countries on elementary and secondary education systems. Many developing countries devote a disproportionate share of their educational spending to higher education, giving much higher subsidies to college and university students than to pupils in primary and secondary education. For example, Malawi in 1997 spent fifteen times its per capita GDP per student on higher education, but only one-twelfth of its per capita GDP per student on primary education. In Jamaica spending per student in higher education was twice the per capita GDP, but spending per student in primary education was only one-eighth of per capita GDP (World Bank, 2002, 87).

Redirecting more funds from higher education to elementary and secondary education systems could be accompanied by more on-the-job training, which could discourage the emigration of professionals. Ronald Dore (1997) has noted that in many African countries employers screen the typically large number of applicants for professional jobs by counting the number of credentials they have, leading to "diploma disease": students engage in an "arms race" to improve their prospects of being hired, and employers hire those with good test-taking skills rather than those who will be most productive. If there were more ports of entry for workers without diplomas and more on-the-job training opportunities, there might be less brain drain migration because the on-the-job skills would be less transferable over borders.

Many developing countries restrict the private provision of higher education, which means that students must enter a government-funded college and university system to get a diploma. The experience of India, the Philippines, and many other countries demonstrates that the private sector can and will provide higher education in developing countries, and that financing mechanisms quickly develop that realistically assess the likely domestic or foreign return on that education. Allowing the private sector to provide higher education in developing countries could help to guide students into fields of study more closely attuned to local labor market needs.

DISTORTION AND DEPENDENCE

The global experience with guest workers is often summarized in a cynical maxim: "There is nothing more permanent than temporary workers." Permanence is a predictable result of the incentives facing employers and migrants. In the absence of mechanization or a change in demand wrought by changing tastes or trade patterns, employers can become comfortable employing migrants while unskilled migrants and their families become dependent on jobs abroad and remittances.

Many industrial countries in the 1990s developed small-scale guest worker programs that took a trust-the-employer approach to foreign worker admissions and employment, reflecting a trend toward deregulating labor markets and shrinking government agencies that deal with employment and labor. The power of employers rises in situations where governments do not have credible information on whether migrants are "truly needed," and government employment agencies that match ever fewer workers and jobs lose their capacity to assess labor supply and demand on an ongoing basis.

Despite the proliferation of small-scale guest worker programs, most industrial democracies have more migrants employed outside official programs than inside them. Most ILO conventions and recommendations apply to legal migrant workers, highlighting the fact that the best way to protect migrants is to ensure that they are legal workers. Reducing illegal entries and employment is a task that falls primarily to host governments, which could do a far better job of discouraging unauthorized worker employment by treating it as a serious offense and developing penalty and inspection systems to enforce labor and immigration laws effectively.[6]

Decisions to hire migrants and to migrate abroad are economic decisions, and guest worker programs are more likely to achieve their goals if they include economic mechanisms that align employer and worker incentives with program rules. One way to align employer incentives with program rules that require employers to seek local workers first and to rotate guest workers out of the country after six to twenty-four months is to equalize the cost of foreign and native workers. Unskilled migrant workers are generally more productive than similar local workers because employers can select the best workers from vast labor pools abroad, while local workers available to fill seasonal jobs in agriculture and similar industries are those with few other job options. One way to minimize distortion in such labor markets is to require employers to pay the usual payroll taxes on the wages of migrants, plus an extra levy or charge, with the extra migrant fee rising over time to encourage the employer to consider alternatives such as mechanization or restructuring work.

Migrant levies encourage employers to consider alternatives, including hiring local workers. Many migrants are employed in competitive sectors marked by relatively low profit margins and little capacity for employer cooperation to mechanize or restructure work. In sectors such as agriculture that depend on migrants, migrant levies could be used to fund research that eventually reduces dependence on migrants.

The California processing-tomato industry demonstrates how such a strategy can work. In the early 1960s more than 80 percent of the workers who handpicked the processing tomatoes used to make catsup in California were Mexican braceros, and growers argued that braceros were necessary to keep the industry in the United States and catsup an everyday product. The bracero program nonetheless ended, and the industry mechanized. The keys to transforming the processing-tomato industry included the cooperation of University of California plant scientists and engineers as well as the government. Scientists developed tomatoes that ripened uniformly and had an oblong shape amenable to mechanical harvesting, while engineers developed a machine capable of harvesting tomatoes in one pass through the field by shaking them off the plant and using an electronic eye to determine which tomatoes were red enough for processing. The once-over harvesting system eliminated 90 percent of the hand-harvesting jobs, and was adopted quickly because of government monitoring of quality. Handpicked tomatoes were delivered in sixty-pound lugs, and with a current value of about $50 a ton or 2.5 cents a pound, a farmer incurred a relatively small loss of $1.50 if a lug was rejected because it had too many green tomatoes. Mechanical harvesting brought tomatoes to processing plants in twenty-five-ton loads worth $1,250, and to overcome perennial disputes between growers and processors, the state of California established quality-control stations that took random samples to determine quality (Martin and Olmstead, 1985).

In the tomato case, research costs were modest relative to consumer savings. Mechanization increased the supply of tomato products and lowered their prices, and the rate of return on the public research funds was estimated at 900–1,000 percent, a very high rate. Mechanization of tomato harvesting occurred at a time of relatively little unauthorized migration and a strong union movement, and the farm worker unions complained that public funds were being used to displace braceros. The result was a series of "mechanization lawsuits" against the University of California that slowed labor-saving research, while rising illegal migration reduced employer pressures to find new labor-saving machines.

Employer-paid migrant levies can reduce distortion and provide funds to help restructure industries so that they are less dependent on migrants over time. The other part of the equation is to encourage migrants to go home when their work permits expire. One return incentive lies in the payroll taxes paid by employers and migrants. To equalize the costs of local and migrant workers, payroll taxes should be the same for both types of workers, but those paid by and on behalf of migrants could be refunded to migrants who return as program rules stipulate. Refunding migrant payroll taxes that are 15–30 percent of earnings can be an incentive to return. It also provides a convenient way to match a portion of returned migrants' savings and encourage investments in such development projects as the three-for-one programs in Mexico, which use government funds to match voluntary migrant contributions to improve infrastructure in their areas of origin.[7]

There are ten million to fifteen million unauthorized foreign workers in industrial countries, and some have been employed for more than a decade. Their presence often contributes to the sense that migration is out of control and forces difficult decisions about how to treat families whose members may have a variety of legal statuses. If illegal migration can be reduced with more effective enforcement of labor and immigration laws and cooperation with sending countries, and guest worker programs are revised to include economic mechanisms to align employer and migrant incentives with rules, a path should be made available for the unauthorized worker who has developed equity stakes in her host country to earn a legal status by finding jobs, paying taxes, and learning the host country's language.

Experience with regularization or amnesty programs suggests that there is never just one program, since legalization always leaves some unauthorized foreigners and may attract more. The United States, which legalized 2.7 million unauthorized foreigners in 1987–1988, did not legalize all the unauthorized foreigners in the country and attracted more during the program and after it ended, including family members of the newly legalized as well as foreigners hoping for another legalization. In southern European countries such as Italy and Spain, regularization means that employed migrants can obtain a temporary work and residence permit, so a foreigner can become unauthorized again if his temporary permit expires before he gets regular or permanent status. Unauthorized foreigners usually become eligible for amnesty on the basis of time and work in the country, and there has been a tendency for the eligibility criteria for amnesty to become "tougher" over time, as governments learn that there can be considerable fraud in legalization programs. Australia, Canada, and the Scandinavian countries have resisted legalization programs; the United States and southern European countries use them most often.

Migrants are people whose aspirations and goals change with experience, which makes managing migration for employment far more complex than managing trade in goods or the movement of capital over borders. Most twentieth-century guest worker programs had unexpected effects that were more important and long lasting than their expected effects. Successful twenty-first-century guest worker programs are likely to be associated with minimal illegal migration, economic mechanisms that align migrant and employer incentives with program rules, and a path to legal status for migrants who develop "roots" in the country in which they work. Deciding when a migrant has developed roots is not easy: some consider it unfair that host societies benefit from the work of seasonal or temporary workers who in theory never acquire the right to bring their families or settle. Even if guest workers know that they are expected to leave after one or two years, many observers argue that only truly temporary jobs should be filled with guest workers (Böhning, 2003).

Guest worker programs that enforce the rotation of workers can mean that migrants have fewer workplace rights, violating the letter and spirit of ILO conventions 97 and 143, since they "make no distinction between workers who have migrated for permanent settlement, and those who have migrated for short-term or even seasonal work. States are not permitted to exempt any category of regular-entry migrant worker not specified in the instruments."[8] ILO conventions 97 and 143, as well as the United Nations' International Convention on the Protection of the Rights of All Migrant Workers and Members of Their Families, give numerous rights to migrant workers, but states may decide to whom they confer settlement rights, as well as the rules for status change of migrant workers.

Most industrial countries prefer to give settlement rights to highly skilled migrants while taking steps to ensure that low- or semiskilled workers remain "guests." Presumably spurred by the thought that future economic competitiveness will be a function of the number of highly skilled people available in the economy, an increasing number of governments have introduced programs, such as the United Kingdom's Highly Skilled Migrant Programme, that allow highly qualified migrants to come to the country as free agents in the labor market and/or with an immediate settlement option. However, if competitiveness depends on successful integration of foreigners at *all* skill levels, countries may make a mistake trying to induce professionals to settle while rotating less-skilled workers. Canada, for example, has switched from a purely supply-based approach of awarding points for education, language, and other factors to including demand-related criteria, including whether a potential migrant has a Canadian job offer.

Part III Developing Countries and Sustainable Migration

The switch from large-scale to small-scale guest worker programs that draw migrants from the top and bottom of the educational ladder concerns primarily migrants from developing to developed countries. But migrants also move from poorer to richer countries within the developing world, and in the past decade many middle-income developing countries had to deal with guest worker issues for the first time. Many of these new labor importers are southeast Asian "tiger economies" that grew rapidly by attracting foreign investment to build factories and export goods. With many local workers taking factory jobs, migrants from poorer countries arrived to fill in as domestic helpers, construction and plantation workers, and factory workers in small and medium-sized enterprises.

About 40 percent of the world's migrant workers are in developing countries, and in Chapter 6 we turn the spotlight on Thailand, a fast-growing country in Southeast Asia that both imports and exports workers. Thailand has more than a million migrants from Myanmar (Burma), Cambodia, and Laos, and there are 300,000 Thai workers in Taiwan, Singapore, and Israel. Thailand exemplifies the challenges facing many middle-income developing countries that are managing labor migration from poorer neighbors while also seeking to protect Thai migrants employed abroad.

In Chapter 7 we ask what labor-sending and labor-receiving countries can do cooperatively to make international migration an exchange that is sustainable. Sustainability requires benefits to all parties concerned, from migrants and employers to labor-sending and labor-receiving countries, and also has the broader goal of promoting respect for the human rights of migrants. The major challenge is to ensure that migration from developing to developed nations is self-stopping, which means that migration must contribute to stay-at-home development in labor-sending countries. Finding a sustainable framework to promote economic convergence is likely to arise in a bottom-up fashion as best practices are extracted from bilateral and regional migration agreements.

6 Thailand: Migration in a Tiger Economy

Thailand is a "tiger economy" that had one of the world's fastest economic growth rates between 1986 and 1996. Per capita income more than tripled from $750 to $2,400 as the economy, primarily agricultural previously, began to include far more industry and services. Thailand adopted an export-oriented economic policy in the mid-1980s and, with foreign direct investment, achieved 10 percent annual economic growth over the next decade, employing first female rural-urban migrants, and later foreign migrants, in export-oriented agriculture, in construction, and in manufacturing industries that produced clothing, textiles, and similar items for export (Archavanitkul, 1998, 12).

The Thai economy experienced a financial shock in July 1997. The economy shrank by 10 percent in 1998 but bounced back to grow by 5 percent in 1999 and 6 percent in 2000. Between 1980 and 2000, Thailand's population rose from 47 million to 62 million, and the labor force rose from 24 million to 34 million, up 500,000 a year. There is significant inequality and poverty; a sixth of Thai residents have incomes below the poverty line, and poverty rose in the late 1990s after the financial crisis, especially in the north and east of the country.

Thailand received 1.2 million refugees in the wake of the Vietnam war, from the mid-1970s to the mid-1980s, but labor migration from neighboring countries accelerated only in the 1990s, as a result of the Thai economic miracle. Thailand made the transition from net labor exporter to net labor importer in the early 1990s, as many Thais with new job options shunned so-called 3-D jobs in agriculture, fisheries, construction, and private households.

Thailand's major immigration laws—the Foreign Employment Act of 1978, the Immigration Act of 1979, and the Investment Promotion Act of 1997—do not permit the admission of unskilled foreign workers, so most of the estimated 1 million unskilled foreign workers in Thailand are unauthorized. The financial crisis was expected to encourage unemployed Thais to replace migrants, who were expected to leave Thailand if they lost their jobs. Many migrants did leave Thailand in 1997–1998—the Ministry of Labor and Social Welfare estimate of migrants fell from almost 1 million in 1998 to 664,000 in 1999. However, the number of migrants soon rebounded, and by 2004 there were about 1.5 million foreign migrants in Thailand.

The Thai experience shows how ad hoc responses to a structural demand for out-of-area workers can lead to a spreading dependence on migrants. As the number of migrants rose, the government's response was to allow an ever-longer list of employers to "register" their unauthorized foreign workers in exchange for fees equivalent to one to two months' wages. But the government never developed a strategy to reduce dependence on migrants or to integrate migrants and their children. Government policy may be changing: in 2004, for the first time, the Thai government explicitly involved the migrants' countries of origin in labor migration management.

THAI MIGRATION POLICY

Thailand is a parliamentary democracy with a constitutional monarchy; the absolute monarchy was abolished in 1932. There were seventeen military coups between 1932 and 1991, in part because coalition civilian governments were often unstable and short lived. In January 2001 elections were held under a new electoral system and were won by the Thai Rak Thai (Thai love Thai, TRT) party, led by Thaksin Shinawatra, who became prime minister and was re-elected in February 2005.

There are three major types of foreigners in Thailand (Archavanitkul, 1998,

7): lifetime migrants who entered Thailand before 1972 and received permanent resident status (85 percent of 270,000 lifetime migrants are Chinese in the Bangkok area); skilled foreign workers employed in professions specified in Royal Decree 281 in 1972; and unskilled migrants from neighboring Myanmar (85 percent of the total), Cambodia, and Laos.[1]

Thai policy toward the Burmese evolved in three distinct phases (Caouette et al., 2000, 37–39). Between 1945 and 1983, Thailand considered the ethnic Burmese minorities on the Thai-Burmese border who were fighting the central government in Rangoon a buffer between Thailand and Myanmar, especially after Myanmar declared itself a socialist country in 1962. Burmese who fled to Thailand before March 9, 1976, were called "displaced persons of Burmese nationality" and issued colored cards to indicate their status in Thailand. From 1984 to 1987 a Thai-Burmese rapprochement led to intensified fighting between ethnic Burmese Karen and Mon and the Myanmar government, resulting in the flight of many Karen and Mon to Thailand. Therese Caouette and colleagues (2000, 42) emphasize that Thailand has not ratified the 1951 Geneva Refugee Convention and note that the Thai government called the Burmese in camps in Thailand "temporarily displaced persons," not refugees. Since the Burmese State Law and Restoration Council came to power in 1988, many countries have banned the import of Burmese goods, which has prompted Thais and foreigners to invest in factories in Thailand on the Burmese border, so that products such as garments can be made with Burmese labor and exported from Thailand, avoiding the sanctions on Burmese exports.

Royal Decree 281 of November 24, 1972, reserves most jobs in Thailand for Thais, but article 12 opens to foreigners twenty-seven occupations, which are also specified in the Foreigner Employment Act (FEA) of 1978. However, article 17 of the FEA allows the Thai cabinet to permit foreigners to enter and stay in Thailand as an exception to the general bar on foreigners. This provision has been the basis for Thailand's policy toward unskilled migrants: exceptions are made to the general bar by allowing Thai employers to register unauthorized foreign workers and thus fix a date for their anticipated removal from Thailand.

Thai policy for unskilled foreign workers represents a reaction to an underground movement that could no longer be ignored. The policy was calculated to identify the migrants by having their employers register them under the threat of stepped-up enforcement. In exchange for registration, which cost the equivalent of one to two months' wages, migrants obtained identification cards that allowed them to work legally in Thailand for six to twenty-four months. This policy has been regarded skeptically by migrant advocates, who emphasize that the government never laid out a plan for the integration of migrants and their children; it only delayed the removal of migrants.

In 1992 the first registration allowed employers in nine provinces along the Burmese border to register their migrants, but only 706 migrants were registered, largely because employers had to pay a 5,000-baht bond or bail fee that was to be returned when employers "turned over" their workers to authorities as their work permits expired (Archavanitkul, 1998, 8). In what Kritaya Archavanitkul calls an "example of unclear policy," another 101,845 unauthorized foreigners received "purple cards" from the Ministry of Interior at no cost, "in order to control the people in a certain area." In 1993 Thai fisheries law was changed to permit migrants registered by their employers to work on Thai fishing boats based in twenty-two coastal provinces.

The first "regular" registration in 1996 allowed employers of unauthorized migrants from Myanmar, Cambodia, and Laos to register them for twenty-four months after paying a 1,000-baht bond, a 1,000-baht fee, and a 500-baht health fee, a total Bt2,500.[2] Only employers in seven sectors (agriculture, fisheries, construction, mining, coal, transportation, and manufacturing) and thirty-nine provinces could register migrants when the program began, but the number of sectors was later expanded to include domestic helpers and several other occupations, and the number of provinces was expanded to forty-three. Between September 1, 1996, and November 29, 1996, some 323,123 migrants were registered, 88 percent Burmese, and 293,652 two-year work permits were issued. Almost 80 percent of the migrants were registered in three sectors—construction (33 percent), agriculture (28 percent), and fisheries (18 percent).[3]

A 1997 study of registered migrants and their employers (Chintayananda, Risser, and Chantavanich) estimated that 45 percent of the migrants in Thailand were registered, implying a total of 652,560. Some of the employers of nonregistered migrants were in industries and provinces not covered by registration, while others did not register all of their migrants to avoid paying what they considered to be high fees. Most employers who registered migrants had fewer than fifteen workers, and most said they registered their migrants to avoid enforcement and bribes. Migrants similarly said they wanted to be registered in order to avoid police harassment.

Registered migrants were to be paid at least the Thai minimum wage, but no offices were established to which migrants could report violations of labor laws. Indeed, labor offices in some provinces announced publicly that registered migrants were not entitled to the Thai minimum wage, as when labor officials in Tak province on the Thai-Burmese border said that wages are "worked out" between employers and migrants rather than regulated by Thai labor law. In a survey of 337 migrants, Archavanitkul (1998, 13) reported that migrants earned an average of $68 a month, which was about half the average Thai worker's salary, and remitted an average $175 a year to their families.[4]

During the 1997–1998 financial crisis, the Thai government tried and largely failed to remove migrants to open up jobs for unemployed Thais.[5] In one of the most publicized examples of the failure to substitute Thais for migrants, the government threatened not to renew the work permits of migrants employed in rice mills after June 1, 1998. Thailand is the world's largest rice exporter, and its one thousand rice mills employed twenty thousand migrants, many to carry bags of rice that weigh 100 kilograms, or 220 pounds. Rice mills asked the Thai Employment Service to provide Thai workers to replace the migrants, but only seventeen Thais responded. To make the rice mill jobs more attractive to Thai workers, the government proposed that the mills raise wages and reduce the weight of the bags to 50 kilograms, or 110 pounds. The mills did not make rice bags smaller, and the government extended registration for migrants employed in rice mills.

Both Thai and migrant workers lost construction jobs in the financial crisis. Many laid-off Thais returned to their villages, but many migrants remained in Bangkok, home to about 10 percent of Thailand's population. For example, some seventeen thousand migrants lost their jobs in Bangkok construction in August 1997, but only one thousand were officially terminated by Thai employers, a procedure that requires the employer to notify the immigration department that the migrant is jobless so that he can be removed from Thailand. One reason some employers did not formally terminate migrants is that some migrants were owed back wages, and termination would require that these back wages be paid. Many migrants remained in Thailand for fear that trying to collect back wages from abroad would be futile.[6]

In November 1997 the National Security Council estimated that 30,000 Cambodians and 800,000 Burmese were in Thailand, and the government soon thereafter announced plans to remove 300,000 migrants. Enforcement was stepped up and accompanied by a border commuter program that allowed Burmese to work on a daily basis in Thai border areas where minimum wage and other laws were said to be routinely violated, reducing Thai worker interest in the jobs. In August 1998 employers were permitted to reregister migrants for another year, then again, and then again, and then again. After each "final" registration, enforcement was stepped up, especially in border areas, but enforcement often took the form of Thai police raiding garment factories and collecting fines from employers and migrants. The Tak Industrial Council in January 2000 complained that Thais were not willing to replace migrants—the council said that 20,000 migrants had been removed, but only 6,000 Thais had applied for their jobs.

In 2001 the newly elected government of Prime Minister Thaksin Shinawatra announced that it would "solve the illegal migrant labor problem." There had been discussion of "social problems" associated with migrants in Thailand, including the charge that migrants were responsible for increasing crime rates and reintroducing communicable diseases that had been eliminated from Thailand. The Thaksin government debated whether to have another registration and decided in an August 28, 2001, cabinet resolution that "owing to the lack of Thai workers' willingness and ability to work in some hazardous jobs . . . [employers will be permitted] to employ illegal foreign workers temporarily prior to deportation in 37 of Thailand's 76 provinces and in 18 types of jobs, such as fisheries and hog farms." However, the 2001 registration was different. It allowed all employers, regardless of industry or province, to register their migrants, and promised the involvement of the military in stepped-up enforcement after registration ended; the Thai military is perceived as less corrupt than the police.

In order to register their migrants, employers had to pay fees of Bt3,250 ($74), including Bt1,200 for health insurance (services are provided at state hospitals), Bt900 for the six-month work permit, Bt150 for a photo ID card, and Bt1,000 as a deposit that is forfeited if the migrant disappears. After six months, migrants could be reregistered for another six months by paying a work permit fee of Bt900 and a health fee of Bt300, for a total of Bt4,450 ($101) for twelve months.[7] Some 568,000 migrants were registered in September–October 2001 (see Table 6.1, 429,000 were reregistered in February–March 2002, and 289,000 were re-registered in 2003).

The declining number of migrants who were registered reflected a variety of complaints about the process. For example, some of the employers who paid the registration fee on behalf of their migrants complained that migrants whose wages were reduced when the fee was deducted from their wages "ran away," and there was no legal way to replace them. Migrants complained that they were paying for registration, but some employers kept their registration papers for "safekeeping," which left the migrants vulnerable to police harassment. Some critics accused the government of having registration exercises every year or two to raise revenue.

Most registered migrants earned less than the minimum wage, which was

Table 6.1. Thai Migrant Registration, 2001 and 2002

	Total 2001	Total 2002	Percent Decline	Burmese		Laotian		Cambodian	
				2001	2002	2001	2002	2001	2002
Agriculture	132,987	98,408	26%	112,571	85,548	9,218	6,247	11,198	6,613
Construction	47,320	35,475	25%	39,856	30,845	2,133	1,382	5,331	3,248
Rice mills	6,195	4,771	23%	5,880	4,565	129	102	186	104
Fisheries	103,375	74,140	28%	80,029	58,794	2,102	1,290	21,244	14,056
Maids	82,389	62,950	24%	61,381	47,359	16,828	12,497	4,180	3,094
Subtotal	372,266	275,744	26%	299,717	227,111	30,410	21,518	42,139	27,115
Total	568,285	429,331	24%	451,335	349,647	59,358	42,085	57,592	37,599

Notes: The 2001 registration was September 24–October 25. The 2002 registration was February 24– March 25.

Source: Yongyuth Chalamwong, "Recent Trends and Policy Initiatives of International Migration and Labor Market in Thailand." Thai Development Research Institute. Mimeo, 2004.

Bt133 a day in most of Thailand in 2001, Bt143 in six southern provinces, and Bt165 in Bangkok and surrounding provinces. Migrants may legally be paid less than the minimum wage if they are employed by employers with fewer than ten workers, or in agriculture, where minimum wage coverage is incomplete. Many migrants also work in seasonal or casual jobs that do not offer work every day, so average monthly earnings for migrants are believed to be Bt1,500–2,000 ($34–45), making the registration fees equivalent to one to two months' wages.[8]

Thailand's labor migration policy evolved into a policy of registering and identifying unauthorized migrants, with the government gradually expanding the number of provinces and sectors whose employers could register migrants and employ them legally for an additional year or two. Contrary to initial plans, migrant reregistration was permitted in response to largely failed efforts to substitute unemployed Thais for migrants removed from the country. In 2004 the Thai government, recognizing that periodically registering migrants to delay their removal was not a successful migration management policy, announced a new policy based on decentralization, bilateral memoranda of understanding (MOUs), and promoting economic development in the border areas of neighboring countries from which many migrants came. Under the new policy a national quota or ceiling is placed on the number of migrant workers and then allocated to provinces based on each province's share of registered migrants in 2001–2003. A committee chaired by the appointed provincial governor allocates each province's quota by industry, and employers register the migrants they employ until the quota is exhausted.

Before this newest quota system was put in place, there was a comprehensive registration of migrants and their employers, and 1,269,074 foreign migrants registered for a fee of Bt3,800 each in July 2004. They included 906,000 Burmese, 182,000 Laotians, and 182,000 Cambodians. Some 337,000 migrants were registered by agricultural employers, 206,000 by construction employers, 154,000 by private households for domestic helpers, and 115,000 by fisheries employers. (Migrants who were self-employed and unemployed were also allowed to register.) Registered foreign workers must pass a physical exam and then can obtain work permits valid for two years that entitle them to Thai labor-law protection.

After all migrant workers are fully registered and the number of migrants employed falls below the quota, Thai employers seeking permission to employ foreign workers can advertise jobs they want to fill with migrants. If no Thais are available, migrants can be admitted under the MOUs with neighboring countries, with the Thai employer specifying the skills needed and the labor-sending country selecting the migrants. Those selected will travel to Thailand without their families to work for an initial two years, with the possibility of a two-year renewal followed by a mandatory three-year stay at home. Migrants admitted under the MOUs are to have 15 percent of their Thai earnings deducted and placed in a savings fund, which is to be refunded with interest if they return home at the end of their contracts; this savings fund is also to be used to cover the cost of deporting unauthorized workers.

MIGRANTS AND LABOR MARKETS

Thailand had a 2002 labor force of thirty-four million, including thirty-three million employed and one million unemployed.[9] About half of the employed Thais are in agriculture, followed by 15 percent each in services, handicrafts, and commerce. The dominance of agriculture is reflected in the facts that twenty-five million Thais are employed outside metropolitan areas and that national employment exhibits marked seasonal variations. Some 80 percent of men and 60 percent of women are in the labor force in the first quarter, the dry season, compared with 85 and 65 percent in the third quarter, the wet season. Agricultural employment is three to four million higher in the third quarter than in the first, so that the size of the labor force varies by two to three million throughout the year.

In the 1990s the labor force participation rate of young people (under twenty-five) fell sharply as more youth stayed in school; for example, the labor force participation rate (LFPR) for males fifteen to nineteen dropped from 68 percent in 1991 to 40 percent in 2001. About 66 percent of Thai workers (twenty-two million) had an elementary school education or less in 2001, down from 81 percent in 1990; the average number of years of education of persons fifteen and older in 2000 was 7.8.

Thai workers are grouped into six categories. The largest group, unpaid family workers, accounted for 11 million, or 37 percent, of employees in 2001, followed by own-account workers, at 9 million, and private-sector employees, at 7.5 million. About half of the workers employed in Thailand are in the informal sector. The Thai Labor Force Survey (LFS) calculates wages for private sector employees as follows. Individuals are asked to report their wages and the payroll period—hourly, daily, weekly, or monthly—and the LFS converts all wages to their monthly equivalents by assuming that private sector workers work eight hours a day for twenty-six days a month, and for 4.2 weeks a month.

Most Thai labor laws, such as minimum wage laws, are gradually being extended to smaller employers; before 2002 only employers with ten or more workers were usually covered, but now even small employers who hire migrants are subject to labor laws.[10] In 2000 there were 251,000 employers with fewer than ten workers, employing a total of 870,000 workers, and 107,000 employers with ten or more workers, employing a total of 5.9 million employees. Thus about 5.9 million of the 33 million employed workers—or 18 percent—were covered fully by minimum wage and other labor laws, and this coverage is expanding. Unions are relatively weak—fewer than 5 percent of workers belong to one of the one thousand unions, most of which represent workers at a single company.

The presence of migrant workers increased Thai employment and economic activity. The TDRI estimated that 700,000 unauthorized migrants in 1995 increased Thai GDP by 0.5 percent and depressed the wages of Thai workers with primary education or less by 3.5 percent. The real income of the poorest 60 percent of households fell by 0.4 percent as a result of migrants, while the real income of the richest 40 percent rose 0.3 percent, according to the National Economic and Social Development Board (NESDB), which concluded that migrants have benefited "only [a] small group of businessmen and corrupt officers" (n.d., 17).

Many Thai employers are critical of the government's migrant policy. The Thai Farmers Research Center (TFRC), for example, thinks that migrant policy is inconsistent with other policies. According to the TFRC, the Board of Investment (BOI) encourages foreign investment that depends on low-wage workers to produce export goods, then tries to prevent migrant employment because of social problems associated with migrants and unemployment among Thai workers.[11] In 2000 the Ministry of Labor and Social Welfare's (MOLSW) National Advisory Council for Labor Development urged a stricter migrant policy, advising the MOLSW to set a clear grace period before banning the employment of illegal foreign workers; allow only registered alien workers, not their families, to stay in Thailand during the grace period; register employers who hire alien labor and increase penalties on employers who hire nonregistered foreign workers; and establish a national database system to obtain information about employers and foreign workers.

CASE STUDIES

Migrants represent a high percentage of workers in agriculture, fishing and fish processing, garments in the Burmese-border area, and construction and domestic service in Bangkok. Case studies of employment in these sectors have found that most employers and migrants know about the registration process and that most once believed that registration would free them from police "harassment."[12] However, many migrants noted that even if they were registered, they were subject to apprehension and deportation if their employer retained the registration card, as many employers do. Some employers, especially farmers who employ workers seasonally, believe that registration fees are too high, while others complained that after they advanced registration fees to their workers, the workers ran away, meaning that the employer lost his payment and was not able to hire another legal migrant.

Agriculture

Agriculture generated about 11 percent of Thailand's $122 billion GDP in 2000 and 10 percent of Thailand's $57 billion in export earnings. An estimated 50 percent of Thailand's workforce depends at least in part on income from farming, and many Thai farmers migrate seasonally to urban areas when there is no farm work; that is, agriculture serves as an employment buffer.

Thailand is the world's fifth-largest producer of rice and the leading exporter of rice, producing twenty-four million tons and exporting a quarter of its production.[13] Most of Thailand's rice is grown on ten million hectares (about twenty-five million acres) of central plains rice paddy, with the main crop harvested between November and January. Another ten million hectares of Thai farmland produces corn, cassava, cotton, and pineapple, as well as sugar in the northeast and rubber and palm oil in the south.

Tak province on the border with Myanmar attracted foreign and local investment in the 1990s to establish garment factories and fruit, vegetable, and flower farms. The unskilled hired farm workforce in Tak is almost 100 percent Burmese—only the supervisors were reported to be Thais. Daily wages are low—Bt60–70 a day ($1.40–1.63) for eight hours a day, six or seven days a week; Thai supervisors are paid Bt100 a day, less than the Bt133 minimum wage. Farm employers provide housing for the migrant workers they hire, some food, and some additional benefits, such as gold chains for Chinese New Year.

Employers reportedly turned to migrants in the 1990s because they could not find Thais, and migrants were cheaper. Both employers and migrants were aware of the registration program, but employers complained that registration was too costly for seasonal workers—a farmer grossing Bt50,000 a year and hiring ten seasonal workers would have to pay Bt44,500 up front for registration. Even though the registration fee could be deducted from the migrants' pay, some employers would have had to borrow money to register their workers, and some feared that migrants would run away before the registration fee was recouped in wage deductions.

Thailand is a major producer and consumer of pork, with many hogs raised in family-owned operations that hire one migrant to care for each 150–200 hogs, or fifty to sixty workers to care for 10,000 hogs. In the provinces surrounding Bangkok, internal migrants from Thailand's northeast were replaced by migrants in the 1990s, in part because working on hog farms often involves living on the farms and working eight to ten hours a day, seven days a week, for Bt120–130 a day. Employers provide very basic housing, some food, and incentives to keep hogs healthy.

Fisheries and Fish Processing

Thailand had 150,000 fishermen and fifty-four thousand vessels in 1995, including eleven thousand commercial boats longer than ten meters or heavier than five tons. Boats smaller than ten meters typically rely on family labor and work close to port, returning daily. There are two major types of boats that employ migrants: those that fish in Thai coastal waters and stay at sea up to fourteen days, and those that fish in foreign waters for two to five years. These larger fishing vessels, which have Thai captains, pilots, and engineers but migrant crews, have refrigeration for catching and storing shrimp, lobster, squid, cuttlefish, and tuna; their catch is taken to port by mother ships that visit periodically. In many cases hired workers receive no guaranteed wages, only a share of the value of the catch, typically 7 percent, which Pongat Boonchuwong and Waraporn Dechboon (2000, 40) estimated gave workers Bt4,600–8,000 ($106–184) a month in 1995.

Internal migrants began to shun jobs on fishing boats after many boats sank in an early 1990s typhoon. Many boat owners assert that with Thai workers from the northeast abandoning fishing, they had to turn to migrants to fill jobs on fishing boats, especially those that stay at sea for extended periods. Labor advocates say that the problem is low and uncertain wages—a crew sharing 7 percent of the value of the catch, they argue, can never be sure of their earnings and could be cheated by price manipulation between the boat owner and fish processors. Interviews conducted by the Asian Research Center for Migration (ARCM) with boat owners emphasize that as days at sea increase, so does the likelihood that the unskilled workers will be migrants. (In a crew of ten, for example, there may be six migrants and four Thais.) ARCM reported that migrants earned an average of Bt200 ($4.65) a day in 2001.[14]

Employers who register migrants typically keep the workers' registration cards, bailing out workers who are apprehended by police because they do not have registration cards with them. Migrants employed in fisheries have the highest "runaway rate," which has prompted the fisheries association to propose that the association, rather than individual boat owners, be responsible for registering migrants. This provision would allow migrants to shift between boats. Most boat owners in 2001 registered their migrants, and most migrants in fisheries did not complain about the cost of registration, believing that it was a reasonable price to pay for "freedom from police harassment." However, "illegality" was widespread in fisheries, because some migrants were not registered and some registered migrants worked for an employer who did not register them. Some migrants noted that the Bt4,450 registration fee was only slightly less than the Bt7,000 smuggling fee to return to Thailand if deported.

Fishery and fish-processing workers differ significantly—fishing crews tend to be male, and fish-processing workers female. Fish-processing workers are sometimes the wives of migrants employed on boats, but moving from the boats to the processing plants can also be seen as a step up because processing workers can live with their family and friends. Thais allegedly shun fish-processing work, which requires getting up at 1 or 2 A.M. to peel shrimp and working irregular hours that depend on the catch for piece-rate wages.

Construction

Bangkok is the economic heart of Thailand, employing a sixth of the Thai labor force and generating a half of Thai GDP, but since the 1997 economic crisis, the government has sought to decentralize industrial activity, encouraging multinationals such as Nike to move to the poorer northern and northeastern provinces. The construction case study noted that most migrants were employed by subcontractors, not general contractors, and that Thais and migrants worked alongside each other, albeit for different wages. The Thais employed in construction were reported to be older, with little education, which made it harder for them to find jobs in manufacturing.

Traditionally, construction workers in Bangkok were internal Thai migrants from the northeast who returned to their farms for one or two months a year. In early 1997, before the financial crisis, Thai construction employers reportedly accepted this seasonal migration by internal Thai migrants, but as Burmese migrants became more readily available, Thais were reportedly fired if they left their construction jobs to return to their farms. The number of migrants employed in Bangkok area construction rose, and some subcontractors came to prefer migrants. Registered Burmese migrants in Bangkok reported working eight or nine hours a day, seven days a week, for Bt150–200 a day. Their employers paid the registration fee, deducting Bt300 a month from their wages to recoup it, but some noted that this was less than the Bt400–500 a month they had to pay to police before registration.

Garments

Textiles are the largest part of the manufacturing sector in Thailand, which employs 4.6 million workers and accounts for about a third of Thai GDP. The growth sectors of Thai manufacturing include autos (two-thirds exported) and the assembly of computers, integrated circuits, and television sets, but textiles and shoes have traditionally dominated employment and exports. The Tak case study, which focused on Burmese migrants employed in sewing shops in Mae Sot, found that most large employers registered most of their Burmese migrants, deducting the Bt3,250 cost from workers' wages at the rate of Bt540–600 a month; migrant earnings were Bt1,200–2,400 a month. Registration helped employers by freeing them from police harassment but was less helpful to migrants, many of whom got only copies of their work permits and were still subject to arrest and deportation if they encountered police away from the workplace. Neither employers nor migrants fully understand the registration process; many migrants, for example, did not understand that registration conferred only six months of legal status with the employer who registered them.

The textile and garment industry in Tak is a "footloose" industry in the sense that it relocated from Bangkok or was developed afresh along the Burmese border, to take advantage of the low wages paid to Burmese migrants. Local sewing shops provide dorm-style housing and food for the migrants, with six to ten workers to a room. Some employers say that the provision of room and board explains why the migrants do not get the Bt133 a day minimum wage the government has set for the area. About 80 percent of the sewing workers were estimated to be migrants, half men and half women.

Domestic Helpers

Many households in Bangkok and other cities employ domestic helpers, and the primary source of labor changed in the 1990s from internal migrants from northern and northeastern Thailand to foreign migrants. According to the Labor Force Survey, the number of maids was 158,000 in the third quarter of 1997, when internal Thai migrants return to their villages during the harvest season, and 250,000 in the first quarter of 2001.

There were 81,405 domestic helpers registered in September–October 2001, up from 34,283 in the 1996 registration. Most were women, but their location shifted—the share of registered maids in Bangkok rose from 38 percent of the total in 1996 to 55 percent in 2001, when they accounted for 30 percent of registered female migrants. Most foreign maids are recruited via brokers, who find them jobs with households via informal networks. Most of the foreign domestic helpers reportedly pay brokers Bt5,000–6,000 for their jobs and receive Bt2,000–4,000 a month in wages. Virtually all live with their employers, and most are provided with housing and food.

The government has tried to train Thais to be housemaids but has had trouble finding applicants and has found that most Thais who were trained did not want to move in with their employers. A 1999 study found that 30 percent of domestic helpers received Bt2,000–3,000 a month, 25 percent received Bt3,000–4,000, and 25 percent received Bt4,000–5,000 a month.

WHICH WAY THAILAND?

Thailand has the problem of managing migrants because its economic success has enabled previously internal migrants who filled 3-D jobs some distance from their homes to find better opportunities in Thailand or abroad. Thai employers turned to migrants from neighboring Myanmar, Cambodia, and Laos to replace internal migrants and to fill newly created jobs, and the government assumed that the need for migrants would be short-lived. Thus Thai migrant policy has been to allow employers to register and thereby defer temporarily the planned removal of unauthorized migrants.

Employers have been encouraged to register their unauthorized migrants by the threat of stepped up enforcement but were given no assurances that they would be allowed to reregister their migrants. Penalties for hiring unauthorized workers seem stiff—employers face a maximum penalty of three years in jail and a Bt60,000 ($1,338) fine, and migrants can be fined Bt5,000 and/or jailed up to three months—but enforcement has never been sustained long enough to persuade employers or migrants to change their behavior.[15] Instead, illegal migration has increased, as employers learned that migrants did not want to have registration fees deducted from their wages, and migrants learned that registration did not necessarily protect them from police harassment.

The Thai Ministry of Labor (MOL) in 2004 estimated there were 1.7 million "irregular" migrants, including unauthorized and quasi-authorized foreigners, "hill tribe" persons born in Thailand but lacking documentation, and refugees. Will the newest registration program, which attracted 1.3 million foreigners, help Thailand to resolve the migrant labor issue? One purpose of registration and having future migrants arrive legally under the terms of MOUs is to combat smuggling and trafficking, and to get the governments of countries such as Myanmar to issue identity documents to their citizens. However, with the decentralization of migration management in Thailand, the rights of migrants are likely to vary from province to province, with a variety of factors determining migrant rights. For example, migrant advocates hailed the order of a Thai court in September 2004 that a Mae Sot garment factory pay Bt1.2 million ($29,250) to eighteen Burmese migrant workers fired from the Nut Knitting factory in October 2002. The Labor Protection Office of Tak province ordered the firm to pay the migrants, but they had to sue for their back wages when the employer did not comply. There are at least 100,000 Burmese migrants in Mae Sot, and this is the first such victory by migrants that resulted in significant back pay.

The Thai experience demonstrates that temporary-worker programs tend to become larger and to last longer than anticipated, as employers and migrants become dependent on one another. If an industry has high worker turnover or expands, the migrant share of employment increases over time. Unless external factors require changes in the labor markets—as, for example, when trade shifts require handling rice in a bulk form that can be mechanized rather than having migrants carry bags, or technology improves to clean shrimp with fewer health risks mechanically than if done by hand—the mutual dependence between migrants and their employers is likely to deepen. Higher minimum wages or improved enforcement could also reduce the economic incentive to hire migrants as employers take steps to mechanize, to reorganize work so that fewer migrants are employed for longer periods, or to shift jobs to the migrants' countries of origin.

The Thai experience shows that migrant labor cannot be turned on and off like a water tap. Instead, labor migration is often like a river that expands from a single channel into a delta of rivulets, making control more difficult over time. There have been suggestions that the Thai government acknowledge that migrant workers are likely to be a medium-term feature of the economy, and develop both clear and transparent migrant worker policies and the socioeconomic justification for employing migrants to overcome union and public opposition. Foreign workers are quite controversial in Thailand, with most unions strongly opposed to their presence, while many Thais blame migrants for rising crime.

The Thai government has deepened ties with labor-sending countries—Myanmar, Cambodia, and Laos—to better manage the flow of migrants, using the carrot of aid to build infrastructure in migrant areas of origin and thus to win cooperation to reduce unauthorized migration and smuggling. However, the central government has not yet aligned employer and migrant incentives with program rules, and it is unlikely that local-level administrators will enforce rules that require employers and migrants to break their relationship after two or four years.

Thailand also exports workers. Some 300,000 were abroad in 2002, including 180,000 in Taiwan; about 200,000 a year depart for one or two years abroad. Thais are employed in Singapore (68,000), Israel (20,000), and Malaysia, Japan, and Hong Kong, and by Gulf oil exporters. The Thai government aims to improve the predeparture orientation of migrants to increase their protections and encourage remittances, which were $1.1 billion in 2002. Thailand allows brokers to recruit workers for overseas jobs with little supervision, and some wind up going into debt to the brokers to get overseas jobs, including up to $4,500 to get a two-year contract to work in Taiwan.

7 Managing Migration in the Twenty-first Century

Migration is a response to differences between areas that encourage individuals to move, usually to take advantage of higher incomes and jobs or more security and improved human rights. Reducing the root causes of such migration is a primary objective of U.N. agencies and national government development programs, as well as private efforts aimed at promoting development. The causes of the inequalities that promote migration are many and complex. Many of the root causes of emigration lie within the developing countries, but the trade, investment, and other economic policies of the industrial nations can increase or decrease emigration pressures. However, since "migration is the most under-researched of the global flows" (World Bank, 2002, 82), the relative importance of domestic and foreign factors contributing to migration pressures is not well understood.

In an ideal world, there would be few barriers to migration and little unwanted migration. This ideal has been largely achieved within the EU, where there is full freedom of movement among most of the twenty-five members, and less migration between, for example, Spain and Germany than many EU leaders desire. However, as the EU expands, fears of "too much" migration loom large, and after the enlargement of 2004 the "old" EU-15 countries restricted migration from new eastern European members for up to seven years.[1] Fears of too much migration are a major obstacle to Turkey's EU entry: accession negotiations were scheduled to begin in fall 2005.

Globally, the question is how to manage migration until differences narrow enough to make migration a nonissue, as among the "old" EU-15 countries. There is clearly a need for more dialogue on migration between emigration, transit, and immigration countries, and a major issue facing the global community is whether that dialogue should occur in a bottom-up fashion, as in bilateral and regional forums, or in a top-down fashion, as might be expected if a World Migration Organization (WMO) analogue to the World Trade Organization were established. Those favoring a WMO say their goal is a "new international regime for the orderly movements of people" (Ghosh, 2000, 6) that would establish rules and open more legal channels for migrants.[2] A WMO, in the best-case scenario outlined by proponents, could substitute more legal migration for today's unauthorized migration.

Many countries oppose establishing a WMO. The United Nations in March 1999 sent letters to its permanent members asking whether a global conference on migration should be convened to discuss the elements of a global migration regime, a precursor to a WMO. Of the seventy-eight governments that responded, forty-seven expressed support for a global conference, twenty-six expressed reservations, and five had mixed views (U.N., 2002, 36). Instead of a global conference, U.N. Secretary General Kofi Annan launched a Global Commission on International Migration (www.gcim.org/), with the support of several governments, to place migration on the global agenda, examine gaps in migration management and linkages between migration and development, and make recommendations to maximize the benefits and reduce the costs of international migration. Annan noted that the U.N. system "still lacks a comprehensive institutional focus at the international level that could protect the rights of migrants and promote the shared interest of emigration, immigration and transit countries." The Global Commission's report, due in fall 2005, was expected to recommend policies that make better use of remittances and other factors associated with migration to reduce migration pressures.

The industrial countries that are the destination for most migrants are among the most skeptical of the push for a World Migration Organization. One reason for industrial country skepticism is that, unlike trade and finance, there is no generally accepted theory showing that countries that refuse to open themselves to migrants suffer economically. By contrast, trade theory makes it clear that voluntary trade helps countries to specialize in the production of the goods in which they have a comparative advantage, which increases the GDPs of trading countries as well as global economic output. Thus the World Bank and IMF can encourage countries to open themselves to trade by arguing that not trading reduces their own as well as the global economic output.

The lack of a comparable theory that highlights the benefits of encouraging migration makes a bottom-up approach to global migration norms more likely. A growing number of bilateral and regional forums deal with migration. For example, the Regional Migration Conference, or Puebla Process (www.rcmvs.org), an initiative launched by the Mexican government in the city of Puebla in 1996 in response to voter approval of Proposition 187 in California in 1994, includes eleven countries that meet at least once a year to discuss migration issues: Canada, the United States, Mexico, and Central American countries plus the Dominican Republic. The discussions cover changes in national migration policies, the link between migration and development, migrant trafficking, cooperation for the return of extraregional migrants, and the human rights of migrants.

Puebla Process consultations are credited with paving the way for the United States to legalize the status of many Central Americans who fled there during civil wars in the 1980s; to grant temporary protected status to Central Americans in the United States when Hurricane Mitch carved a path of destruction in 1998 and after El Salvador had severe earthquakes in 2001; and to encourage cooperation to improve safety at the Mexican-U.S. and Mexican-Guatemalan borders. There are many other regional migration forums, including those between the EU and North African countries, between African countries, and between the Andean countries of South America. These forums discuss such economic issues as remittances and development as well as such migration management issues as traffickers and criminals.

REMITTANCES AND DEVELOPMENT

Remittances, the portion of migrant incomes that are sent home, can reduce poverty and incentives to migrate. Remittances have risen with the number of migrants and have surpassed official development assistance in developing countries in the mid-1990s (see Figure 7.1). In recent years, foreign direct investment in developing countries has decreased, so that remittances constitute the only financial flow to developing countries that is still on an upward path.

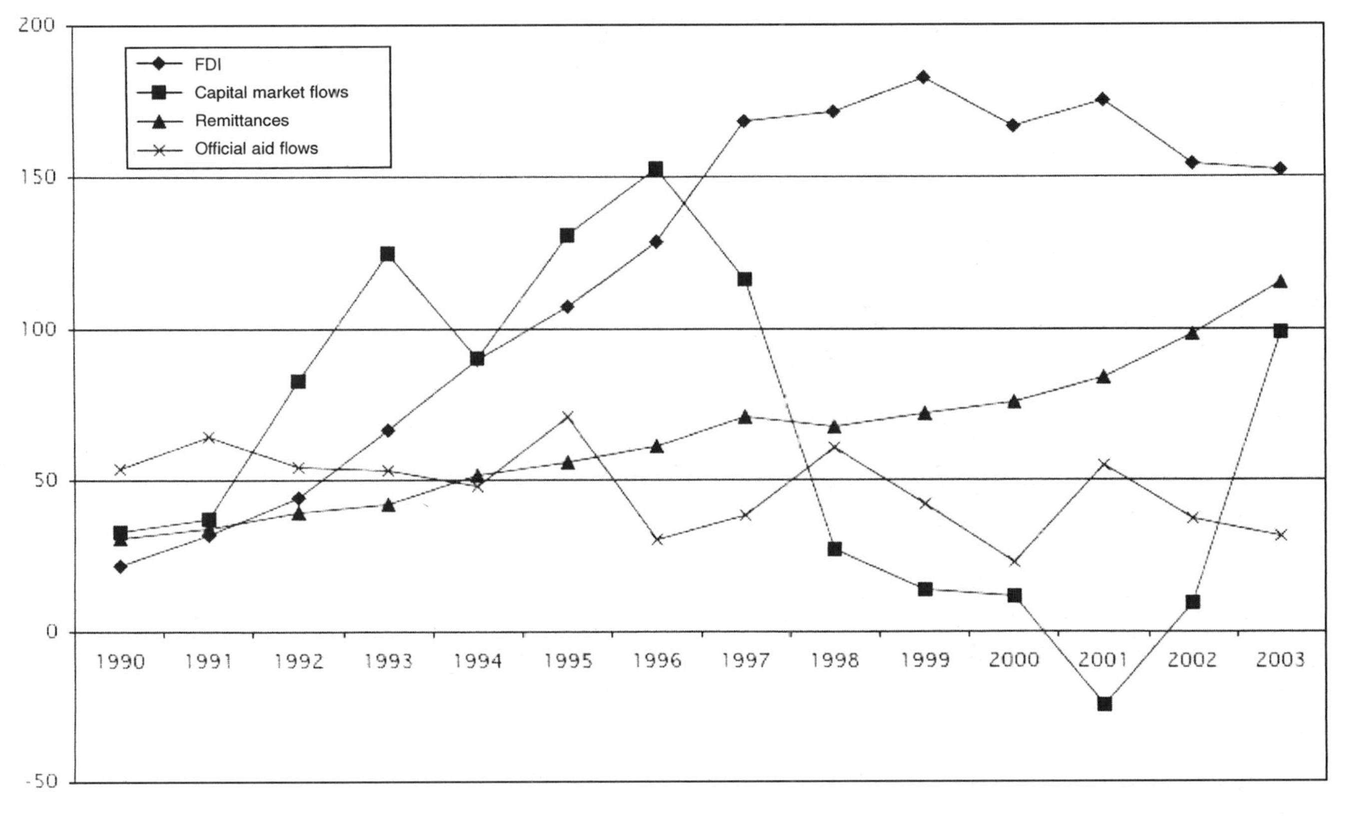

Figure 7.1. Remittances and Other Flows to Developing Countries (in billions of dollars). *Source:* Ratha (2003)

The growth of remittances has stirred hopes that they can become an alternative source of foreign capital to reduce poverty and stimulate development. The IMF estimates remittances for each country in its *Balance of Payments Statistics Yearbook,* distinguishing between worker remittances (the wages and salaries that are sent home by migrants abroad for twelve or more months) and compensation of employees (the wages and benefits of migrants abroad less than twelve months, called labor income until 1995).[3] The volume of remittances received by an emigration country depends on the number of migrants, their earnings, and their willingness and ability to remit. Remittances to developing countries more than doubled between the late 1980s and the late 1990s, after experiencing drops in 1991 (Gulf war) and in 1998 (Asian financial crisis; see Table 7.1).

A handful of developing countries receive most remittances. The three largest recipients, India, Mexico, and the Philippines, received a third of total remittances to developing countries in recent years. The top six recipients, these three plus Morocco, Egypt, and Turkey, received half of all remittances to developing countries (see Table 7.2). However, remittances are most important in smaller nations, where they can be equivalent to 20–40 percent of GDP; in 2001, for example, remittances were 37 percent of GDP in Tonga, 26 percent in Lesotho, 23 percent in Jordan, and 15–17 percent in Albania, Nicaragua, Yemen, and Moldova. The major sources of remittances were the United States ($28 billion), Saudi Arabia ($15 billion), and Germany, Belgium, and Switzerland ($8 billion each).

The World Bank's Global Development Finance (GDF) report estimated that remittances to developing countries reached $80 billion in 2002 and $115 billion in 2003. In order to increase their development payoff, the GDF investigated how to increase the access of workers to official banking channels, which can allow governments to borrow against expected remittances, as well as how to lower the fees charged to migrants, which average 13 percent of the amount transferred.[4] Many countries with migrants are making it easier for migrants to open bank accounts, which has the side effect of increasing competition in the money-transfer business.[5]

Studies demonstrate convincingly that the best way to maximize the volume of remittances is to have an appropriate exchange rate and economic policies that promise growth in sending countries (Ratha, 2003). Regardless of how much migrants remit, many governments have since the September 11, 2001, terrorism attacks tried to reduce transfers through informal channels and shift them to formal channels, such as banks. Migrants have demonstrated a will-

Table 7.1. Financial Flows to Developing Countries, 1990–2003 (billions of dollars)

	1990	1991	1992	1993	1994	1995	1996	1997	1998	1999	2000	2001	2002	2003
FDI[a]	22	32	44	67	90	107	129	168	171	182	166	175	154	152
Capital market flows	33	38	83	125	90	131	153	117	27	14	12	−25	10	99
Remittances	31	34	40	42	52	56	61	71	68	72	76	84	98	115
Official aid flows	54	65	54	53	48	71	30	38	61	42	23	55	37	32

[a]Foreign direct investment.

Source: Ratha, 2003.

Table 7.2. Remittances to Developing Countries, 1995–2001

	1995	1996	1997	1998	1999	2000	2001
Total (billions of dollars)	48	53	63	60	65	65	72
India (% share)	6.2 (13%)	8.8 (17%)	10.3 (16%)	9.5 (16%)	11.1 (17%)	9.2 (14%)	10 (14%)
Mexico (% share)	4.4 (9%)	5.0 (10%)	5.5 (9%)	6.5 (11%)	6.6 (10%)	7.6 (12%)	9.9 (14%)
Philippines (% share)	5.4 (11%)	4.9 (9%)	6.8 (11%)	5.1 (9%)	6.9 (11%)	6.2 (10%)	6.4 (9%)
Morocco (% share)	2.0 (4%)	2.2 (4%)	1.9 (3%)	2.0 (3%)	1.9 (3%)	2.2 (3%)	3.3 (5%)
Egypt (% share)	3.2 (7%)	3.1 (6%)	3.7 (6%)	3.4 (6%)	3.2 (5%)	2.9 (4%)	2.9 (4%)
Turkey (% share)	3.3 (7%)	3.5 (7%)	4.2 (7%)	5.4 (9%)	4.5 (7%)	4.6 (7%)	2.8 (4%)
Six-country subtotal	24.5 (51%)	27.5 (52%)	32.4 (52%)	31.9 (54%)	34.2 (53%)	32.7 (51%)	35.3 (49%)

Source: www.worldbank.org/prospects/gdf2003/gdf_statApp_web.pdf (198).

ingness to transfer money via official channels, especially if bank transfers are easy and cheap, but this usually requires banking outlets in migrant communities at home and abroad and competition to lower transfer costs.

There has been considerable progress on both fronts. In one of the largest transfer markets, that between the United States and Mexico, there were 25 million consumer money transfers in 2000 averaging $300 each. The Mexican government has sought to increase access to formal banking channels and lower the cost of transferring funds.[6] For example, on April 23, 2001, when the interbank exchange rate was $1 to 9.3 pesos, the fee charged by most money transfer firms in Los Angeles was $15, and the rate at which dollars were converted to pesos was about 1 to 9, making the total costs of a transfer $5–20, or 2–7 percent of the $300 typically sent.

The U.S.-Mexican remittance market is unregulated, in the sense that Mexicans in the United States decide how and how much to remit. Several Asian countries, by contrast, have specified both the amount of remittances migrants must send and the form in which they are remitted. For example, many Korean migrants in the Middle East in the late 1970s and early 1980s were considered employees of their Korean construction company and had their earnings sent to their families in Korea while receiving a stipend in local currency abroad. Many Chinese and Vietnamese migrants today who go abroad as employees of Chinese and Vietnamese firms are paid their wages in a similar way—most wages go to the migrant's family or home bank account in local currency. The Philippines, in a policy unpopular with migrants, attempted to specify how much should be remitted in the 1980s, but later abandoned the policy.

Forced savings programs are unpopular with migrants. Migrants from Jamaica, Barbados, Saint Lucia, and Dominica have been recruited by U.S. farmers since 1943 under the auspices of the British West Indies Central Labor Organization (BWICLO). The BWICLO required migrants to sign a contract in which they agreed to pay a fee of 5 percent of their earnings for BWICLO services, and the BWICLO contract additionally required U.S. employers to deposit 20 percent of each worker's earnings in a Jamaican savings bank. When migrants complained that they had difficulty getting access to these forced savings or received them with no interest, the Jamaican bank began to pay interest.

Between 1942 and 1946 Mexican braceros had 10 percent of their earnings sent from U.S. employers directly to the Bank of Mexico. Many wartime braceros complain that they never received these forced savings, and the Mexican government says that it has no records of what happened to the money. Suits filed in the United States prompted the Mexican government to accept claims for the unpaid forced savings, a case that persists sixty years after the labor migration occurred. Eighty thousand to ninety thousand former braceros registered with the Mexican Interior Ministry allege that they did not receive wages withheld during World War II, and the Mexican government has created a $26 million fund (*fideicomiso*) to compensate them, but payments had not yet begun by 2005, sixty years after the wages were deducted.

Remittances improve the lives of recipients and can under some circumstances accelerate development that reduces poverty for nonmigrants as well. Most remittances are used for consumption, helping to explain their stability in the face of changing exchange rates and investment outlooks.[7] In an effort to attract remittances and spur development, many developing countries made their exchange rates more realistic in the 1990s, and some took steps to encourage migrants to remit by creating government bonds that migrants could buy with their foreign currency earnings.

The spending of remittances generate jobs and thus benefits nonmigrants. Most studies suggest that each $1 of remittances flowing into an emigration area generates a $2–3 increase in economic output, as recipients buy goods or invest in housing, education, or health care. These additional jobs can reduce poverty, since the remittances act as an external source of capital for the place in which they are received. A study of seventy-four low- and middle-income developing countries found that a 10 percent increase in the share of remittances in a country's GDP was associated with a 1.2 percent decline in the share of people living on less than $1 per person per day (Adams and Page, 2003).

Classical theories of migration suggested that the emigration of men in the prime of their working lives would reduce economic output in migrant areas of origin, or leave output unchanged in Lewis-type economic development models in which surplus labor was trapped in agriculture.[8] Empirical research suggests that while emigration may initially reduce output in local economies, remittances can also lead to adjustments so that output is maintained, as when migrant families that lose males to migration shift from crops to less-labor-intensive livestock or hire labor to continue to produce crops. In some cases, the exit of men and the return of remittances can increase output in agricultural areas, as when farm productivity was kept low by the unavailability of credit to buy machinery or construct irrigation systems, and remittances provide the funds to buy the machinery or construct the irrigation facilities that increase output.

Remittances have many other effects in the communities in which they arrive. A very visible effect is to allow the families receiving them to build or improve their homes. Many migrant families often build more housing than they need, introducing rental housing in areas that previously had none, which produces other socioeconomic consequences, as when newlyweds began to live away from in-laws in rural Turkey (Martin, 1991). Women often assume new roles in the absence of migrant husbands, and some became moneylenders in their villages, a remarkable change in often traditional areas. There is a growing literature on the risk and relativity of remittances, as when a farmer is more likely to try new seeds or crops if he is receiving remittances from abroad that cushion the risk of crop failure. Other theories emphasize that if one family uses remittances to buy a television and satellite dish, there is pressure on other families to send out migrants and get remittances to keep up with their neighbors (Taylor and Martin, 2001).

TRADE, INVESTMENT, AND DEVELOPMENT

Goods have labor embodied in them, so trade can be a substitute for migration. This is what has occurred in countries that have gone through the migration transition from labor senders to receivers, such as Italy and South Korea. Between 1950 and 2000, world GDP increased fourfold to $30 trillion, while world trade in goods increased seventeenfold to $13 trillion, meaning that goods worth 40 percent of the value of global output crossed national borders by 2000.[9] Increased trade was stimulated by economic growth and reductions in the average tariff on manufactured goods, which fell from 40 percent in 1950 to 4 percent in 2000. Services, which are normally produced and consumed at the same time, as with medical care and tourism, involved global exports worth $1.4 trillion and imports worth $1.4 trillion. Most trade in goods and services is between high-income countries, more than 80 percent in 2000 (see Table 7.3).

Most global trade involves goods, and trade in goods means that something is produced in one country, taken over borders, and consumed in another. Economic theory suggests that if countries specialize in producing those goods in which they have a comparative advantage, most residents of countries that trade will be better off.[10] Even if the United States can produce both television sets and corn cheaper than Mexico can, but is relatively better at corn production, comparative advantage advises the United States to devote resources to corn production and buy televisions from Mexico so that Americans have cheaper TVs and Mexicans cheaper tortillas. With trade accelerating economic and job growth in both countries, trade can become a substitute for migration, and Mexican-U.S. migration would be expected to fall as trade narrows wage differences.

Table 7.3. Global Trade and Service Flows, 1990 and 2000

Merchandise	2000 (billions of dollars)	Food	Agriculture and Raw Materials	Manufactured Goods	1990	1990–2000 Increase
Exports						
Total trade	6,356	7%	1%	78%	3,433	85%
High income (%)	4,612 (73%)	6%	2%	82%	2,423 (71%)	90%
Low-middle income	1,743	9%	2%	61%	702	148%
Imports						
Total trade	6,565	7%	2%	74%	3,516	87%
High income	4,949	7%	2%	75%	2,846	74%
Low-middle income	1,616	8%	3%	71%	663	144%

Commercial Services	2000 (billions of dollars)	Transport	Travel	1990	1990–2000 Increase
Exports					
Total trade	1,431	23%	32%	750	91%
High income (%)	1,170 (82%)	23%	30%	647 (86%)	81%
Low-middle income	261	23%	43%	103	153%
Imports					
Total trade	1,400	28%	31%	775	81%
High income	1,103	27%	32%	643	72%
Low-middle income	297	33%	28%	131	127%

Notes: Services are produced and consumed at the same time. Transport services are performed by residents of one country for residents of another. Travel services include goods and services consumed by travelers while abroad.

Source: World Bank, World Development Indicators, 2002.

Migration and trade were substitutes across the Atlantic and within Europe in the nineteenth and early twentieth centuries. When European growth rates in the 1950s and 1960s rose above U.S. rates, the gaps in wages and incomes across the Atlantic narrowed, and migration slowed even though the United States reopened opportunities for European immigration. A similar story of narrowing wage and income gaps due to freer trade and aid explains why labor migration from southern European nations such as Italy and Spain practically stopped in the 1970s and 1980s just as Italians and Spaniards got the right to live and work anywhere in the European Union.

The U.S. Commission for the Study of International Migration and Cooperative Economic Development studied the links between trade and migration and concluded that "expanded trade between the sending countries and the United States is the single most important remedy" for unwanted migration (1990, xv). However, the commission emphasized that when countries suddenly embrace freer trade and investment, there can be labor-displacing adjustments in emigration countries that temporarily increase migration. For example, Mexican farmers who were protected from imported corn may quit growing corn as imports rise. Since Mexicans were migrating to the United States from rural areas before there was freer trade in corn, migration may temporarily increase so that "the economic development process itself tends in the short to medium term to stimulate migration," producing a migration hump when flows are charted over time (1990, xvi).

The migration hump can be relatively smaller and shorter lived if foreign direct investment accelerates job creation in emigration countries that globalize, as when foreign investment creates jobs for former corn farmers in TV factories in Mexico. However, in Mexico and many other places where foreign investment created jobs in manufacturing, the jobs were far from the areas in which workers were being displaced. Most of the foreign investment in Mexico, for example, is just across the U.S. border, while most of the displaced farmers are in western and central Mexico, and much of the foreign investment in China is in the southeastern coastal provinces, far from the northern and western provinces where workers are being displaced in part because of freer trade.

FDI rose rapidly in the 1990s, peaking in 1997 at $196 billion, reflecting in part widespread privatization programs that allowed foreign investors to buy previously state-owned operations. The top ten developing-country recipients of FDI between 1992 and 2001 received 70–80 percent of the total: China, Brazil, Mexico, Argentina, Poland, Chile, Malaysia, Thailand, the Czech Republic, and Venezuela, with China alone accounting for almost 40 percent.

The incentive to invest in developing countries is driven by expected profits, not by the need for jobs to reduce emigration, and much FDI goes to low- and middle-income countries that are net immigration areas, including Argentina, Malaysia, Thailand, and the Czech Republic. In the case of Malaysia and Thailand, for example, foreign investors may create jobs that are filled by migrants.

Trade and investment often seem to be the slow road to stay-at-home development, but the world has found no other path that promises sustained economic and job growth. The new globalizers, as the World Bank (2002) termed the Chinese and Indian states that attracted foreign investment to produce manufactured goods for export, have had the fastest rate of poverty reduction, and they often attract internal migrants to the areas that attract investors. At least parts of developing countries with about three billion residents have experienced substantial poverty reduction as a result of more trade and investment, but other parts of developing countries with about two billion residents seem to be falling farther behind, "in danger of becoming marginal to the world economy" except as sources of migrants (World Bank, 2002, x).

AID, FARM SUBSIDIES, AND MIGRATION

Official Development Assistance (ODA) monies are grants and low-interest loans given by one government to assist development in another. In 2000 the OECD nations that are members of the Development Assistance Committee provided $54 billion in ODA, about the same as the $53 billion in 1990, but a smaller percentage of donor GDP. (The net official aid flow data in Table 7.1 reflect the fact that some of ODA must be spent on donor country goods and experts.)[11] Some countries, notably France, call their bilateral aid programs "codevelopment" to stress their cooperation in both economic development and other areas of mutual interest with the countries receiving their aid, including migration. Since 2000, for example, the annual Mali-France Consultation on Migration has dealt with the integration of Malians who want to stay in France; comanagement of migration flows; and cooperative development in emigration areas of Mali to reduce migration pressures.

The stability of ODA contrasts sharply with other global flows. During the 1990s, for example, remittances to developing countries more than doubled, trade increased 1.5 times, and FDI rose almost sixfold. This raises a question: if there must be a choice, which is more important, more aid or reforms in the richer donor countries that would permit developing nations to expand their exports of farm commodities and labor-intensive goods? The World Bank (2002,

131) has concluded that freer trade in farm commodities is the most promising avenue for poverty reduction: "Trade reform in both industrial and developing countries would have a larger impact on improving welfare in developing countries than any of the increases in aid. . . . Industrial countries spend more than $300 billion a year in agricultural subsidies, more than six times the amount they spend on foreign aid." If developing countries had unrestricted access to industrial country markets, their GDPs would rise 5 percent, according to the World Bank, five times more than their current gain from remittances.

In most developing countries, 40–60 percent of the labor force is employed in agriculture, and farm goods are a major share of exports. Most migrant-receiving countries protect their farm sectors, usually by guaranteeing their farmers higher-than-world prices for the commodities they produce. Richer countries often donate or subsidize the sale of the surplus in world markets, depressing world prices for farm commodities and limiting incentives for developing country farmers to stay on the farm.[12] Farm subsidies in rich countries have been rising: between the late 1980s and late 1990s, the producer support equivalent (PSE) level of subsidy for the farm sector in the United States, Japan, and the EU rose from about four times their level of aid to five times.

Freer trade promises reduction of poverty and pressure to emigrate more than an increase of aid, but could more aid alone reduce migration pressures? An ambitious study concluded "not necessarily." After examining the role that aid played in the various countries and regions that sent large numbers of economic migrants and political refugees over borders in the 1970s and 1980s, experts concluded that the most important aid would open up markets to developing-country products, effectively buying off the protests of industries and workers that currently restrict developing countries' exports of garments and farm commodities (Böhning and Schloeter-Paredes, 1993). Experts studying the role of aid in refugee situations have concluded that the superpowers gave aid as they jockeyed for position in ways that often led to longer conflicts and more refugees. There may be ways to reconfigure aid to reduce the number of economic migrants and political refugees, but the record of the 1970s and 1980s is not encouraging.

THE ILO, THE UNITED NATIONS, AND MIGRANTS

Most of the world's workers are in developing countries. The industrial countries, with 12 percent of the world's workers and 60 percent of the world's migrants, face a future in which their labor forces will shrink without immigration. The movement of migrants from south to north seems like a natural fit, but the question is whether south-north migration will speed or slow the convergence of wages that promises to reduce what are now rising migration pressures. And until migration is reduced, how should migrants be protected?

Persons outside their country of citizenship have long been a special concern of the international community, with the ILO taking the lead to protect migrant workers. ILO Convention 97 (1949), ratified by forty-two mostly emigration countries, defines a "migrant for employment" as "a person who migrates from one country to another with a view to being employed otherwise than on his own account." Its bedrock principle is that migrant wage and salary workers should be treated like other workers in the countries in which they work, and Convention 97 is designed to protect migrants and ensure their equal treatment by encouraging countries to sign bilateral agreements governing labor migration.[13] In an ideal world, these bilateral agreements would spell out procedures for private and public recruitment, lead to the exchange of information on migration policies and regulations, and foster cooperation to ensure that employers have accurate information on migrants and migrants have complete information on wages and working conditions abroad.

The ILO's second migrant-specific convention is 143 (1975), ratified by eighteen countries. Enacted after oil-price hikes led to recessions in the European countries that had been importing large numbers of guest workers, it emphasizes steps governments can take to minimize illegal migration and to promote the integration of settled migrants. For example, Convention 143 calls for sanctions on employers who hire unauthorized migrants and encourages international cooperation to reduce the smuggling of migrants, including prosecution of smugglers in both source and destination countries. Convention 143 also calls for "equality of treatment" in wages and other benefits for employed migrants, regardless of legal status.[14]

Both ILO migrant conventions have fewer-than-average ratifications, which is often attributed to provisions that conflict with national legislation.[15] For example, even when member states ratify the ILO migrant conventions, they often make exceptions for occupations dominated by migrants, such as farm workers and maids, that are excluded from national labor laws.[16] However, migrants may still be protected by national laws that conform to other ILO conventions, including Convention 87, Freedom of Association and Protection of the Right to Organize (1948), and Convention 98, the Right to Organize and Collective Bargaining (1949). However, migrants "protected" by national laws that conform to other ILO conventions can still be denied effective remedies if their rights are violated. For example, U.S. labor law gives practically all private-sector workers the right to form or join unions without employer interference, but if an employer unlawfully fires an unauthorized worker in retaliation for union activities, the worker can be denied the normal remedy of reinstatement with back pay.[17]

The ILO could not find consensus among employers, workers, and governments for additional migrant conventions in the 1980s, but on December 18, 1990, the United Nations General Assembly approved the International Convention on the Protection of the Rights of all Migrant Workers and Members of their Families. This eight-part, ninety-three-article U.N. convention, which went into force in July 2003, is designed to "contribute to the harmonization of the attitudes of States through the acceptance of basic principles concerning the treatment of migrant workers and members of their families."[18] The U.N. convention, ratified as of 2005 only by net emigration countries, includes most of the protections of ILO conventions and goes beyond them to cover all migrants, including seafarers and the self-employed. It calls on states to adhere to basic human rights standards in their dealings with authorized and unauthorized migrants, including guaranteeing migrants freedom of religion and freedom from arbitrary arrest or imprisonment.

The major employment-related protections of the U.N. convention are in part III, particularly articles 25–27, which prescribe equality in wages and working conditions for authorized and unauthorized migrant and national workers, assert that migrants should be allowed to join unions, and call for migrant workers to receive benefits under social security systems to which they contribute, or to receive refunds of their social security contributions on departure. Authorized migrants should have additional rights set out in part IV, including the right to information about jobs abroad as well as a list of "equal treatments," including freedom of movement within the host country, freedom to form unions and participate in the political life of the host country, and equal access to employment services, public housing, and educational institutions.[19]

Other international instruments and declarations also call for equal treatment for migrants. The Vienna Declaration and Programme of Action on Human Rights (1993) and the Cairo Programme of Action of the International Conference on Population and Development (1994) affirmed the importance of promoting and protecting the human rights of migrant workers and their families, while the Beijing Platform of Action of the Fourth World Conference on Women (1995) paid special attention to the rights of women migrants and urged that migrants be protected from violence and exploitation. The United Nations Commission on Human Rights in 1999 appointed a special rapporteur to investigate violations of the human rights of migrants, and the World Conference on Racism, Racial Discrimination, Xenophobia, and Related Intolerance in 2001 issued the Durban Declaration and Programme of Action, including a call for countries to allow migrants to unify their families and for active efforts to reduce the discriminatory treatment of migrant workers. The U.N. General Assembly in 2000 adopted the Convention against Transnational Organized Crime, which has two additional protocols: the U.N. Protocol to Prevent, Suppress, and Punish Trafficking in Persons, Especially Women and Children, and the Protocol against the Smuggling of Migrants by Land, Sea, and Air.

The ILO's ninety-second conference in June 2004 concluded that the best policy to protect migrants is a rights-based approach sensitive to labor market needs and the sovereign rights of countries to determine who can enter and stay. The ILO's goal is to encourage lawful migration for employment and to ensure that receiving countries treat migrants like other workers regardless of their legal status. To do this, the ILO is developing a nonbinding multilateral framework that will highlight and recommend best practices and policies; identify the actions needed to gain adherence to international labor standards; provide technical assistance to new countries sending and receiving migrant workers; strengthen social dialogue between employers, unions, and governments; and improve the knowledge base on trends in labor migration and conditions of migrant workers.[20] The ILO's report, "A Fair Deal for Migrant Workers in the Global Economy," emphasized that labor migration is likely to increase for the foreseeable future and that migration can be a plus-plus relationship for sending and receiving countries.[21]

WHITHER LABOR MIGRATION?

Migration is generally a force for individual and global betterment. Individuals moving to take advantage of higher wages and more opportunities generally benefit themselves, their host countries, and sometimes the countries they left, as when their remittances and returns lead to an economic takeoff. However, there is no scientific basis for calculating an optimal rate of migration, which means that there is no agreement on whether the current 3 percent of the world's residents who are migrants is optimal. The migrant shares of the global population and of the workforce have been rising, but there are sharp variations from country to country that reflect history as well as economic, social, and political conditions.

A continuing dialogue that honestly evaluates the trade-offs inherent in migration is the foundation for effective migration management. However, migration dialogues must deal with a fundamental contradiction. Differences prompt migration, but most international and many national standards call for equal treatment of migrants.[22] This complicates the discussion because the number of migrants tends to fall as rights and equal treatment rise. Globally, the fastest growth in migrant employment is outside established channels designed to admit and protect foreign workers—that is, in unauthorized migration—and raises a fundamental challenge for governments and international organizations: should they try to put unauthorized migrants and their jobs into established and legal channels by stepping up enforcement and having legalization programs, or should they accept a layered labor market and society in which rights and conditions for migrants vary with legal status and other factors?

Most worker and migrant advocates believe strongly that there can be only one labor market and one set of rights and privileges, and that all migrants—regardless of legal status—should enjoy fundamental labor and human rights. Many advocates reject a trade-off of numbers and rights; the AFL-CIO in the United States, for example, calls for legalization for unauthorized workers as well as an end to the enforcement of laws sanctioning employers, arguing instead for stepped-up enforcement of labor laws so that migrants receive minimum wages and other workplace protections.

Most economists and employers, on the other hand, acknowledge the relationship between numbers and rights by emphasizing that if wages were truly equal, there would probably be fewer migrant workers because trade, mechanization, and other changes would reduce the demand for them. Freer trade in farm commodities, for example, would probably reduce the demand for migrant farm workers, since lower global prices would force some local farmers who hire migrants to mechanize or change crops.

There is no easy way to balance migrant numbers and rights. However, in thinking about the trade-offs, we must be mindful of the fact that the perfect can be the enemy of the good. The quest for comprehensive international migration conventions, for example, can lead to a panoply of theoretical rights for migrants but a dearth of ratifications and limited government efforts to enforce these rights. Finding the proper balance between numbers and rights is a difficult and complex challenge for migrants, employers, and governments in the twenty-first century.

Appendix: ILO Conventions on Migrants

CONVENTION 97

Migration for Employment (Revised) (1949; into force, 1952)

The General Conference of the International Labour Organisation,

Having been convened at Geneva by the Governing Body of the International Labour Office, and having met in its Thirty-second Session on 8 June 1949, and

Having decided upon the adoption of certain proposals with regard to the revision of the Migration for Employment Convention, 1939, adopted by the Conference at its Twenty-fifth Session, which is included in the eleventh item on the agenda of the session, and

Considering that these proposals must take the form of an international Convention,

adopts the first day of July of the year one thousand nine hundred and forty-nine, the following Convention, which may be cited as the Migration for Employment Convention (Revised), 1949:

Article 1

Each Member of the International Labour Organisation for which this Convention is in force undertakes to make available on request to the International Labour Office and to other Members—

(a) information on national policies, laws and regulations relating to emigration and immigration;
(b) information on special provisions concerning migration for employment and the conditions of work and livelihood of migrants for employment;
(c) information concerning general agreements and special arrangements on these questions concluded by the Member.

Article 2

Each Member for which this Convention is in force undertakes to maintain, or satisfy itself that there is maintained, an adequate and free service to assist migrants for employment, and in particular to provide them with accurate information.

Article 3

1. Each Member for which this Convention is in force undertakes that it will, so far as national laws and regulations permit, take all appropriate steps against misleading propaganda relating to emigration and immigration.
2. For this purpose, it will where appropriate act in co-operation with other Members concerned.

Article 4

Measures shall be taken as appropriate by each Member, within its jurisdiction, to facilitate the departure, journey and reception of migrants for employment.

Article 5

Each Member for which this Convention is in force undertakes to maintain, within its jurisdiction, appropriate medical services responsible for—

(a) ascertaining, where necessary, both at the time of departure and on arrival, that migrants for employment and the members of their families authorised to accompany or join them are in reasonable health;
(b) ensuring that migrants for employment and members of their families enjoy adequate medical attention and good hygienic conditions at the time of departure, during the journey and on arrival in the territory of destination.

Article 6

1. Each Member for which this Convention is in force undertakes to apply, without discrimination in respect of nationality, race, religion or sex, to immigrants lawfully within its territory, treatment no less favourable than that which it applies to its own nationals in respect of the following matters:
   (a) in so far as such matters are regulated by law or regulations, or are subject to the control of administrative authorities—
      (i) remuneration, including family allowances where these form part of remunera-

tion, hours of work, overtime arrangements, holidays with pay, restrictions on home work, minimum age for employment, apprenticeship and training, women's work and the work of young persons;

(ii) membership of trade unions and enjoyment of the benefits of collective bargaining;

(iii) accommodation;

(b) social security (that is to say, legal provision in respect of employment injury, maternity, sickness, invalidity, old age, death, unemployment and family responsibilities, and any other contingency which, according to national laws or regulations, is covered by a social security scheme), subject to the following limitations:

(i) there may be appropriate arrangements for the maintenance of acquired rights and rights in course of acquisition;

(ii) national laws or regulations of immigration countries may prescribe special arrangements concerning benefits or portions of benefits which are payable wholly out of public funds, and concerning allowances paid to persons who do not fulfil the contribution conditions prescribed for the award of a normal pension;

(c) employment taxes, dues or contributions payable in respect of the person employed; and

(d) legal proceedings relating to the matters referred to in this Convention.

2. In the case of a federal State the provisions of this Article shall apply in so far as the matters dealt with are regulated by federal law or regulations or are subject to the control of federal administrative authorities. The extent to which and manner in which these provisions shall be applied in respect of matters regulated by the law or regulations of the constituent States, provinces or cantons, or subject to the control of the administrative authorities thereof, shall be determined by each Member. The Member shall indicate in its annual report upon the application of the Convention the extent to which the matters dealt with in this Article are regulated by federal law or regulations or are subject to the control of federal administrative authorities. In respect of matters which are regulated by the law or regulations of the constituent States, provinces or cantons, or are subject to the control of the administrative authorities thereof, the Member shall take the steps provided for in paragraph 7(b) of Article 19 of the Constitution of the International Labour Organisation.

Article 7

1. Each Member for which this Convention is in force undertakes that its employment service and other services connected with migration will co-operate in appropriate cases with the corresponding services of other Members.
2. Each Member for which this Convention is in force undertakes to ensure that the services rendered by its public employment service to migrants for employment are rendered free.

Article 8

1. A migrant for employment who has been admitted on a permanent basis and the members of his family who have been authorised to accompany or join him shall not be returned to their territory of origin or the territory from which they emigrated because the migrant is

unable to follow his occupation by reason of illness contracted or injury sustained subsequent to entry, unless the person concerned so desires or an international agreement to which the Member is a party so provides.

2. When migrants for employment are admitted on a permanent basis upon arrival in the country of immigration the competent authority of that country may determine that the provisions of paragraph 1 of this Article shall take effect only after a reasonable period which shall in no case exceed five years from the date of admission of such migrants.

Article 9

Each Member for which this Convention is in force undertakes to permit, taking into account the limits allowed by national laws and regulations concerning export and import of currency, the transfer of such part of the earnings and savings of the migrant for employment as the migrant may desire.

Article 10

In cases where the number of migrants going from the territory of one Member to that of another is sufficiently large, the competent authorities of the territories concerned shall, whenever necessary or desirable, enter into agreements for the purpose of regulating matters of common concern arising in connection with the application of the provisions of this Convention.

Article 11

1. For the purpose of this Convention the term migrant for employment means a person who migrates from one country to another with a view to being employed otherwise than on his own account and includes any person regularly admitted as a migrant for employment.
2. This Convention does not apply to—
   (a) frontier workers;
   (b) short-term entry of members of the liberal professions and artistes; and
   (c) seamen.

Article 12

The formal ratifications of this Convention shall be communicated to the Director-General of the International Labour Office for registration.

Article 13

1. This Convention shall be binding only upon those Members of the International Labour Organisation whose ratifications have been registered with the Director-General.
2. It shall come into force twelve months after the date on which the ratifications of two Members have been registered with the Director-General.
3. Thereafter, this Convention shall come into force for any Member twelve months after the date on which its ratifications has been registered.

Article 14

1. Each Member ratifying this Convention may, by a declaration appended to its ratification, exclude from its ratification any or all of the Annexes to the Convention.
2. Subject to the terms of any such declaration, the provisions of the Annexes shall have the same effect as the provisions of the Convention.
3. Any Member which makes such a declaration may subsequently by a new declaration notify the Director-General that it accepts any or all of the Annexes mentioned in the declaration; as from the date of the registration of such notification by the Director-General the provisions of such Annexes shall be applicable to the Member in question.
4. While a declaration made under paragraph 1 of this Article remains in force in respect of any Annex, the Member may declare its willingness to accept that Annex as having the force of a Recommendation.

Article 15

1. Declarations communicated to the Director-General of the International Labour Office in accordance with paragraph 2 of Article 35 of the Constitution of the International Labour Organisation shall indicate—
   (a) the territories in respect of which the Member concerned undertakes that the provisions of the Convention shall be applied without modification;
   (b) the territories in respect of which it undertakes that the provisions of the Convention shall be applied subject to modifications, together with details of the said modifications;
   (c) the territories in respect of which the Convention is inapplicable and in such cases the grounds on which it is inapplicable;
   (d) the territories in respect of which it reserves its decision pending further consideration of the position.
2. The undertakings referred to in subparagraphs (a) and (b) of paragraph 1 of this Article shall be deemed to be an integral part of the ratification and shall have the force of ratification.
3. Any Member may at any time by a subsequent declaration cancel in whole or in part any reservation made in its original declaration in virtue of subparagraph (b), (c) or (d) of paragraph 1 of this Article.
4. Any Member may, at any time at which the Convention is subject to denunciation in accordance with the provisions of Article 17, communicate to the Director-General a declaration modifying in any other respect the terms of any former declaration and stating the present position in respect of such territories as it may specify.

Article 16

1. Declarations communicated to the Director-General of the International Labour Office in accordance with paragraph 4 or 5 of Article 35 of the Constitution of the International Labour Organisation shall indicate whether the provisions of the Convention will be applied in the territory concerned without modification or subject to modifications; when the declaration indicates that the provisions of the Convention will be applied subject to modifications, it shall give details of the said modifications.

2. The Member, Members or international authority concerned may at any time by a subsequent declaration renounce in whole or in part the right to have recourse to any modification indicated in any former declaration.
3. The Member, Members or international authority concerned may, at any time at which the Convention is subject to denunciation in accordance with the provisions of Article 17, communicate to the Director-General a declaration modifying in any other respect the terms of any former declaration and stating the present position in respect of the application of the Convention.

Article 17

1. A Member which has ratified this Convention may denounce it after the expiration of ten years from the date on which the Convention first comes into force, by an Act communicated to the Director-General of the International Labour Office for registration. Such denunciation should not take effect until one year after the date on which it is registered.
2. Each Member which has ratified this Convention and which does not, within the year following the expiration of the period of ten years mentioned in the preceding paragraph, exercise the right of denunciation provided for in this Article, will be bound for another period of ten years and, thereafter, may denounce this Convention at the expiration of each period of ten years under the terms provided for in this Article.
3. At any time at which this Convention is subject to denunciation in accordance with the provisions of the preceding paragraphs any Member which does not so denounce it may communicate to the Director-General a declaration denouncing separately any Annex to the Convention which is in force for that Member.
4. The denunciation of this Convention or of any or all of the Annexes shall not affect the rights granted thereunder to a migrant or to the members of his family if he immigrated while the Convention or the relevant Annex was in force in respect of the territory where the question of the continued validity of these rights arises.

Article 18

1. The Director-General of the International Labour Office shall notify all Members of the International Labour Organisation of the registration of all ratifications and denunciations communicated to him by the Members of the Organisation.
2. When notifying the Members of the Organisation of the registration of the second ratification communicated to him, the Director-General shall draw the attention of the Members of the Organisation to the date upon which the Convention will come into force.

Article 19

The Director-General of the International Labour Office shall communicate to the Secretary-General of the United Nations for registration in accordance with Article 102 of the Charter of the United Nations full particulars of all ratifications and acts of denunciation registered by him in accordance with the provisions of the preceding Articles.

Article 20

At the expiration of each period of ten years after the coming into force of this Convention, the Governing Body of the International Labour Office shall present to the General Conference a report on the working of this Convention and shall examine the desirability of placing on the agenda of the Conference the question of its revision in whole or in part.

Article 21

1. Should the Conference adopt a new Convention revising this Convention in whole or in part, then, unless the new Convention otherwise provides:
   (a) the ratification by a Member of the new revising Convention shall ipso jure involve the immediate denunciation of this Convention, notwithstanding the provisions of Article 17 above, if and when the new revising Convention shall have come into force;
   (b) as from the date when the new revising Convention comes into force this Convention shall cease to be open to ratification by the Members.
2. This Convention shall in any case remain in force in its actual form and content for those Members which have ratified it but have not ratified the revising Convention.

Article 22

1. The International Labour Conference may, at any session at which the matter is included in its agenda, adopt by a two-thirds majority a revised text of any one or more of the Annexes to this Convention.
2. Each Member for which this Convention is in force shall, within the period of one year, or, in exceptional circumstances, of eighteen months, from the closing of the session of the Conference, submit any such revised text to the authority or authorities within whose competence the matter lies, for the enactment of legislation or other action.
3. Any such revised text shall become effective for each Member for which this Convention is in force on communication by that Member to the Director-General of the International Labour Office of a declaration notifying its acceptance of the revised text.
4. As from the date of the adoption of the revised text of the Annex by the Conference, only the revised text shall be open to acceptance by Members.

Article 23

The English and French versions of the text of this Convention are equally authoritative.

Annex I

Recruitment, placing and conditions of labour of migrants for employment recruited otherwise than under government-sponsored arrangements for group transfer.

Article 1

This Annex applies to migrants for employment who are recruited otherwise than under Government-sponsored arrangements for group transfer.

Article 2

For the purpose of this Annex:

(a) the term recruitment means:

(i) the engagement of a person in one territory on behalf of an employer in another territory, or

(ii) the giving of an undertaking to a person in one territory to provide him with employment in another territory, together with the making of any arrangements in connection with the operations mentioned in (i) and (ii) including the seeking for and selection of emigrants and the preparation for departure of the emigrants;

(b) the term introduction means any operations for ensuring or facilitating the arrival in or admission to a territory of persons who have been recruited within the meaning of paragraph (a) of this Article; and

(c) the term placing means any operations for the purpose of ensuring or facilitating the employment of persons who have been introduced within the meaning of paragraph (b) of this Article.

Article 3

1. Each Member for which this Annex is in force, the laws and regulations of which permit the operations of recruitment, introduction and placing as defined in Article 2, shall regulate such of the said operations as are permitted by its laws and regulations in accordance with the provisions of this Article.
2. Subject to the provisions of the following paragraph, the right to engage in the operations of recruitment, introduction and placing shall be restricted to:
   (a) public employment offices or other public bodies of the territory in which the operations take place;
   (b) public bodies of a territory other than that in which the operations take place which are authorised to operate in that territory by agreement between the Governments concerned;
   (c) any body established in accordance with the terms of an international instrument.
3. In so far as national laws and regulations or a bilateral arrangement permit, the operations of recruitment, introduction and placing may be undertaken by:
   (a) the prospective employer or a person in his service acting on his behalf, subject, if necessary in the interest of the migrant, to the approval and supervision of the competent authority;
   (b) a private agency, if given prior authorisation so to do by the competent authority of the territory where the said operations are to take place, in such cases and under such conditions as may be prescribed by:
      (i) the laws and regulations of that territory, or
      (ii) agreement between the competent authority of the territory of emigration or any body established in accordance with the terms of an international instrument and the competent authority of the territory of immigration.
4. The competent authority of the territory where the operations take place shall supervise the activities of bodies and persons to whom authorisations have been issued in pursuance

of paragraph 3 (b), other than any body established in accordance with the terms of an international instrument, the position of which shall continue to be governed by the terms of the said instrument or by any agreement made between the body and the competent authority concerned.

5. Nothing in this Article shall be deemed to permit the acceptance of a migrant for employment for admission to the territory of any Member by any person or body other than the competent authority of the territory of immigration.

Article 4

Each Member for which this Annex is in force undertakes to ensure that the services rendered by its public employment service in connection with the recruitment, introduction or placing of migrants for employment are rendered free.

Article 5

1. Each Member for which this Annex is in force which maintains a system of supervision of contracts of employment between an employer, or a person acting on his behalf, and a migrant for employment undertakes to require:
   (a) that a copy of the contract of employment shall be delivered to the migrant before departure or, if the Governments concerned so agree, in a reception centre on arrival in the territory of immigration;
   (b) that the contract shall contain provisions indicating the conditions of work and particularly the remuneration offered to the migrant;
   (c) that the migrant shall receive in writing before departure, by a document which relates either to him individually or to a group of migrants of which he is a member, information concerning the general conditions of life and work applicable to him in the territory of immigration.
2. Where a copy of the contract is to be delivered to the migrant on arrival in the territory of immigration, he shall be informed in writing before departure, by a document which relates either to him individually or to a group of migrants of which he is a member, of the occupational category for which he is engaged and the other conditions of work, in particular the minimum wage which is guaranteed to him.
3. The competent authority shall ensure that the provisions of the preceding paragraphs are enforced and that appropriate penalties are applied in respect of violations thereof.

Article 6

The measures taken under Article 4 of the Convention shall, as appropriate, include:
(a) the simplification of administrative formalities;
(b) the provision of interpretation services;
(c) any necessary assistance during an initial period in the settlement of the migrants and members of their families authorised to accompany or join them; and
(d) the safeguarding of the welfare, during the journey and in particular on board ship, of migrants and members of their families authorised to accompany or join them.

Article 7

1. In cases where the number of migrants for employment going from the territory of one Member to that of another is sufficiently large, the competent authorities of the territories concerned shall, whenever necessary or desirable, enter into agreements for the purpose of regulating matters of common concern arising in connection with the application of the provisions of this Annex.
2. Where the members maintain a system of supervision over contracts of employment, such agreements shall indicate the methods by which the contractual obligations of the employers shall be enforced.

Article 8

Any person who promotes clandestine or illegal immigration shall be subject to appropriate penalties.

Annex II

Recruitment, placing and conditions of labour of migrants for employment recruited under government-sponsored arrangements for group transfer

Article 1

This Annex applies to migrants for employment who are recruited under Government-sponsored arrangements for group transfer.

Article 2

For the purpose of this Annex:

(a) the term recruitment means:
   (i) the engagement of a person in one territory on behalf of an employer in another territory under a Government-sponsored arrangement for group transfer, or
   (ii) the giving of an undertaking to a person in one territory to provide him with employment in another territory under a Government-sponsored arrangement for group transfer, together with the making of any arrangements in connection with the operations mentioned in (i) and (ii) including the seeking for and selection of emigrants and the preparation for departure of the emigrants;

(b) the term introduction means any operations for ensuring or facilitating the arrival in or admission to a territory of persons who have been recruited under a Government-sponsored arrangement for group transfer within the meaning of subparagraph (a) of this paragraph; and

(c) the term placing means any operations for the purpose of ensuring or facilitating the employment of persons who have been introduced under a Government-sponsored arrangement for group transfer within the meaning of subparagraph (b) of this paragraph.

Article 3

1. Each Member for which this Annex is in force, the laws and regulations of which permit the operations of recruitment, introduction and placing as defined in Article 2, shall regulate such of the said operations as are permitted by its laws and regulations in accordance with the provisions of this Article.
2. Subject to the provisions of the following paragraph, the right to engage in the operations of recruitment, introduction and placing shall be restricted to:
   (a) public employment offices or other public bodies of the territory in which the operations take place;
   (b) public bodies of a territory other than that in which the operations take place which are authorised to operate in that territory by agreement between the Governments concerned;
   (c) any body established in accordance with the terms of an international instrument.
3. In so far as national laws and regulations or a bilateral arrangement permit, and subject, if necessary in the interest of the migrant, to the approval and supervision of the competent authority, the operations of recruitment, introduction and placing may be undertaken by:
   (a) the prospective employer or a person in his service acting on his behalf;
   (b) private agencies.
4. The right to engage in the operations of recruitment, introduction and placing shall be subject to the prior authorisation of the competent authority of the territory where the said operations are to take place in such cases and under such conditions as may be prescribed by:
   (a) the laws and regulations of that territory, or
   (b) agreement between the competent authority of the territory of emigration or any body established in accordance with the terms of an international instrument and the competent authority of the territory of immigration.
5. The competent authority of the territory where the operations take place shall, in accordance with any agreements made between the competent authorities concerned, supervise the activities of bodies and persons to whom authorisations have been issued in pursuance of the preceding paragraph, other than any body established in accordance with the terms of an international instrument, the position of which shall continue to be governed by the terms of the said instrument or by any agreement made between the body and the competent authority concerned.
6. Before authorising the introduction of migrants for employment the competent authority of the territory of immigration shall ascertain whether there is not a sufficient number of persons already available capable of doing the work in question.
7. Nothing in this Article shall be deemed to permit the acceptance of a migrant for employment for admission to the territory of any Member by any person or body other than the competent authority of the territory of immigration.

Article 4

1. Each Member for which this Annex is in force undertakes to ensure that the services rendered by its public employment service in connection with the recruitment, introduction or placing of migrants for employment are rendered free.

2. The administrative costs of recruitment, introduction and placing shall not be borne by the migrants.

Article 5

In the case of collective transport of migrants from one country to another necessitating passage in transit through a third country, the competent authority of the territory of transit shall take measures for expediting the passage, to avoid delays and administrative difficulties.

Article 6

1. Each Member for which this Annex is in force which maintains a system of supervision of contracts of employment between an employer, or a person acting on his behalf, and a migrant for employment undertakes to require:
   (a) that a copy of the contract of employment shall be delivered to the migrant before departure or, if the Governments concerned so agree, in a reception centre on arrival in the territory of immigration;
   (b) that the contract shall contain provisions indicating the conditions of work and particularly the remuneration offered to the migrant;
   (c) that the migrant shall receive in writing before departure, by a document which relates either to him individually or to a group of migrants of which he is a member, information concerning the general conditions of life and work applicable to him in the territory of immigration.
2. Where a copy of the contract is to be delivered to the migrant on arrival in the territory of immigration, he shall be informed in writing before departure, by a document which relates either to him individually or to a group of migrants of which he is a member, of the occupational category for which he is engaged and the other conditions of work, in particular the minimum wage which is guaranteed to him.
3. The competent authority shall ensure that the provisions of the preceding paragraphs are enforced and that appropriate penalties are applied in respect of violations thereof.

Article 7

The measures taken under Article 4 of this Convention shall, as appropriate, include:
(a) the simplification of administrative formalities;
(b) the provision of interpretation services;
(c) any necessary assistance, during an initial period in the settlement of the migrants and members of their families authorised to accompany or join them;
(d) the safeguarding of the welfare, during the journey and in particular on board ship, of migrants and members of their families authorised to accompany or join them; and
(e) permission for the liquidation and transfer of the property of migrants for employment admitted on a permanent basis.

Article 8

Appropriate measures shall be taken by the competent authority to assist migrants for employment, during an initial period, in regard to matters concerning their conditions of employment; where appropriate, such measures may be taken in co-operation with approved voluntary organisations.

Article 9

If a migrant for employment introduced into the territory of a Member in accordance with the provisions of Article 3 of this Annex fails, for a reason for which he is not responsible, to secure the employment for which he has been recruited or other suitable employment, the cost of his return and that of the members of his family who have been authorised to accompany or join him, including administrative fees, transport and maintenance charges to the final destination, and charges for the transport of household belongings, shall not fall upon the migrant.

Article 10

If the competent authority of the territory of immigration considers that the employment for which a migrant for employment was recruited under Article 3 of this Annex has been found to be unsuitable, it shall take appropriate measures to assist him in finding suitable employment which does not prejudice national workers and shall take such steps as will ensure his maintenance pending placing in such employment, or his return to the area of recruitment if the migrant is willing or agreed to such return at the time of his recruitment, or his resettlement elsewhere.

Article 11

If a migrant for employment who is a refugee or a displaced person and who has entered a territory of immigration in accordance with Article 3 of this Annex becomes redundant in any employment in that territory, the competent authority of that territory shall use its best endeavours to enable him to obtain suitable employment which does not prejudice national workers, and shall take such steps as will ensure his maintenance pending placing in suitable employment or his resettlement elsewhere.

Article 12

1. The competent authorities of the territories concerned shall enter into agreements for the purpose of regulating matters of common concern arising in connection with the application of the provisions of this Annex.
2. Where the Members maintain a system of supervision over contracts of employment, such agreements shall indicate the methods by which the contractual obligations of the employer shall be enforced.
3. Such agreements shall provide, where appropriate, for co-operation between the competent authority of the territory of emigration or a body established in accordance with the terms of an international instrument and the competent authority of the territory of immigration, in respect of the assistance to be given to migrants concerning their conditions of employment in virtue of the provisions of Article 8.

Article 13

Any person who promotes clandestine or illegal immigration shall be subject to appropriate penalties.

Annex III

Importation of the personal effects, tools and equipment of migrants for employment

Article 1

1. Personal effects belonging to recruited migrants for employment and members of their families who have been authorised to accompany or join them shall be exempt from customs duties on arrival in the territory of immigration.
2. Portable hand-tools and portable equipment of the kind normally owned by workers for the carrying out of their particular trades belonging to recruited migrants for employment and members of their families who have been authorised to accompany or join them shall be exempt from customs duties on arrival in the territory of immigration if such tools and equipment can be shown at the time of importation to be in their actual ownership or possession, to have been in their possession and use for an appreciable time, and to be intended to be used by them in the course of their occupation.

Article 2

1. Personal effects belonging to migrants for employment and members of their families who have been authorised to accompany or join them shall be exempt from customs duties on the return of the said persons to their country of origin if such persons have retained the nationality of that country at the time of their return there.
2. Portable hand-tools and portable equipment of the kind normally owned by workers for the carrying out of their particular trades belonging to migrants for employment and members of their families who have been authorised to accompany or join them shall be exempt from customs duties on return of the said persons to their country of origin if such persons have retained the nationality of that country at the time of their return there and if such tools and equipment can be shown at the time of importation to be in their actual ownership or possession, to have been in their possession and use for an appreciable time, and to be intended to be used by them in the course of their occupation.

CONVENTION 143

Migrations in Abusive Conditions and the Promotion of Equality of Opportunity and Treatment of Migrant Workers (1975; in force, 1978)

The General Conference of the International Labour Organisation,

Having been convened at Geneva by the Governing Body of the International Labour Office, and having met in its Sixtieth Session on 4 June 1975, and

Considering that the Preamble of the Constitution of the International Labour Organisation assigns to it the task of protecting the interests of workers when employed in countries other than their own, and

Considering that the Declaration of Philadelphia reaffirms, among the principles on which the Organisation is based, that labour is not a commodity, and that poverty anywhere constitutes a danger to prosperity everywhere, and recognises the solemn obligation of the ILO to further programmes which will achieve in particular full employment through the transfer of labour, including for employment, . . .

Considering the ILO World Employment Programme and the Employment Policy Convention and Recommendation, 1964, and emphasising the need to avoid the excessive and uncontrolled or unassisted increase of migratory movements because of their negative social and human consequences, and

Considering that in order to overcome underdevelopment and structural and chronic unemployment, the governments of many countries increasingly stress the desirability of encouraging the transfer of capital and technology rather than the transfer of workers in accordance with the needs and requests of these countries in the reciprocal interest of the countries of origin and the countries of employment, and

Considering the right of everyone to leave any country, including his own, and to enter his own country, as set forth in the Universal Declaration of Human Rights and the International Covenant on Civil and Political Rights, and

Recalling the provisions contained in the Migration for Employment Convention and Recommendation (Revised), 1949, in the Protection of Migrant Workers (Underdeveloped Countries) Recommendation, 1955, in the Employment Policy Convention and Recommendation, 1964, in the Employment Service Convention and Recommendation, 1948, and in the Fee-Charging Employment Agencies Convention (Revised), 1949, which deal with such matters as the regulation of the recruitment, introduction and placing of migrant workers, the provision of accurate information relating to migration, the minimum conditions to be enjoyed by migrants in transit and on arrival, the adoption of an active employment policy and international collaboration in these matters, and

Considering that the migration of workers due to conditions in labour markets should take place under the responsibility of official agencies for employment or in accordance with the relevant bilateral or multilateral agreements, in particular those permitting free circulation of workers, and

Considering that evidence of the existence of illicit and clandestine trafficking in labour calls for further standards specifically aimed at eliminating these abuses, and

Recalling the provisions of the Migration for Employment Convention (Revised), 1949, which require ratifying Members to apply to immigrants lawfully within their territory treatment not less favourable than that which they apply to their nationals in respect of a variety of matters which it enumerates, in so far as these are regulated by laws or regulations or subject to the control of administrative authorities, and

Recalling that the definition of the term "discrimination" in the Discrimination (Employment and Occupation) Convention, 1958, does not mandatorily include distinctions on the basis of nationality, and

Considering that further standards, covering also social security, are desirable in order to promote equality of opportunity and treatment of migrant workers and, with regard to matters regulated by laws or regulations or subject to the control of administrative authorities, ensure treatment at least equal to that of nationals, and

Noting that, for the full success of action regarding the very varied problems of migrant workers, it is essential that there be close co-operation with the United Nations and other specialised agencies, and

Noting that, in the framing of the following standards, account has been taken of the work of the United Nations and of other specialised agencies and that, with a view to avoiding duplication and to ensuring appropriate co-ordination, there will be continuing co-operation in promoting and securing the application of the standards, and

Having decided upon the adoption of certain proposals with regard to migrant workers, which is the fifth item on the agenda of the session, and

Having determined that these proposals shall take the form of an international Convention supplementing the Migration for Employment Convention (Revised), 1949, and the Discrimination (Employment and Occupation) Convention, 1958,

adopts the twenty-fourth day of June of the year one thousand nine hundred and seventy-five, the following Convention, which may be cited as the Migrant Workers (Supplementary Provisions) Convention, 1975:

Part I. Migrations in Abusive Conditions

Article 1

Each Member for which this Convention is in force undertakes to respect the basic human rights of all migrant workers.

Article 2

1. Each Member for which this Convention is in force shall systematically seek to determine whether there are illegally employed migrant workers on its territory and whether there depart from, pass through or arrive in its territory any movements of migrants for employment in which the migrants are subjected during their journey, on arrival or during their period of residence and employment to conditions contravening relevant international multilateral or bilateral instruments or agreements, or national laws or regulations.
2. The representative organisations of employers and workers shall be fully consulted and enabled to furnish any information in their possession on this subject.

Article 3

Each Member shall adopt all necessary and appropriate measures, both within its jurisdiction and in collaboration with other Members—

(a) to suppress clandestine movements of migrants for employment and illegal employment of migrants, and

(b) against the organisers of illicit or clandestine movements of migrants for employment departing from, passing through or arriving in its territory, and against those who employ workers who have immigrated in illegal conditions, in order to prevent and to eliminate the abuses referred to in Article 2 of this Convention.

Article 4

In particular, Members shall take such measures as are necessary, at the national and the international level, for systematic contact and exchange of information on the subject with other States, in consultation with representative organisations of employers and workers.

Article 5

One of the purposes of the measures taken under Articles 3 and 4 of this Convention shall be that the authors of manpower trafficking can be prosecuted whatever the country from which they exercise their activities.

Article 6

1. Provision shall be made under national laws or regulations for the effective detection of the illegal employment of migrant workers and for the definition and the application of administrative, civil and penal sanctions, which include imprisonment in their range, in respect of the illegal employment of migrant workers, in respect of the organisation of movements of migrants for employment defined as involving the abuses referred to in Article 2 of this Convention, and in respect of knowing assistance to such movements, whether for profit or otherwise.
2. Where an employer is prosecuted by virtue of the provision made in pursuance of this Article, he shall have the right to furnish proof of his good faith.

Article 7

The representative organisations of employers and workers shall be consulted in regard to the laws and regulations and other measures provided for in this Convention and designed to prevent and eliminate the abuses referred to above, and the possibility of their taking initiatives for this purpose shall be recognised.

Article 8

1. On condition that he has resided legally in the territory for the purpose of employment, the migrant worker shall not be regarded as in an illegal or irregular situation by the mere fact of the loss of his employment, which shall not in itself imply the withdrawal of his authorisation of residence or, as the case may be, work permit.
2. Accordingly, he shall enjoy equality of treatment with nationals in respect in particular of guarantees of security of employment, the provision of alternative employment, relief work and retraining.

Article 9

1. Without prejudice to measures designed to control movements of migrants for employment by ensuring that migrant workers enter national territory and are admitted to employment in conformity with the relevant laws and regulations, the migrant worker shall, in cases in which these laws and regulations have not been respected and in which his po-

sition cannot be regularised, enjoy equality of treatment for himself and his family in respect of rights arising out of past employment as regards remuneration, social security and other benefits.

2. In case of dispute about the rights referred to in the preceding paragraph, the worker shall have the possibility of presenting his case to a competent body, either himself or through a representative.
3. In case of expulsion of the worker or his family, the cost shall not be borne by them.
4. Nothing in this Convention shall prevent Members from giving persons who are illegally residing or working within the country the right to stay and to take up legal employment.

Part II. Equality of Opportunity and Treatment

Article 10

Each Member for which the Convention is in force undertakes to declare and pursue a national policy designed to promote and to guarantee, by methods appropriate to national conditions and practice, equality of opportunity and treatment in respect of employment and occupation, of social security, of trade union and cultural rights and of individual and collective freedoms for persons who as migrant workers or as members of their families are lawfully within its territory.

Article 11

1. For the purpose of this Part of this Convention, the term migrant worker means a person who migrates or who has migrated from one country to another with a view to being employed otherwise than on his own account and includes any person regularly admitted as a migrant worker.
2. This Part of this Convention does not apply to—
   (a) frontier workers;
   (b) artistes and members of the liberal professions who have entered the country on a short-term basis;
   (c) seamen;
   (d) persons coming specifically for purposes of training or education;
   (e) employees of organisations or undertakings operating within the territory of a country who have been admitted temporarily to that country at the request of their employer to undertake specific duties or assignments, for a limited and defined period of time, and who are required to leave that country on the completion of their duties or assignments.

Article 12

Each Member shall, by methods appropriate to national conditions and practice—

(a) seek the co-operation of employers' and workers' organisations and other appropriate bodies in promoting the acceptance and observance of the policy provided for in Article 10 of this Convention;

(b) enact such legislation and promote such educational programmes as may be calculated to secure the acceptance and observance of the policy;
(c) take measures, encourage educational programmes and develop other activities aimed at acquainting migrant workers as fully as possible with the policy, with their rights and obligations and with activities designed to give effective assistance to migrant workers in the exercise of their rights and for their protection;
(d) repeal any statutory provisions and modify any administrative instructions or practices which are inconsistent with the policy;
(e) in consultation with representative organisations of employers and workers, formulate and apply a social policy appropriate to national conditions and practice which enables migrant workers and their families to share in advantages enjoyed by its nationals while taking account, without adversely affecting the principle of equality of opportunity and treatment, of such special needs as they may have until they are adapted to the society of the country of employment;
(f) take all steps to assist and encourage the efforts of migrant workers and their families to preserve their national and ethnic identity and their cultural ties with their country of origin, including the possibility for children to be given some knowledge of their mother tongue;
(g) guarantee equality of treatment, with regard to working conditions, for all migrant workers who perform the same activity whatever might be the particular conditions of their employment.

Article 13

1. A Member may take all necessary measures which fall within its competence and collaborate with other Members to facilitate the reunification of the families of all migrant workers legally residing in its territory.
2. The members of the family of the migrant worker to which this Article applies are the spouse and dependent children, father and mother.

Article 14

A Member may—
(a) make the free choice of employment, while assuring migrant workers the right to geographical mobility, subject to the conditions that the migrant worker has resided lawfully in its territory for the purpose of employment for a prescribed period not exceeding two years or, if its laws or regulations provide for contracts for a fixed term of less than two years, that the worker has completed his first work contract;
(b) after appropriate consultation with the representative organisations of employers and workers, make regulations concerning recognition of occupational qualifications acquired outside its territory, including certificates and diplomas;
(c) restrict access to limited categories of employment or functions where this is necessary in the interests of the State.

Part III Final Provisions

Article 15

This Convention does not prevent Members from concluding multilateral or bilateral agreements with a view to resolving problems arising from its application.

Article 16

1. Any Member which ratifies this Convention may, by a declaration appended to its ratification, exclude either Part I or Part II from its acceptance of the Convention.
2. Any Member which has made such a declaration may at any time cancel that declaration by a subsequent declaration.
3. Every Member for which a declaration made under paragraph 1 of this Article is in force shall indicate in its reports upon the application of this Convention the position of its law and practice in regard to the provisions of the Part excluded from its acceptance, the extent to which effect has been given, or is proposed to be given, to the said provision and the reasons for which it has not yet included them in its acceptance of the Convention.

Article 17

The formal ratifications of this Convention shall be communicated to the Director-General of the International Labour Office for registration.

Article 18

1. This Convention shall be binding only upon those Members of the International Labour Organisation whose ratifications have been registered with the Director-General.
2. It shall come into force twelve months after the date on which the ratifications of two Members have been registered with the Director-General.
3. Thereafter, this Convention shall come into force for any Member twelve months after the date on which its ratification has been registered.

Article 19

1. A Member which has ratified this Convention may denounce it after the expiration of ten years from the date on which the Convention first comes into force, by an Act communicated to the Director-General of the International Labour Office for registration. Such denunciation should not take effect until one year after the date on which it is registered.
2. Each Member which has ratified this Convention and which does not, within the year following the expiration of the period of ten years mentioned in the preceding paragraph, exercise the right of denunciation provided for in this Article, will be bound for another period of ten years and, thereafter, may denounce this Convention at the expiration of each period of ten years under the terms provided for in this Article.

Article 20

1. The Director-General of the International Labour Office shall notify all Members of the International Labour Organisation of the registration of all ratifications and denunciations communicated to him by the Members of the Organisation.
2. When notifying the Members of the Organisation of the registration of the second ratification communicated to him, the Director-General shall draw the attention of the Members of the Organisation to the date upon which the Convention will come into force.

Article 21

The Director-General of the International Labour Office shall communicate to the Secretary-General of the United Nations for registration in accordance with Article 102 of the Charter of the United Nations full particulars of all ratifications and acts of denunciation registered by him in accordance with the provisions of the preceding Articles.

Article 22

At such times as may consider necessary the Governing Body of the International Labour Office shall present to the General Conference a report on the working of this Convention and shall examine the desirability of placing on the agenda of the Conference the question of its revision in whole or in part.

Article 23

1. Should the Conference adopt a new Convention revising this Convention in whole or in part, then, unless the new Convention otherwise provides:
   (a) the ratification by a Member of the new revising Convention shall ipso jure involve the immediate denunciation of this Convention, notwithstanding the provisions of Article 19 above, if and when the new revising Convention shall have come into force;
   (b) as from the date when the new revising Convention comes into force this Convention shall cease to be open to ratification by the Members.
2. This Convention shall in any case remain in force in its actual form and content for those Members which have ratified it but have not ratified the revising Convention.

Article 24

The English and French versions of the text of this Convention are equally authoritative.

Notes

1. WHY INTERNATIONAL MIGRATION?

1. The U.N. migrant estimate for 1990 was raised from 120 million to 154 million in 2002, largely to reflect the break-up of the Soviet Union, which increased the number of migrants as people crossed borders (for example, Russians returning to Russia), and added to the stock of migrants even with no movement (Russians who became foreigners in the newly independent Baltic states). Some sources put the number of international migrants at 145 million and add 30 million for the Soviet Union.
2. Convention 97 excludes border-crossing commuters (frontier workers), seamen (covered by other ILO conventions), and artists and similar professionals abroad for a short time.
3. Both historically and today middleman recruiters and transporters have been involved in the migration process. Today these understudied middlemen—the merchants of labor who act as arbitrageurs of differences between international labor markets—play a growing role in facilitating legal and unauthorized labor migration, extracting a fee from migrant workers or their employers equivalent to 25 to 100 percent of what the migrants will earn in their first year abroad. See Martin, 2005.
4. The 1951 Geneva Convention obliges nations not to "refoul" or return persons who fear persecution in their countries of origin based on race, religion, nationality, membership in a particular social group, or political opinion (www.unhcr.org).

5. The average woman in developing countries (excluding China) has 3.5 children, compared with 1.5 children per woman in developed countries. According to the Population Reference Bureau (www.prb.org), the world's fastest-growing population is in Gaza, where the population growth rate is 4.5 percent a year, and the fastest-shrinking population is in Russia, where the population is declining by 0.5 percent a year.
6. For example, Portugal and South Korea moved from middle- to high-income status between 1985 and 1995, while Zimbabwe and Mauritania moved from middle- to low-income status.
7. Taxes are extracted from agriculture via monopoly input suppliers, who sell seeds or fertilizers at high prices, or via monopoly purchasers of farm commodities, who buy from farmers at less-than-world prices and pocket the difference when the coffee or cocoa is exported. In high-income countries, farmers' incomes are generally higher than those of nonfarmers, in part because high-income countries transfer funds to producers of food and fiber.
8. The CIA factbook lists 191 "independent states," plus 1 "other" (Taiwan), and 6 miscellaneous entities, including the Gaza Strip, the West Bank, and Western Sahara (www.cia.gov/cia/publications/factbook/index.html).
9. Even if migrants know that movies and television portray exaggerated lifestyles, some who had found themselves in slavelike conditions abroad have said that they did not believe that conditions in rich countries could be "that bad."

2. GLOBAL MIGRATION PATTERNS AND ISSUES

1. Bade (2000, 142) concludes that the most likely number of emigrants was sixty million to sixty-five million, of whom ten million to fifteen million returned to Europe.
2. Germany changed its citizenship law in 2000 to give children born to foreign parents legally residing in the country automatic German citizenship.
3. The models assumed that Polish and other nationals of new EU states could seek jobs anywhere in the enlarged EU. Of those moving from eastern to western Europe, 80 percent were projected to move to Austria and Germany. Tito Boeri and Herbert Brucker, "The Impact of Eastern Enlargement on Employment and Labour Markets in the Member States," *Financial Times,* June 27, 2000, P15.
4. However, fewer than fifteen thousand green cards were issued, suggesting that the shortage figure of seventy-five thousand may have been exaggerated. Philip L. Martin and Heinz Werner, Anwerbung von IT-Spezialisten: Der amerikanische Weg -ein Modell für Deutschland? *Kurzbericht,* no. 5 (2000), http://www.iab.de/iab/publikationen/kb2000.htm/
5. At the end of 2000, 22 percent of the 2.7 million welfare recipients in Germany were foreigners; foreigners were 8.9 percent of residents.
6. The Dublin Convention entered into force on September 1, 1997 (www.europaworld.org/DEVPOLAWAR/Eng/Refugees/Refugees_DocC_eng.htm).
7. Many asylum applicants destroy their documents and say they are from a country to which it is difficult to return rejected asylum seekers, as when governments refuse to is-

sue passports and identity documents to foreigners until French or German authorities prove that a person is from Ghana or Sri Lanka.

8. A constitution is adopted by states, while a treaty is an agreement between states.
9. France, Netherlands, Belgium, *Migration News* 9, no. 12 (December 2002), http://migration.ucdavis.edu/
10. Quoted in EU: Asylum, Immigration, Guest Workers, *Migration News* 10, no. 4 (October 2003), http://migration.ucdavis.edu/
11. Le Pen received 18 percent of the vote in French presidential elections in May 2002, comparable to the 19 percent of the vote won by Ross Perot in the United States in 1992. Pim Fortuyn, a former sociology professor, was killed a week before the May 15, 2002, elections, but his List Pim Fortuyn received 18 percent of the vote and 24 seats in the 150-seat Parliament, making it the second-largest party in Parliament.
12. The economic stream included 118,000 skilled workers (including families), 6,200 entrepreneurs, and 2,500 self-employed (http://www.cic.gc.ca/english/).
13. In 1998 an independent commission urged a series of changes to Canadian immigration policy, including requiring immigrants admitted under the point system to speak English or French before their arrival, and requiring that immigrants who were arriving to join settled family members speak English or French or pay fees to learn English or French after arrival. Measures were aimed at facilitating the entry of immigrants into the Canadian labor market.
14. The exceptions are Native Americans, slaves, and those who became U.S. citizens by purchase or conquest, such as French nationals who became Americans with the Louisiana Purchase, Mexicans who became Americans with the settlement ending the Mexican War, and Puerto Ricans who became U.S. citizens as a result of the American victory over Spain in 1898.
15. In November 2004 Arizona voters approved a similar Proposition 200. See Prop. 187 Approved in California, *Migration News* 1, no. 12 (December 1994), http://migration.ucdavis.edu/ and Bush, Congress, States, *Migration News* 12, no. 1 (January 2005), http://migration.ucdavis.edu/
16. Quoted in Fox Visits Bush, *Migration News* 8, no. 10 (October 2001), http://migration.ucdavis.edu/ Bush was encouraged to propose policies to turn unauthorized workers into legal guest workers by such groups as the Essential Worker Coalition.
17. Diversity immigrants are persons who applied for a U.S. immigrant visa in a lottery open to those from countries that sent fewer than fifty thousand immigrants to the United States in the previous five years.
18. Almost 100,000 of the foreign students were enrolled in two-year community colleges.
19. The sharpest year-to-year drop was in Thai students, which is explained in part by a reduction in government scholarships available to Thais who want to study abroad.
20. Huffman Aviation in Venice, Florida, was notified in March 2002 that two of the hijackers who crashed planes into the World Trade Center had been approved for student visas. The two hijackers were already in the United States when Huffman submitted I-20 forms to change their status to student in August 2001. President Bush was reportedly furious, saying that immigration control "needs to be modernized so we know who's com-

ing and who's going out and why they're here." INS: Reorganize, Police, Sanctions, *Migration News* 9, no. 4 (April 2002), http://migration.ucdavis.edu/

21. Apprehensions record the event of capturing an unauthorized alien and are not a count of individuals; one alien apprehended five times is recorded as five apprehensions.
22. This gap, with elites more open to immigration than the public at large, appeared in earlier polls as well. Chicago Council on Foreign Relations, *Worldviews 2002: American Public Opinion and Foreign Policy,* accessed online at www.worldviews.org/detailreports/usreport/html/ch5s5.html, on March 26, 2003.
23. The National Bureau of Statistics estimated there were 130 million Chinese living away from the place in which they were registered to live in June 2001; not all of them were migrant workers. Most migrants had moved from inland rural areas to coastal urban areas. China: Rural, Tourism, Hong Kong, *Migration News* 8, no. 9 (August 2001), http://migration.ucdavis.edu/
24. The Prime Minister's Commission on Japan's Goals in the Twenty-first Century recommended on January 18, 2000, that Japan "should set up an explicit immigration and permanent-residence system to encourage foreigners who can be expected to contribute to the development of Japanese society to move in and possibly take up permanent residence here." This recommendation has not been implemented.
25. These are the countries from which most foreign students violate the terms of their visas. Japan, Korea, *Migration News* 11, no. 2 (April 2004), http://migration.ucdavis.edu/
26. Quoted in Labor Exporters, *Migration News* 8, no. 5 (May 2001), http://migration.ucdavis.edu/
27. The survey of migrants, based on interviews with sixty-nine thousand families in seventy-one hundred villages in thirty-one provinces, found that two-thirds of migrants come from grain producing areas, 56 percent worked outside their home provinces, and 70 percent worked in eastern coastal provinces. About 86 percent of migrants were under forty; 47 percent were under twenty-five.
28. Details of each of these smuggling incidents are available in *Migration News.* http://migration.ucdavis.edu/
29. The United Nations High Commissioner for Refugees (UNHCR) reported that there were 1.2 million Afghan refugees in Pakistan in 2001, some of whom had been there since the Soviet Union invaded Afghanistan in 1979, and another 1.3 million Afghani refugees in Iran. There are more than 4 million Palestinians, including those in Jordan, Lebanon, and the West Bank. Gaza has the world's highest population growth rate—4.5 percent a year—and families of ten are common.
30. Middle East: Renationalization, *Migration News* 8, no. 11 (November 2001), http://migration.ucdavis.edu/ The Saudi government has also implemented training programs to teach Saudis to be more efficient service workers.
31. Irin Carmon, "Israel Rounds Up Migrants in Deportation Campaign," *Boston Globe,* July 25, 2004.
32. The United Nations imposed sanctions in 1992 after Libya refused to turn over two men suspected in the 1988 bombing of a Pan Am plane over the Scottish town of Lockerbie. Libya eventually turned over the suspects and compensated the families of the victims, after which the sanctions were lifted.

33. Many of the killings were in western Libya. Ade Obisesan, "Deportees: Widespread Killing of Black Africans in Libya," *Agence France Presse,* October 5, 2000.
34. There has been discussion of opening "reception centers" funded by European countries in northern African nations so that those headed to Europe to apply for asylum could have housing, food, and hearings in North Africa. Sophie Arie, "Italy and Libya in Joint Offensive on Migrants," *Guardian,* August 12, 2004.
35. Professionals have freedom of movement rights in east and west Africa in recognition of the regional educational institutions established by colonial powers.
36. Barbara Crossette, "What It Takes to Stop Slavery," *New York Times,* April 22, 2001.
37. Celia W. Dugger, "In Africa, an Exodus of Nurses," *New York Times,* July 12, 2004. The African Union estimates that poor African countries subsidize rich industrial countries with $500 million a year through the migration of health workers.
38. Robyn Dixon and Peta Thornycroft, "Minister Says Zimbabwe Plans to Nationalize Land," *Los Angeles Times,* June 9, 2004. The government called land reform a success on its fifth anniversary in 2005, but the World Food Program warned that about 40 percent of the population, especially in rural areas, needed food assistance.
39. Quoted in President Bush's letter to Congress, May 1, 1991, p. 17.
40. Quoted in Guest Workers, Legalization, *Migration News* 8, no. 9 (August 2001), http://migration.ucdavis.edu/ Foreign Minister Jorge Castaneda in June 2001 said that Mexico's four-pronged immigration agenda included legalization, a guest worker program, an end to border violence, and exemption of Mexico from visa quotas; Castaneda added, "It's the whole enchilada or nothing." In September 2001, however, he said: "It's not an all-or-nothing deal."
41. During the 1960s and 1970s, many former Caribbean colonies became independent countries. Since 1983 most islands have voted against independence, including Puerto Rico in 1998.
42. In 1996 about 40 percent of Puerto Rican families received some form of federal welfare assistance.
43. Quoted in Australia: Legal, Asylum, *Migration News* 8, no. 6 (June 2001), http://migration.ucdavis.edu/
44. Kalinga Seneviratne, "Global Con Men Target Cash-strapped Islands," *Straits Times,* July 4, 2000.

3. HIGHLY SKILLED GUEST WORKERS

1. Some studies are restricted to a subset of PTKs, often scientists and engineers, also known as human resources devoted to science and technology, or HRST (OECD, 2002). Other studies focus on all those with postsecondary or tertiary education.
2. During the 1990s the number of migrants in more-developed countries rose by twenty-three million, or 28 percent, and immigration accounted for two-thirds of industrial country population growth.
3. Migrants tend to be younger than other local residents, and thus may have higher-than-average labor force participation rates (LFPRs). In the United States, for example, about twenty million of the thirty-four million foreign-born residents, almost 60 percent, were

in the labor force in 2002. These foreign-born workers included immigrants, temporary workers, and an estimated number of unauthorized workers. One reason for the LFPR of more than 50 percent is that the children of migrants born in the United States are U.S. citizens.

4. In today's global labor force, average years of schooling are 6.4–7.2 years for men and 5.2 for women.
5. The actual "mapping" between years of education recorded on the U.S. census and the educational groups was as follows: less than nine years corresponded to no or primary schooling, nine to twelve years corresponded to secondary schooling, and thirteen or more years corresponded to high school graduates and beyond. In the United States many adults would be classified in the nine-to-twelve category of the U.S. census, the high school–graduate category in Barro and Lee (1993, 12).
6. Note that other studies consider professionals to be those with sixteen or more years of schooling, not thirteen or more years as in Carrington and Detragiache, 1998.
7. The data cannot say where the person obtained the education and do not record the legal status of the foreigner, who may be an immigrant or a graduate student, although Carrington and Detragiache tried to subtract graduate students.
8. In the United States in 1990, 75 percent of adults had a high school diploma or more and thus would have been considered PTK by Carrington and Detragiache. However, only 20 percent had a college degree or more. Another 25 percent had education beyond high school but no college degree.
9. Their estimate was based on 1 million scientists and engineers employed in U.S. research-and-development activities, including 23 percent who were foreign born (230,000), with 72 percent of the foreign born from developing countries (166,000).
10. Barro and Sala-i-Martin (1995) used data from 111 countries to conclude that a workforce with an average of one more year of education than workforces in other countries was 5–15 percent more productive.
11. It is hard to assess the volume of PTK flows. The OECD (2002) has concluded that "while it is difficult to measure . . . there is every reason to believe that [PTK] flows rose substantially during the 1990s" (7).
12. Some 35 percent of doctors who graduated from the University of the Witwatersrand's medical school in the 1990s emigrated by 2002. James Lamont, "S. African Leaders Do Little to Stem Exodus of Skills," *Financial Times,* July 24, 2002, 9. Reasons for leaving included violent crime (some 250,000 people were murdered in South Africa in the 1990s), a falling currency, and opportunities for travel that were not available during apartheid. Some 800,000 South Africans, many skilled, hold British passports.
13. The ILO papers are available online (http://www.ilo.org/public/english/protection/migrant/publ/imp-list.htm).
14. Narrower definitions produced smaller numbers: for example, there were 8 million scientists and engineers, including 2 million each in Germany and the United Kingdom (OECD, 2002, 20). The U.S. Scientists and Engineers Statistical Data System (SESTAT) found 12 million scientists and engineers in 1997, but only 3.3 million of them were employed in science and engineering (OECD, 2002, 23).
15. Half of the foreign students in 2025 were projected to be Chinese and Indian when

China and India were expected to account for 35 percent of the world's 7.9 billion residents (Bohm et al., 2002).

16. In practice, employers rarely find local workers, in part because employers requesting foreign workers usually have identified the migrant(s) that they want to hire.
17. The American Competitiveness and Work Force Improvement Act of 1998 raised the ceiling by 142,500 over three years and required employers to pay $500 per H-1B application to provide scholarships for U.S. residents to encourage them to study science and engineering and thus head off persisting shortages. The American Competitiveness in the Twenty-first Century Act of 2000 raised the ceiling to 195,000 a year and the fee to $1,000 per H-1B application but exempted foreigners employed in universities and nonprofits from the ceiling and their U.S. employers from the fee. The 65,000 quota for FY2005 was reached on the first day of the new fiscal year, October 1, 2004.
18. Deborah Billings, "Audit by DOL Inspector General Faults Employment-based Immigration Programs," *Daily Labor Report,* April 15, 1996. Once a foreigner receives an immigrant visa, she is no longer required to work for the employer who sponsored her. About 10 percent of the foreigners who received employment-related immigration visas never worked for the U.S. employers who sponsored them, and 17 percent worked for less than six months with the sponsoring employer.
19. Jim Sprecht, "Government Has Little Control over Job-based Immigration," Gannett News Service, August 4, 1996. In most cases, employers sponsor housekeepers for immigrant visas as a reward for faithful service to their families; the cook and chef visas often went to relatives of the owners of ethnic restaurants.
20. Only H-1B-dependent employers—those with 15 percent or more H-1B workers—must certify that they did not lay off U.S. workers to hire H-1B workers.
21. H-1B IT workers between jobs are considered "benched," and there are frequent disputes over the allowances they should receive when they incur living costs but do not earn wages.
22. Jobs, H-1Bs, Students, *Migration News* 6, no. 12 (December 1999), http://migration.ucdavis.edu
23. Rachel Emma Silverman, "Visiting Workers Are Forced to Leave the U.S. as Tech Jobs Don't Materialize," *Wall Street Journal,* June 21, 2001. This particular H-1B worker had appropriate training, but the incentive to collect recruitment fees means that not all H-1B workers have appropriate credentials. The U.S. Department of State reported in 1999 that 45 percent of a sample of the H-1B applicants in Chennai, India (formerly Madras), presented credentials that could not be authenticated; 21 percent were clearly fraudulent.
24. The International Council of Nurses issued similar recruitment guidelines in 2001 (http://www.icn.ch/psrecruit01.htm).
25. Celia W. Dugger, "In Africa, an Exodus of Nurses," *New York Times,* July 12, 2004. PHR did not recommend that African governments try to prevent the emigration of health care workers but did recommend that industrial countries not recruit actively in Africa.
26. One recruiter promises Filipino nurses that their U.S. hospital employers will sponsor them for immigrant visas (http://www.nursestousa.com/).
27. Abella notes that governments can play important indirect roles in labor migration, such as negotiating cheaper airfares for migrants and passing some of the savings on to the migrants (1997, 85).

28. Quoted in Latin America, *Migration News* 8, no. 10 (October 2001), http://migration.ucdavis.edu/
29. People of Indian origin abroad have incomes totaling $160 billion a year, a third of the GDP generated by 1 billion Indians in India. Estimates of Indians abroad include 2.2 million in the United Kingdom; 1.7 million each in the United States and Malaysia; 850,000 in Canada; 700,000 in Mauritius; 500,000 in Trinidad and Tobago; 400,000 in Guyana; and 340,000 in Fiji. See South Asia, *Migration News* 10, no. 2 (April 2003), http://migration.ucdavis.edu/ Harvard's Mihir Desai put the number of Indians in the United States at 1 million, 0.1 percent of India's population, and their income at 10 percent of India's GDP.
30. *Diaspora* is a Greek word first applied to Jews dispersed outside of Israel in the sixth century B.C., after Nebuchadnezzar of Babylon destroyed the first Jewish temple.
31. These students were highly motivated to pursue advanced studies. Before they could go abroad, they had to complete two years of military service and obtain private or overseas financing.
32. Shanghai reportedly has thirty thousand returned professionals, 90 percent with master's or doctoral degrees earned abroad, who are employed or starting businesses (Jonathan Kaufman, "China Reforms Bring Back Executives Schooled in US," *Wall Street Journal,* March 6, 2003; Rone Tempest, "China Tries to Woo Its Tech Talent Back Home," *Los Angeles Times,* November 25, 2002).
33. Quoted in Alan Beattie, "Seeking Consensus on the Benefits of Immigration," *Financial Times,* July 22, 2002, 9.
34. *Temporary* is not defined in GATS, but the agreement explicitly does not apply to permanent migration. Most WTO members limit service providers to less than five years in their country.
35. Countries may also deregulate the provision of services, but limit competition to national suppliers—for example, introduce vouchers and charter or private schools, but allow only national firms employing citizens to provide educational services.
36. In the United States, preadmission ENTs are called labor certification, and postadmission ENTs are called employer attestation.
37. Some countries, including the United Kingdom, already allow the admission of "independent service providers." In the United Kingdom they are non-EU foreigners who achieve at least 75 points in five personal areas: education (maximum 30 points for a Ph.D.), work experience (maximum 25 points for five years), past earnings (25 points for $65,000 a year, 35 points for $165,000), work achievements (15 or 25 points for publications and honors), and skills in U.K. "priority areas," such as general practice medicine (www.workpermits.gov.uk/).
38. The EU's mutual recognition system applies only to EU nationals, so that a Turk recognized as a doctor in Germany does not have to be recognized as a doctor by France. In countries such as the United States and Canada, credentials may be state- or province-specific, so that a doctor or lawyer accredited to practice in one place may not be licensed to practice in another within the same country.
39. Winters et al. (2002, 57) conclude that subcontracting and using intracompany transfers "offers the greatest chance of extending Mode 4 [migration] to lower-skilled workers."

4. GUEST WORKER PROGRAMS

1. Germany remains the major source of immigrants to the United States after 182 years of recorded immigration. Of the 67 million immigrants whose arrival was recorded in the United States between 1820 and 2001, some 7.2 million, or 11 percent, were from Germany, followed by 6.3 million from Mexico, 5.4 million from Italy, and 5.3 million from the United Kingdom (INS Statistical Yearbook, 2001, 19). In the 1980 U.S. census some 60 million Americans, or 1 in 4, reported German roots.

   Prussia had developed an elaborate system of controlling foreign labor that differentiated according to nationalities and occupations. For details on the migration history of the German Empire and the Republic of Weimar see Jochen Oltmer's "Deutsche Migrationsverhältnisse: neuere Forschungsergebnisse zur Wanderungsgeschichte imKaiserreich und in der Weimarer Republik," http://www.bpb.de/refdb/refdb_pdf_openshow.php?rid=122&pid=48

   In August 1944 some 2 million war prisoners and 5.7 million non-German civilian workers made up about one-third of the German labor force (Herbert, 1997).
2. Greece became a member of the EC in 1981, and Spain and Portugal became members in 1986. Greeks had to wait seven years, until 1988, for full freedom-of-movement rights. Spain and Portugal, scheduled to have freedom-of-movement rights after seven years, in 1993, got mobility rights one year early in 1992.
3. The challenge as seen by Jean-Jacques Servan-Schreiber was that major European firms would become subsidiaries of U.S. multinationals, such as Opel, a General Motors subsidiary in Germany.
4. Some 30 to 40 percent of Turkish guest workers were considered to be skilled workers in Turkey, but most worked as manual laborers in Germany.
5. Then–Foreigners Commissioner Liselotte Funke reported that employers and the labor ministry in 1973 wanted continued recruitment, and they proposed tighter restrictions on family unification to avoid schooling and other integration issues as a way to offset "out-of-control" fears and keep guest workers coming. *Die Zeit,* February 17, 1989, 19.
6. Today ONI is called the Office for International Migration (Office des migrations internationales, OMI).
7. The agreement with Algeria was special since it was concluded in the context of decolonization. To a certain extent it included an accord on establishment.
8. As a former colonial power France experienced increased immigration during the wars of liberalization and decolonization in the 1950s and 1960s. In particular, there were unregulated entries from Algeria in the period up to and following Algerian independence in 1962, with new arrivals including former French colonialists as well as Algerians who had sided with France. Numbers went up from 350,000 in 1962 to 470,000 in 1968. Kimberly Hamilton and Patrick Simon, "The Challenge of French Diversity," *Migration Information Source,* May 2002, http://www.migrationinformation.org/Profiles
9. For a detailed description and analysis of the Swiss quota system see Piguet and Mahnig, 2000.
10. "Man hat Arbeitskräfte gerufen, und es kamen Menschen." Max Frisch, www.migration.bl.bs.ch/tgv/themen-2.htm

11. For about fifty years the Florida sugarcane industry relied on legal foreign workers from the Caribbean to hand-cut sugarcane grown in south-central Florida. The number of foreign cane cutters rose with cane production from the 1960s, after the Cuban embargo, and peaked in the late 1980s, when a suit was filed alleging that cutters were being underpaid.

    The suit was based on the job offer filed by employers seeking U.S. workers, the so-called clearance order (the job offer was "cleared" through U.S. employment offices) that had twenty items an employer must complete, ranging from the name of the employer to the wages, hours, and job specifications. The item that led to lawsuits and mechanization was the task rate described in item 9 of the order. The government set the minimum hourly wage workers had to earn at $5.30 in the late 1980s. The sugar companies set the task rate or piece rate for cutting a foot of cane and a task or productivity standard—U.S. and H-2A workers who could not satisfy the productivity standard could be and sometimes were fired.

    The workers' suit alleged that the job offer promised workers $5.30 a ton but that workers were in fact paid only about $3.75 a ton. The basis for the suit was the minimum wage of $5.30 an hour, a promise to workers that piece rates would be set so that "the average cane cutter [can] earn more than the minimum wage rate," and the statement that "a worker would be expected to cut an average of 8 tons of harvest cane per day throughout the season." Thus, worker attorneys argued, if cutting eight tons of cane in an eight-hour day satisfies the productivity standard, and workers must earn at least $5.30 an hour, a worker cutting a ton of cane an hour must be a satisfactory worker, and can expect to receive $5.30 a ton.

    Three juries rejected this argument, siding with employers who argued that if a contract is ambiguous, what each party believes it means is important. The employers convinced the juries that they never intended to pay workers $5.30 a ton, and some workers testified that they did not believe they were being offered $5.30 a ton.
12. U.S. professionals have reciprocal rights to enter Canada and Mexico.
13. Between 1992 and 1995 foreign students with F-1 visas could work off-campus for U.S. employers who attested that they had tried to hire U.S. workers at the prevailing wage for at least sixty days and had failed to find any, and the F-1 students could work for any such U.S. employers for up to twenty hours a week, or full-time when school was not in session. The U.S. Senate–approved Agricultural Job Opportunity Benefits and Security Act of 1998 (AgJOBS), which was not enacted into law, would have allowed legal guest workers to seek jobs with U.S. farm employers who filed attestations that they had tried and failed to recruit U.S. workers.
14. The Italian interior minister in August 2003 asserted that a bilateral deal between Italy and Sri Lanka, allowing one thousand young Sri Lankans to enter for work and training, had reduced the flow of illegal Sri Lankan migrants.
15. Half of the eastern Europeans employed in Germany in the mid-1990s were admitted under the new programs (Hönekopp, 1997, 15).
16. Participating countries are Albania, Bulgaria, Croatia, the Czech Republic, Estonia, Hungary, Latvia, Lithuania, Poland, Romania, Russia, Slovakia, and Slovenia. France

and Switzerland have almost identical programs. Switzerland concluded thirty bilateral agreements for training purposes, and both France and Switzerland keep adding new ones; for example, France signed an agreement with Romania in December 2003 which went into force in the summer of 2004.

17. Many have observed that the German green card is unlike the U.S. immigrant visa, which is also known colloquially as a green card; in U.S. terminology, the German green card is a nonimmigrant visa entitling a foreigner to remain in Germany for a specific time and purpose.
18. Then–Labor Minister Walter Riester (SPD) objected, saying: "We cannot allow a general international opening of the job market. We have over four million unemployed people, among them very qualified people in the information technology field." Thirty-one thousand IT workers were unemployed in December 1999. Quoted in Germany: Green Cards? *Migration News* 7, no. 4 (April 2000), http://migration.ucdavis.edu
19. The commission recommended that Germany admit fifty thousand more foreigners a year than currently arrive via family unification, including twenty thousand foreign professionals selected on the basis of a point system, another twenty thousand admitted temporarily with five-year permits that could lead to settlement, and ten thousand trainees and foreign graduates of German universities, who would receive two-year work visas but be allowed to settle. The commission's report, Organizing Immigration: Fostering Integration, can be found at http://www.bmi.bund.de/dokumente/Artikel/ix_46876.htm
20. As self-employed carpenters or bricklayers, workers were exempt from high German payroll taxes, but critics noted that these self-employed EU nationals often took instructions from on-site supervisors, and argued that they should have been considered employees.
21. Surveys suggest that remittances were used primarily for consumer goods and housing, with 20 percent devoted to investments that could create self-employment in the migrants' area of origin (Hönekopp, 1997, 20).
22. The European Economic Area includes twenty-five EU nations and non-EU nations Iceland, Liechtenstein, and Norway.
23. Home Office Press Release 252/2004, July 22, 2004.
24. Home Office, 2004. This scheme is explained at http://www.workingintheuk.gov.uk/working_in_the_uk/en/homepage/schemes_and_programmes.html?
25. Home Office Announcement, June 18, 2004, http://www.workingintheuk.gov.uk/
26. Home Office Press Releases 191/2004, May 19, 2004; Release 252/2004, July 22, 2004.
27. Labor Secretary Robert B. Reich in 1995 testified, "We have seen numerous instances in which American businesses have brought in foreign skilled workers after having laid off skilled American workers, simply because they can get the foreign workers more cheaply. [The H-1B program] has become a major means of circumventing the costs of paying skilled American workers or the costs of training them." Nonimmigrants: High-Tech, *Migration News* 5, no. 2 (February 1998), http://migration.ucdavis.edu

    H-1B workers with master's degrees or more or earning $60,000 or more are not included in calculating dependency.

28. One worker could fill more than one H-2B job, and a worker who left the United States and returned within one year counts as two admissions.
29. For example, Amigos Labor Solutions (www.amigos-inc.com/) in Dallas says that it provided two thousand H-2B workers to employers in thirty-four states in 2002.
30. In 2000 and 2001 there were about two thousand admissions a year of Mexicans with TN visas.
31. Quoted in Canada: Migrants, *Migration News* 12, no. 1 (January 2005), http://migration.ucdavis.edu/
32. FARMS began to play this role in 1987, when the program was changed and the private sector assumed a greater role in program administration. Transportation is arranged by CAN-AG Travel Services.
33. About 75 percent of the Mexican migrants are from four Mexican states: Tlaxcala, Guanajuato, Mexico, and Hidalgo.
34. Caribbean migrants have 25 percent of their pay deducted in a forced savings program.
35. Since 2004 others have been able to apply to become scheme operators, and in September 2004 there were nine. Operators charge farmers and/or SAWS workers for their services, and fees vary. Harvesting Opportunity Permit Scheme, HOPS, the largest operator, with eight thousand SAWS workers in 2002, uses seventy-five recruiting agents in agricultural colleges to find students (www.nfyfc.org.uk/HOPS.htm).
36. The number of permits issued exceeds the ceiling in most years because some of the students receiving permits do not report for work in the United Kingdom.
37. There have been calls to prevent illegal and exploitative employment by better regulating gangmasters. There are two approaches: (1) penalizing violators by, for example, requiring them to register and withholding licenses from those who violate laws (and perhaps penalizing employers on the farms where gangmaster violations are discovered) and (2) rewarding gangmasters who abide by laws with seals of approval. http://www.ethicaltrade.org/pub/publications/2003/04-gangmstr/index.shtml
38. Raising the quota would presumably leave less reason for hiring unauthorized workers. See White Paper, Secure Borders, Safe Haven (2002), http://www.official-documents.co.uk/document/cm53/5387/cm5387.htm
39. A May 2002 review of the SAWS program "suggests that shortages in the supply of labor are increasingly being met by non-EU citizens working in the UK illegally and by UK nationals working illegally whilst in receipt of benefit" (5).
40. If seasonal foreign workers are employed less than two months in Germany, the workers and their employers do not have to pay social security taxes on their wages.
41. A third of foreigners, compared with 20 percent of Swiss, had only compulsory education in 2000, suggesting that foreigners were being "negatively selected" for permanent residence (Liebig, 2003; de Wild and Sheldon, 2000, 4).
42. Swiss voters have refused liberalization in two previous referenda in the past twenty-one years. Opponents of liberalizing naturalization in the 2004 campaign put Osama bin Laden's photo on a Swiss ID card and claimed that if the new law were enacted, Switzerland could be taken over by Muslims. About 20 percent of the 7.2 million people living in Switzerland were born in another country, with the largest groups born in Italy and the Balkans.

5. MANAGING GUEST WORKERS

1. Lowell (2002, 24) concluded that "the direct impact of significant outflows of highly educated persons . . . is to reduce economic growth in the source country."
2. Since most overseas Americans are exempt from income taxes and most plan to return, the U.S. policy is an exception to the rule that taxing nationals abroad rarely works.
3. The richest OECD countries have a combined GDP of about $25 trillion, and they currently provide $55 billion a year in ODA. If they were to reach the 0.7 percent ODA goal, they would add $120 billion in ODA.
4. President George Bush proposed to increase U.S. foreign aid from $16 billion to $18 billion in FY2004, but to add the $2 billion to a new Millennium Challenge Account that targets countries with per capita annual incomes below $1,435 that meet performance standards in human rights, democracy, and lack of corruption.
5. Professionals also migrate between developed nations, and to avoid replenishment assistance when Canadians migrate to the United States or vice versa (DeVoretz and Laryea, 1998), HCRA could be made available only when per capita income differences are at least 5–1.
6. New enforcement strategies such as joint liability may also be needed. Joint liability is the concept that the beneficiaries of work done are jointly liable for labor law, tax, and other violations committed by contractors who bring workers to the job site. The intent of joint liability laws is to have farmers and construction firms, for example, police the contractors whose market share of work in sectors with a high percentage of migrants is rising. However, in many cases, the willingness of contractors to serve as risk absorbers for violations of tax, labor, and immigration laws is becoming a comparative advantage.
7. An estimated 50 percent of those born in Zacatecas are in the United States, the highest per capita emigration rate in Mexico. Federal, state, and local governments match the remittance savings sent back to Zacatecas by hometown associations in the United States, and $20 million was spent on 308 three-for-one projects, including building bridges, paving roads, and providing drinking water. One assessment concluded that three-for-one projects have improved the quality of life but not stimulated the Zacatecan economy. Ken Bensinger, "Mexico's Other Migrant Wave," *Christian Science Monitor,* October 8, 2004.
8. This is one of the reasons that some countries cite for not ratifying these ILO conventions. ILO, *Migrant workers,* General Survey: Report of the Committee of Experts on the Application of Conventions and Recommendations, International Labour Conference, 87th Session (Geneva: ILO, 1999), para. 107.

6. THAILAND

1. The Office of Foreign Workers Administration on January 18, 2001, reported that there were 99,656 legal foreign workers in Thailand, that most were professionals living in Bangkok, and that 25 percent were Japanese.
2. Mid-1990s studies of migrants in the provinces of Chiang Rai, Tak, Kanchanaburi, and Ranong found that most migrants walked across the Burmese-Thai border, sometimes

with help from Thai or Burmese agents, and that most local residents thought that migrants increased crime and helped to spread contagious diseases.

3. The registration exercise was later extended through March 7, 1997.
4. Foreign sex workers earned and remitted more—$125 a month and $385 a year. Most of the Burmese migrants surveyed were from Shan state, the area that has some of the strongest opponents to the Burmese government. Burmese and Thai agents reportedly have very strong networks to move migrants from Burmese villages to Thai workplaces because of weak controls and corruption on both sides of the border.
5. The financial crisis had its origins in a property price bubble that was sustained by foreign capital flowing into the country that spread to the stock market. The baht appreciated, reducing the competitiveness of exports (there was no growth in exports in 1996), and the bubble burst and resulted in capital flight in 1997.
6. Thailand: Crisis and Migrants, *Migration News* 4, no. 11 (November 1997), http://migration.ucdavis.edu
7. Migrants are covered by the Bt30 health plan (most services at hospitals require a Bt30 co-payment). Hospitals receive about Bt1,253 a year for each person covered by the plan, which has generated controversy over the financial viability of the program. The Ministry of Labor and Social Welfare (MOLSW) and health authorities are debating what to do about migrants who test positive for communicable diseases such as tuberculosis—if they are simply deported, they are not likely to get treatment.
8. A migrant working full-time (twenty-four days a month) at the minimum wage would earn Bt3,960 ($90) a month in Bangkok, Bt3,192 ($73) in most of Thailand.
9. These data are from the Thai Labor Force Survey, conducted since 1963 by the National Statistical Office. It interviews sixty-one thousand households each quarter to obtain data on persons thirteen and older who were employed (one hour or more of work for wages or in family businesses during the survey week) or unemployed but actively seeking work.
10. The Social Security Act of 1990 created retirement benefits that began paying the current equivalent of Bt300 a month in 2003. Employers, workers, and the government each contribute 1.5 percent of wages for medical, maternity, death, and disability benefits.
11. The BOI offers investors a combination of corporate tax exemptions—typically for five to eight years—and waivers of import duties on raw materials and machinery. These incentives are to be phased out as Thailand complies with World Trade Organization commitments, but BOI says that some investment incentives may be retained for agriculture, furniture, and other labor-intensive industries.
12. The case studies summarized here utilized focus groups of eight to ten registered and unregistered migrants, interviews with at least five employers, and interviews with provincial officials.
13. China, Indonesia, Vietnam, and Bangladesh produced more rice than Thailand in 1997–1998 but exported less. Vietnam is the world's second-leading exporter of rice, exporting about four million metric tons a year. Half of the Thai rice exported was fragrant and parboiled; parboiled rice is soaked in water, steamed under pressure, and dried before milling, and thus needs minimal cooking. Glutinous or sticky rice as well as jasmine rice are produced in the north and northeast of Thailand.

14. Some boats reportedly advance funds to the migrants, then deduct these wage advances from the workers' pay.
15. Thailand's Immigration Bureau had a 2001 budget of Bt80 million ($1.8 million) to remove unauthorized foreign workers and reported arresting twenty thousand migrants a month in 2001.

7. MANAGING MIGRATION IN THE TWENTY-FIRST CENTURY

1. The fifteen senior EU members may block freedom of movement for up to seven years—that is, until April 30, 2011—from Poland, the Czech Republic, Hungary, Slovakia, Slovenia, Lithuania, Latvia, and Estonia. Studies have suggested that net migration from these new EU countries to the fifteen that previously constituted the EU could be 70,000–150,000 a year. Many migration researchers have noted that when Spain and Portugal joined the EU in 1986, their citizens had to wait seven years for freedom-of-movement rights in order to avoid a migration hump. In 1995 there were 100,000 fewer Spaniards and 110,000 fewer Portuguese living in "old" EU countries than there had been in 1986.
2. Ghosh calls for "regulated openness," with participating countries sharing "common objectives," a "harmonized normative framework," and a "monitoring mechanism" (Ghosh, 2000, 227).
3. Remittances are listed under current transfers and compensation of employees in a country's current account. Many countries do not know how long the migrants remitting funds have been abroad, so most analyses combine workers' remittances and compensation of employees. For example, Mexico reports most money inflows under worker remittances, while the Philippines reports most under compensation of employees.

   A third item not generally included in discussions of remittances comprises migrants' transfers, which measure the net worth of migrants who move from one country to another. For example, if a person with stock migrates from one country to another, the value of the stock owned moves from one country to another in international accounts.
4. When the risk premium for borrowing funds abroad is very high, some countries have been able to float bonds secured by the anticipated future flow of remittances, as Brazil did in 2001.
5. The money transfer business tends to have high fixed and low marginal costs. Thus if banks with branches in migrant areas in sending and receiving countries form alliances, they can attract migrant customers to use their services.
6. Since December 1998 Mexico's federal consumer protection agency, Profeco, has compared the cost of transferring $300 from the United States to Mexico weekly in six U.S. cities: Chicago, Los Angeles, New York, Dallas, Miami, and Houston (http://www.profeco.gob.mx/enviodinero/enviomnu.htm). The costs vary by city or origin and destination as well as by services provided with the transfer. Converting $300 to pesos at an exchange rate of 1 to 9.3 yields 2,790 pesos; at 1 to 9, the yield is 2,700 pesos, or almost $10 less. The total cost to send money is $25, or 8.3 percent of the amount sent.
7. Automatic stabilizers in developed countries, such as unemployment insurance, help to

stabilize the flow of remittances to developing countries that have the same economic cycles as the countries in which their migrants work. Thus if unemployment rises in both the United States and Mexico, Mexican migrants can continue to send some remittances to their families if they receive unemployment insurance payments in the United States.

Ratha (2003) noted that remittances to high-debt and less transparent countries were more stable than those to middle-income open economies because the latter include more remittances destined for investment.

8. Lewis (1954) assumed that the traditional agricultural sector of developing countries had an unlimited supply of labor that could be absorbed in an expanding modern industrial sector with no loss of farm output. Ranis and Fei (1961) extended the Lewis model so that, once the marginal product of labor and wages are equal in the traditional and modern sector, rural-urban migration stops; Johnson (1967) noted that rural-urban migrants could take capital with them.

   Todaro (1969) took a micro perspective, showing that rural and urban wages did not converge as expected in Lewis-style models because, with high and rigid urban wages, rural migrants continued to pour into cities despite high unemployment because their expected earnings (higher wages times the probability of employment) were higher in the cities. Todaro argued that the solution to unwanted rural-urban migration was urban wage subsidies and migration restrictions; Bhagwati and Srinivasan (1974) showed that tax and subsidy schemes could yield optimal migration levels without migration restrictions.

9. Average world per capita annual GDP doubled from $2,500 to $5,000 between 1950 and 2000.

10. Comparative advantage advises countries to specialize in producing goods in which they have a relative advantage because of their resources, location, or capital-labor costs. Even if one country can produce all goods cheaper than another, both countries are still better off specializing in the production of the goods they can produce most efficiently, exporting some, and importing goods they cannot produce as efficiently. Trade can also lead to economies of scale, which lower the cost of production as output increases for a larger market.

11. Another $6.9 billion in official aid was provided to so-called Part II countries, most in eastern Europe and the former Soviet Union. About a quarter of ODA is provided via technical cooperation grants, as when donors pay consultants to advise developing country governments.

12. In the late 1990s, when global exports of manufactured goods were about $3.5 trillion a year, global exports of farm goods were less than $500 billion a year, including a third from developing countries. Another comparison is with global arms sales: some $26 billion in 2001, down from $40 billion in 2000; two-thirds of global arms sales are to developing countries.

13. Convention 97 excludes border-crossing commuters (frontier workers), seamen (covered by other ILO conventions), and artists and similar professionals abroad for a short time.

    ILO Recommendation No. 86 includes a model bilateral agreement for migrant workers, and has been used as a model for many of the bilateral agreements that have been established.

14. Conventions 97 and 143 exempt seafarers, frontier workers, the self-employed, artists, and trainees.
15. Many other ILO conventions cover migrants (for example, Freedom of Association and Protection of the Right to Organize Convention [87, 1948]) or consider migrants as a group of special concern, as in the Equal Treatment under Social Security Convention (118). The Employment Promotion and Protection against Unemployment Convention, 1988 (168) calls for equality of treatment of all workers and for special measures to support certain workers, including regular migrant workers; it also calls attention to the difficulties of returning migrants who would be unemployed in their home country. The Private Employment Agencies Convention (181, approved in 1997) calls for member states to penalize private employment agencies that defraud or abuse migrant workers and urges bilateral agreements to prevent such abuses.
16. For example, article 8 of Convention 97 says that foreign workers injured at work should not be subject to removal just because they are not employed, but most countries tie legal residence to legal employment. Article 8 of Convention 143 calls for protection for migrants who lose their jobs, and article 14(a) says that migrant workers should have the right to occupational mobility—most countries do not allow migrants to change employers.
17. The U.S. Supreme Court in a 5–4 decision in *Hoffman Plastics* (2002) held that requiring back pay would "encourage the successful evasion of apprehension by immigration authorities, condone prior violations of the immigration laws, and encourage future violations." In effect, the court ruled that a worker's violation of immigration laws was more serious than an employer's violation of labor laws. http://caselaw.lp.findlaw.com/scripts/getcase.pl?court=us&navby=year&year=2002
18. ILO Convention 97 is about 5,600 words; 143 is 3,000 words; and the U.N. convention is more than 14,000 words.
19. Part IV, article 44 was one of the most contentious parts of the migrant convention. It says that "recognizing that the family is the natural and fundamental group unit of society" obligates states to "take appropriate measures to ensure the protection of the unity of the families of migrant workers . . . to facilitate the reunification of migrant workers with their spouses . . . as well as with their minor dependent unmarried children." Migrant family members are to have "equality of treatment with nationals" in access to education and social and health services, and "states of employment shall endeavor to facilitate for the children of migrant workers the teaching of their mother tongue and culture."
20. The activities to be undertaken include assessing demographic and labor market trends in the global labor market; promoting "managed migration for employment" sensitive to aging populations that include bilateral agreements dealing with issues from admissions and family unification to social security; devoting special attention to recruitment agencies and Convention 181 and Recommendation 188; and promoting decent work for migrants, ensuring that they are informed of their rights, and minimizing abuse and smug-

gling. The framework is also intended to deal with policies to combat irregular migration and to promote return migration, and to reduce the cost of remitting funds and increase their development payoff to migrant areas of origin.

21. The report is available at http://www.ilo.org/public/english/protection/migrant/new/index.htm
22. Roger Böhning acknowledged this trade-off when he concluded that guest worker programs must "balance nationals' legitimate expectation of some preferential treatment against human, economic and social rights that foreigners can justifiably claim to be theirs" (1996, 87). Some analysts have come down clearly on the side of rights, even if the result is fewer migrants. For example, a famous study published in the United States in the early 1950s concluded that "the brightest hope for the welfare of seasonal agricultural workers [in the United States] lies with the elimination of the jobs upon which they now depend" (Fisher, 1953, 148)—that is, the best way to improve conditions for migrant and seasonal workers was to eliminate their jobs. However, others argue that developing countries need access to jobs and remittances that migrant workers earn abroad, and that numbers are more important than rights, as exemplified by the familiar riddle: What is worse than being exploited abroad? Not being exploited abroad.

References

Abella, Manolo. 1995. "Asian Migrant and Contract Workers in the Middle East." Pp. 418–423 in Robin Cohen, ed., *Cambridge Survey of World Migrations.* Cambridge.

———. 1997. *Sending Workers Abroad.* ILO. Geneva.

———. 2004. "The Recruiter's Share in Labour Migration." In Massey Douglas and Edward Taylor, eds., *International Migration: Prospects and Policies in a Global Market.* Oxford.

Abella, Manolo, Philip Martin, and Elizabeth Midgley. 2004. "Best Practices to Manage Migration: The Philippines." *International Migration Review* 38, no. 4, 1544–1564.

Adams, R. H., Jr., and John Page. 2003. The Impact of International Migration and Remittances on Poverty. Paper prepared for DFID/World Bank Conference on Migrant Remittances, London, October 9–10.

Arbeitsagentur.de (Employment Service, Germany). 2004. Saisonbeschäftigte. Übergreifende Informationen. http://www.arbeitsagentur.de/vam/vamController/CMSConversation/anzeigeContent

Archavanitkul, Kritaya. 1998. Transnational Population and Policy Options for Importation of Foreign Labour into Thailand. May. Mimeo.

Bade, Klaus J. 2000. *Europa in Bewegung. Migration vom späten 18. Jahrhundert bis zur Gegenwart.* Munich.

Baguioro, Luz. 2002. "Emigration of Nurses Hurts Philippines' Health Services." *Straits Times.* September 7.

Barro, Robert, and Lee Jong-Wha. 1993. "International Comparisons of Educational Attainment." *Journal of Monetary Economics,* no. 32, 363–394.

Barro, Robert, and Xavier Sala-i-Martin. 2003. *Economic Growth.* McGraw Hill. 2nd ed.

Basok, Tanya. 2002. *Tortillas and Tomatoes: Transmigrant Mexican Harvesters in Canada.* Montreal.

Beach, Charles M., Alan G. Green, and Jeffrey G. Reitz, eds. 2003. *Canadian Immigration Policy for the 21st Century.* Kingston, Ont.

Beine, Michel, Frederic Docquier, and Hillel Rapoport. 2001. "Brain Drain and Economic Growth: Theory and Evidence." *Journal of Development Economics* 64, no. 1, 275–289.

Berlan, Jean-Pierre. 1984. "Labor in Southern French Agriculture." Pp. 61–71 in Philip L. Martin, ed., *Migrant Labor in Agriculture: An International Comparison.* Berkeley.

Bhagwati, Jagdish. 1976. "The Brain Drain." *International Social Science Journal* 28, 691–729.

———. 2003. "Borders Beyond Control." *Foreign Affairs* 82, no. 1, 98–104.

Böhning, W. R. 1972. *The Migration of Workers in the United Kingdom and the European Community.* Oxford.

———. 1996. *Employing Foreign Workers: A Manual on Policies and Procedures of Special Interest to Middle- and Low-Income Countries.* ILO. Geneva.

Böhning, W. R., and M. Schloeter-Paredes. 1993. *Economic Haven or Political Refugees: Can Aid Reduce the Need for Migration?* ILO. Geneva.

Boonchuwong, Pongat, and Waraporn Dechboon. 2000. *Sustainable Management of Coastal Fish Stock in Asia: Thailand.* Department of Fisheries. Bangkok.

Borjas, George J. 1994. "The Economics of Immigration." *Journal of Economic Literature* 32, no. 4, 1167–1717.

———. 1999. *Heaven's Door: Immigration Policy and the American Economy.* Princeton.

———. 2002. An Evaluation of the Foreign Student Program. Center for Immigration Studies Backgrounder. June. www.cis.org/articles/index.html#backgrounders

Caouette, Therese, Kritaya Archavanitkul, and Hnin Hnin Pyne. 2000. *Sexuality, Reproductive Health, and Violence: Experiences of Migrants from Burma in Thailand.* Bangkok.

Carrington, William, and Enrica Detragiache. 1998. How Big Is the Brain Drain? IMF working paper 98/102. July. http://www.imf.org/external/pubs/ft/wp/wp98102.pdf

Castles, Stephen, and Mark Miller. 2003. *The Age of Migration: International Population Movements in the Modern World.* New York.

Chalamwong, Yongyuth. 2001. *Country Report: Thailand.* Bangkok.

Chintayananda, Sudthichitt, Gary Risser, and Supang Chantavanich. 1997. *The Monitoring of the Registration of Immigrant Workers from Myanmar, Cambodia, and Laos in Thailand.* Bangkok.

Clark, Nick. 2003. *Overworked, Underpaid, Over Here: Migrant Workers in Britain.* London.

Clarke, James, and John Salt. 2003. "Work Permits and Foreign Labour in the UK: A Statistical Review." *Labour Market Trends,* November, pp. 563–574.

CODETRAS (Collectif de défense des travailleurs étrangers dans l'agriculture). 2004. *Les travailleurs étrangers dans l'agriculture. Salariés, serfs ou esclaves?* Le memorandum du collectif. http://espace.asso.fr/doc/doc_them_1.htm

Cornelius, Wayne A., Thomas J. Espenshade, and Idean Salehyan, eds. 2001. *International*

Migration of the Highly Skilled: Demand, Supply, and Development Consequences in Sending and Receiving Countries. San Diego.

Cornelius, Wayne, Takeyuki Tsuda, Philip Martin, and James Hollifield, eds. 2004. *Controlling Immigration: A Global Perspective.* Stanford.

Craig, Richard B. 1971. *The Bracero Program: Interest Groups and Foreign Policy.* Austin.

CRS (Congressional Research Service). 1980. Temporary Worker Programs: Background and Issues. Prepared for the Senate Committee on the Judiciary. February.

Crush, Jonathan, and Vincent Williams, eds. 1999. *The New South Africans? Immigration Amnesties and Their Aftermath.* Cape Town.

Degler, Carl N. 1970. *Out of Our Past: The Forces That Shaped Modern America.* New York. 2nd ed.

DeVoretz, D. J., and S. Laryea. 1998. Canadian Human Capital Transfers: USA and Beyond. RIIM working paper series, 98–18. www.riim.metropolis.net

de Wild, David, and George Sheldon. 2000. "Entstehung und volkswirtschaftliche Auswirkungen der ausländischen Erwerbsbevölkerung der Schweiz" (Establishment and economic effects of foreign workers in Switzerland). Paper prepared for the symposium Migration and Change in the World of Work. May 26, Bern. Basel.

Dore, Ronald. 1997. *The Diploma Disease: Education, Qualification, and Development.* London. 2nd ed.

Economist. 2002. "Do Developing Countries Gain or Lose when Their Brightest Talents Go Abroad?" September 26.

Ellerman, David. 2003. Policy Research on Migration and Development. Washington, D.C. Mimeo.

Fisher, Lloyd. 1953. *The Harvest Labor Market in California.* Cambridge, Mass.

Futo, Peter, and Michael Jandl, eds. 2004. *Yearbook on Illegal Immigration, Human Smuggling, and Trafficking in Central and Eastern Europe.* Vienna.

Ghosh, Bimal, ed. 2000. *Managing Migration: Time for a New International Regime?* New York.

Hatton, Timothy J., and Jeffrey G. Williamson. 1998. *The Age of Mass Migration: Causes and Economic Impact.* Oxford.

Hillmann, Felicitas. 2003. "Rotation Light? Oder: wie die ausländische Bevölkerung in den bundesdeutschen Arbeitsmarkt integriert ist." *Sozialer Fortschritt* 5–6, 140–151.

Hönekopp, Elmar. 1997. "Labor Migration from Central and Eastern Europe: Old and New Trends." *IAB Labor Market Research Topics,* no. 23.

HRDC/CIC (Human Resources Development Canada/Citizenship and Immigration Canada). 2003. Caribbean and Mexican Seasonal Agricultural Workers Program. http://www.on.hrdc-drhc.gc.ca/english/ps/agri/overview_e.shtml and http://www.cic.gc.ca/english/pub/facts2002-temp/index.html

IMES (Federal Office of Immigration, Integration and Emigration, Switzerland). 2004. http://www.auslaender.ch/news_info/migrationsthemen/Statements_d.asp

International Organization for Migration. 2001. Return of Qualified African Nationals. Fact Sheet. Geneva.

Johnson, Jean M., and Mark C. Rogers. 1998. "International Mobility of Scientists and Engineers to the United States: Brain Drain or Brain Circulation?" National Science Foundation. November 10.

Kindleberger, Charles P. 1967. *Europe's Postwar Growth: The Role of Labor Supply.* Cambridge, Mass.

Krugman, Paul. 2003. *The Great Unraveling: Losing Our Way in the New Century.* New York.

Kuptsch, Christiane. 1995. "Short-term Migration as a Means of Training." In Christiane Kuptsch and Nana Oishi, eds., *Training Abroad: German and Japanese Schemes for Workers from Transition Economies or Developing Countries.* ILO. Geneva.

Kwong, Peter. 1998. *Forbidden Workers: Illegal Chinese Immigrants and American Labor.* New York.

Kyle, David, and Rey Koslowski, eds. 2001. *Global Human Smuggling: Comparative Perspectives.* Baltimore.

Lee, Joseph. 2004. The Developments of Taiwan's Economy and Its Labor Market in 2003. Taipei. Mimeo.

Liebig, Thomas. 2002. Switzerland's Immigration Policy: Lessons for Germany? Forschungsinstitut für Arbeit und Arbeitsrecht FAA-HSG. DP 76. www.faa.unisg.ch/publikationen/publikationen_site.htm

———. 2003. Recruitment of Foreign Labour in Germany and Switzerland. Paper presented at the Seminar on Bilateral Labour Agreements and other Forms of Recruitment of Foreign Workers, OECD, IMES, Montreux, June 19–20.

Lowell, B. Lindsay. 2002. Some Developmental Effects of the International Migration of Highly Skilled Persons. International Migration Papers (IMP-46). http://www.ilo.org/public/english/protection/migrant/publ/imp-list.htm

Lowell, B. Lindsay, and Alan M. Findlay. 2002. Migration of Highly Skilled Persons from Developing Countries: Impact and Policy Responses. International Migration Papers (IMP-44). http://www.ilo.org/public/english/protection/migrant/publ/imp-list.htm

Lucas, Robert. 2004. International Migration Regimes and Economic Development. Stockholm.

Luo, Yu Ling, and Wei-Jen Wang. 2002. High-skill Migration and Chinese Taipei's Industrial Development. In OECD, *International Mobility of the Highly Skilled.* Paris.

Martin, Philip L. 1991. *The Unfinished Story: Turkish Labor Migration to Western Europe, with Special Reference to the Federal Republic of Germany.* ILO. Geneva.

———. 1993. *Trade and Migration: NAFTA and Agriculture.* Washington, D.C.

———. 2004. "Germany: Managing Migration in the 21st Century." Pp. 221–252 in Cornelius et al., 2004.

———. 2005. *Merchants of Labor: Agents of the Evolving Migration Infrastructure.* IILS. Geneva.

Martin, Philip L., and Elizabeth Midgley. 2003. *Immigration: Shaping and Reshaping America.* Washington, D.C. Population Reference Bureau. Vol. 58, no. 2. www.prb.org/pdf/p-58.2Bulletin_Immigration.pdf

Martin, Philip L., and Alan L. Olmstead. 1985. "The Agricultural Mechanization Controversy." *Science* 227, no. 4687, 601–606.

Martineau, T., K. Decker, and P. Bundred. 2002. *Briefing Note on International Migration of*

Health Professionals: Leveling the Playing Field for Developing Country Health Systems. Liverpool.

Massey, Douglas S., Joaquin Arango, Graeme Hugo, Ali Kouaouci, Adela Pellegrino, and J. Edward Taylor. 1998. *Worlds in Motion: Understanding International Migration at the End of the Millennium.* New York.

Mattoo, Aaditya, and Antonia Carzaniga, eds. 2002. *Moving People to Deliver Services: Labor Mobility and the WTO.* New York.

Meyer, Jean-Baptiste, and Mercy Brown. 1999. *Scientific Diasporas: A New Approach to the Brain Drain.* Paris. http://www.unesco.org/most/meyer.htm

Migration News. Since 1994. http://migration.ucdavis.edu

Miller, Mark. 1991a. Foreign Agricultural Labor Programs. Testimony before a hearing held by the Commission on Agricultural Workers. March. Washington, D.C.

———. 1991b. Seasonal Foreign Worker Policies in France and Switzerland. Paper prepared for the Commission on Agricultural Workers, Washington, D.C., and printed in Appendix II to the Report of the CAW, 855–869.

———. 2002. "Continuity and Change in Postwar French Legalization Policy." In A. Messina, ed., *West European Immigration and Immigrant Policy in the New Century* Westport, CT.

Mountford, Andrew. 1997. "Can a Brain Drain Be Good for Growth in the Source Economy?" *Journal of Development Economics* 52, no. 2, 287–303.

National Economic and Social Development Board. N.d. THA/93/P10. A Policy Study on the Management of Undocumented Migrant Workers in Thailand. Part B. Bangkok. Mimeo.

Nielson, Julia. 2002. Labour Mobility in Regional Trade Agreements. April 11–12. Paris. Mimeo.

North, David. 2003. Immigration Policy at the Edges: International Migration to and Through the U.S. Island Territories. Center for Immigration Studies Backgrounder. February. www.cis.org/articles/index.html#backgrounders

OECD. Annual. *Trends in International Migration (SOPEMI).* Paris. www.oecd.org

———. 1995. *Manual on the Measurement of Human Resources Devoted to S&T* (Canberra Manual). Paris.

———. 2002. *International Mobility of the Highly Skilled: From Statistical Analysis to the Formulation of Policies.* Paris.

Piguet, Etienne, and Hans Mahnig. 2000. Quotas d'immigration: l'expérience suisse. International Migration Papers, no. 37. ILO. Geneva.

Plewa, Piotr, and Mark J. Miller. 2004. Postwar and Post–Cold War Generations of European Temporary Worker Policies: Continuities and Discontinuities. Paper prepared for Immigration in a Cross-National Context: What Are the Implications for Europe? Luxembourg Income Study, EU Center of the Maxwell School, Syracuse University. Bourlingster, Luxembourg, June 21–22.

Ratha, Dilip. 2003. "Workers' Remittances: An Important and Stable Source of External Development Finance." Chapter 7 in *Global Development Finance 2003.* World Bank. http://www.worldbank.org/prospects/gdf2003/

Ruhs, Martin. 2003. *Temporary Foreign Worker Programmes: Policies, Adverse Consequences, and the Need to Make Them Work.* Perspectives on Labour Migration, no. 6. ILO. Geneva.

Schiller, Guenter, Emmanuel Drettakis, and Roger Böhning. 1967. *Ausländische Arbeitnehmer und Arbeitsmarkt* (Foreign workers and the labor market). Nuremberg. Institut für Arbeitsmarkt- und Berufsforschung der Bundesanstalt für Arbeit. Beitrag 7.

Smith, James, and Barry Edmonston, eds. 1997. *The New Americans: Economic, Demographic, and Fiscal Effects of Immigration.* Washington.

Sontisakyothin, Sakdina. 2000. Major Factors Affecting Policy Changes on Illegal Migrant Workers in Thailand. Ph.D. thesis, National Institute of Development Administration.

Stalker, Peter. 1999. *Workers Without Frontiers: The Impact of Globalization on International Migration.* Boulder, Colo.

Statistisches Bundesamt (Federal Office for Statistics, Switzerland). 2004. Table T2.2.1 Arbeitslose und Arbeitslosenquote nach Staatsangehörigkeit und Geschlecht, 1993–2002, Ende 2. Quartal, Wohnbevölkerung.

Straubhaar, Thomas. 2000. International Mobility of the Highly Skilled: Brain Gain, Brain Drain, or Brain Exchange. HWWA Discussion Paper 88. Hamburg.

Tapinos, Georges. 1984. "Seasonal Workers in French Agriculture." Pp. 47–60 in Philip L. Martin, ed., *Migrant Labor in Agriculture: An International Comparison.* Berkeley.

Taylor, J. Edward, and Philip L. Martin. 2001. "Human Capital: Migration and Rural Population Change." Pp. 457–511 in Bruce Gardener and Gordon Rausser, eds., *Handbook of Agricultural Economics,* vol. 1. Amsterdam.

Teitelbaum, Michael. 2003. "Do We Need More Scientists?" *Public Interest,* no. 153, 40–53. www.thepublicinterest.com/

Teitelbaum, Michael S., and Philip L. Martin. 2003. "Is Turkey Ready for Europe?" *Foreign Affairs* 82, no 3, 97–111.

Thomas-Hope, Elizabeth. 2002. Skilled Labor Migration from Developing Countries: Study on the Caribbean Region. International Migration Papers (IMP-50). http://www.ilo.org/public/english/protection/migrant/publ/imp-list.htm

Thorogood, David, and Karin Winqvist. 2003. Women and Men Migrating to and from the European Union. *Eurostat. Statistics in Focus.* February.

Torpey, John. 1999. *The Invention of the Passport: Surveillance, Citizenship, and the State.* Cambridge.

U.K. Work Permits. 2002. Review of the Seasonal Agricultural Workers' Scheme. May. http://www.ind.homeoffice.gov.uk/file.asp?fileid=481

UNHCR. 2004. 2003 Global Refugee Trends. June 15. http://www.unhcr.ch/statistics/

U.N. Population Division. 2002. International Migration Report 2002. ST/ESA/SER.A/220.

U.S. Commission for the Study of International Migration and Cooperative Economic Development. 1990. *Unauthorized Migration: An Economic Development Response.* Washington, D.C.

Waldinger, Roger, and Michael I. Lichter. 2003. *How the Other Half Works: Immigration and the Social Organization of Labor.* Berkeley.

Weinberg, Dana Beth, and Suzanne Gordon. 2003. *Code Green: Money-Driven Hospitals and the Dismantling of Nursing.* Ithaca, N.Y.

Weiner, Myron. 1995. *The Global Migration Crisis: Challenge to States and to Human Rights.* Reading, Mass.

Winters, Alan, Terrie Walmsley, Zhen Kun Wang, and Roman Grynberg. 2002. *Negotiating the Liberalization of the Temporary Movement of Natural Persons.* Sussex.

Workpermit.com. 2004a. "British Government Announces Plan to Allow More Short-term Foreign Workers to Work in the United Kingdom." 24 May 2002. http://www.workpermit.com/news/uk25.htm

———. 2004b. "UK: Worker Registration Scheme Statistics Announced." 07 July 2004. http://www.workpermit.com/news/2004_07_07/uk/worker_registration_scheme_statistics

———. 2004c. "UK HSMP to Get Tougher." 21 July 2004. http://www. workpermit.com/news/2004_07_21/uk/hsmp_news.htm

World Bank. 2002. *Globalization, Growth, and Poverty.* Washington, D.C.

———. 2003. *World Development Indicators.* Washington, D.C.

Zahniser, Steven. 1999. *Mexican Migration to the United States: The Role of Migration Networks and Human Capital Accumulation.* New York.

ZAV (Zentralstelle für Arbeitsvermittlung; Central Placement Office, Germany). 2004. Merkblatt zur Vermittlung von Krankenpflegepersonal aus Kroatien und Slowenien nach Deutschland—Hinweise für Bewerber und Arbeitgeber (Regulations on the recruitment of nurses from Croatia and Slovenia for Germany). July 2004. Frankfurt.

Index

Note: f indicates figure; *t* indicates table.